Yukon Wildlife

Yukon Wildlife

A Social History

Robert G. McCandless

 The University of Alberta Press

First published by
The University of Alberta Press
Athabasca Hall
Edmonton, Alberta, Canada
T6G 2E8

ISBN 0-88864-093-5

Canadian Cataloguing in Publication Data

McCandless, Robert G. (Robert George), 1942-
    Yukon wildlife

    Bibliography: p.
    ISBN 0-88864-093-5

    1. Wildlife management—Yukon Territory—History. 2. Wildlife
conservation—Yukon Territory—History. 3. Wildlife conservation—Law and
legislation—Yukon Territory—History. I. Title.
SK471.Y8M23 1985.   333.95'4'097191
                        C85-091265-2

Typesetting by Pièce de Résistance, Edmonton, Alberta, Canada
Printed by D.W. Friesen & Sons Ltd., Altona, Manitoba, Canada

In memoriam

John Gilmore McCandless
1909 - 1975

Contents

Acknowledgements

A year of research for this book was supported by a Canada Council Explorations Program grant. It grew out of four months of work by the writer for the Wildlife Branch of the Yukon Territorial Government in the fall of 1976. Research for the most part relied on materials in the Yukon Archives in Whitehorse, especially the rich documentation contained in Yukon Record Group 1, Series 3 (formerly Temporary Series 3), the commissioner's file on wildlife matters since 1900. Yukon Record Group 1, Series 1 (formerly Federal Government Record Group 91) was another essential source. The Yukon Archives has acquired a very large collection of material from a private collector, Mr. Bob Coutts. This collection and other holdings of the Archives have made it the leading depository of Yukon material. The historical resources cited in this book may be useful to other researchers interested in the history of this part of the continent.

The second source has been the verbal histories of some of the Territory's oldest residents. Their observations have added leavening to an otherwise lifeless history. The writer was fortunate indeed to be able to work with Mr. John Joe of Marsh Lake, born in 1884, Mr. Frank Goulter of Carmacks, born in 1877, and Mr. Johnny Taku Jack, born in 1903. Mr. George Dawson, Mr. Johnny Johns, Miss Victoria Faulkner, and Mr. G.I. Cameron also provided essential facts and viewpoints; their assistance is gratefully acknowledged. Finally, to secure secondary sources on related topics such as game law, the writer was able to read materials at the Vancouver Public Library, Vancouver, the British Museum, London, and the University Library, Cambridge. Where secondary sources have been cited the intention is not so much to make a scholarly historical analysis as it is to make a firm and broad setting for some aspect of Yukon history. However, the treatment made of this material and the bibliography should be useful for those making more detailed analyses for other jurisdictions.

I wish to acknowledge with my sincerest thanks the interest and time given to me and the manuscript by Professor Morris Zaslow and Dr. Manfred Hoefs. Other people who have helped me in this work are Professor Andrew Thompson, Marian Ridge, Peter Munsche, Ken Coates, M. Jean Houston, Jane C. Fredeman, and my editor, Mary Mahoney-Robson at The University of Alberta Press. Betty Gautier, Myrna Clift, and Wendy Hartell typed the drafts of this book and I am grateful for their efforts on my behalf. The map appearing in Chapter 2 was drawn by Stephanie Kucharyshyn of the Cartographic section, Department of Geography at the University of Alberta. I am happy to acknowledge and give special thanks to the opinions and encouragement of Julie M. Cruikshank during the preparation of the manuscript.

This book has been published with the help of a grant from the Social Science Federation of Canada, using funds provided by the Social Sciences and Humanities Research Council of Canada.

Introduction

Even today, Canada's Yukon Territory contains an abundance of wildlife. This has more to do with the small number of people living in the Yukon, than it does to sound game management. The animals have simply persisted. The abundance and diversity of the Yukon's wildlife have absorbed the efforts made to manage it. Game laws have changed their focus many times in this century, reacting to the public attitudes toward game management of populations elsewhere in Canada and the United States. The laws that have evolved concerning wildlife in the Yukon reflect these changing attitudes which in turn have had an influence on the social development of the Yukon. The intent of this work is to analyze the way wildlife was utilized and managed by the inhabitants of this isolated part of North America for the first fifty years of the twentieth century. This work is not a study of the animals themselves. It is about the people who used the animals and made the game laws, a human story. One must look elsewhere for the natural history of the Yukon's animals.

The focus of this book is on the small number of politicians and administrators who made wildlife policies for the Yukon Territory. Like their counterparts in other areas of Canada, they did not make their decisions in isolation. They had neighbors, business associates, and many other influences from their communities, which affected their decisions along what might be called racial or socio-economic lines. It needs to be pointed out that the administrators were not Indian people. One could predict that game management decisions did not favor the Indian wildlife users. Beyond the Yukon community as a whole were other sources of influence coming from the world "outside," from game managers in other jurisdictions, fur buyers, big game hunters, and conservation groups. Surprisingly, these attitudes could sometimes outweigh local concerns, if they carried enough momentum to overcome the barriers of distance and found reception with the Yukon's wildlife administrators.

The path of the wildlife administrators through fifty years is seen in changes to the Yukon's game laws during that time. Each influence, local or beyond the Yukon's borders, is seen in some change to the law. Thus the evolution of the Game Ordinance from 1900 to 1950 is the skeleton of a body of events that make up a history of Yukon game management. But rather than start by quoting the 1900 Game Ordinance, the first chapter will trace the history of game laws from the earliest times to the turn of the century, to provide a broad setting for the policies of the day. An introduction to the Yukon's game laws will be followed by a splitting of the history into two themes, big game and fur. The final chapter will examine the reasons behind the success or failure of influences on the wildlife managers through the technology of communications in the same fifty year period. The Yukon's laws about wildlife had more to do with the barriers of distance than with the animals themselves.

Wild animals have held a special place in man's thinking about nature since time began. It would seem that no culture, regardless of place, antiquity or modernity, is without some reference to wildlife in its art, laws, and customs. But in western European and North American societies in the past one hundred years a deep division has appeared between those people who view wildlife as a utility—something useful to man for its hides, meat, fur, and even entertainment—and those who are passionately concerned with what they see to be the very survival of the animals. This same period has witnessed an enormous increase in human populations and the expansion of agriculture and settlement over new territories. Some animal species have been reduced to near-extinction. The continued survival of other species is threatened because men keep hunting them. There would seem to be no disagreement over the question of species preservation. However, policies to achieve this become entangled in emotional arguments and in opposing interpretations of often meager biological evidence. Inevitably the casualties in such debates are people who have used the animals as a utility, whether or not they were the main agents in the decline. They must find another livelihood.

Today most people would consider it a waste to kill a large wild animal such as a moose. Even more would consider it shocking, even criminal behavior to kill such animals solely for the horns, or the personal pleasure it might give the hunter. Europeans and North Americans derive some comfort in believing that large wild animals continue to live in their natural habitats, even though they realize they may never actually see one. These observations are virtually clichés, but they explain the financial and media support given to conservation groups whose aims include the preservation of wild animals. Everyone feels some sense of responsibility—but there is a contradiction here. Affluent classes which give substantial aid to conservation groups are, in turn, prime users of end products of those animals in furs, exotic leathers, ivory, or the special privilege of hunting or photographing them. Discussions of animal conservation tend to shift their emphasis to matters of economics or biology, then to politics. Alternatively, conservationists draw from the modern media arsenal to wage a television and print war against the status quo using largely emotional arguments. In these debates the animals are merely bystanders; the casualties are the traditional users of the animals. Inevitably they must learn to support themselves in other ways and the animals are enclosed in wildlife refuges, their custody entrusted to others. Today this seems to be the only workable solution to the problem. The dominant society cherishes wildlife because it satisfies and reassures some deeply-felt concerns about the health of the wilderness, so it creates and enforces laws to apply to those who are perhaps the least part of that society. It seems unfair, but it works. The animals are preserved.

Wild animals are a renewable resource. They provide livelihoods for thousands of people in North America. Everyone knows how the continent was settled from east to west and how the various animals were hunted out of existence in one place after another. Points of settlement became patches, interconnected by railways and roads, soon isolating those wilderness enclaves where the animals had found temporary refuge. Those enclaves then became national parks, or they vanished into the hands of farmers, loggers, and miners. Earning a living from wild animals became an anachronism everywhere except in the farthest north and yet today we know that wildlife can be harvested safely, without necessarily diminishing the size or wealth of the resource. In fact, one could argue convincingly that long-wearing and functional garments made from wild fur consume fewer of the world's natural resources and less labor over time than would outer clothing made from petroleum-based polymers and agricultural products. Similarly, meat from moose, caribou (reindeer), or deer is better meat than beef or pork because it is higher in protein and lower in fat. Yet millions of people in the continent would prefer that no hunting or trapping be carried on at all, save by the Indians and Inuit, who are always afforded special status in this matter. The public, popular attitude is to see animals preserved, meaning not hunted. The economic use of wild animals is no longer an acceptable way to make a living.

Wildlife conservation and management issues received a great deal of attention in Canada during the late 1970s, especially regarding hunting rights for Indians and Inuit. Much of this controversy found expression in the *Report of the Mackenzie Valley Pipeline Inquiry* of May 1977 by Mr. Justice Thomas Berger. The report made a strong defense of the Indian economy in the Mackenzie Valley based partially on wildlife use; but beyond that, it nourished all the attitudes Canadians had about northern peoples and the frail nature of northern ecology. The report's political success came from public belief that permanent damange might occur to wildlife populations along the pipeline route. It did not succeed to the same extent in educating the public to the fact that one can make a living, and often a very good living, by hunting, killing, and using wild animals in northern Canada. It was for this reason that northern peoples, Indian, Inuit, and European, insisted to the Inquiry that they and they alone were to be the custodians of northern wildlife, that they will resist any attempts by "outside" agencies to impose on them other concepts and philosophies of game and land management. So for the Canadian north it seems a new solution to the problem of wildlife preservation must be found, one that lays the burden of trust on wildlife users and not on professionally-trained managers of northern wildlife refuges and national parks.

The example provided by the history of the Yukon Territory can help to illuminate problems of wildlife management which may be encountered by other jurisdictions. This history is an anomalous one because of its origins in the Gold Rush and the years of decline which followed, but it is one which throws wildlife issues into sharp relief. Every step in its evolution can be seen more clearly than perhaps any other jurisdiction in the continent, including Alaska. By contrast, Alaska's wildlife laws were made in Washington where legislators were subject to great pressure from a powerful conservation lobby. The Northwest Territories' laws were made in Ottawa until fairly recently. The Yukon gained responsibility for its wildlife on the day it became a separate jurisdiction, with power to elect its legislators. In the Yukon from 1900 to 1940, wild animals provided considerable government revenues, employment, and meat for every household, bought and sold in shops alongside beef, mutton, and pork. The Yukon's production of furs was small compared to other jurisdictions, but the value of those furs through export taxes together with other game licenses provided nearly a quarter of the Territorial Government's direct revenues. The big game shooting there was long regarded as among the best obtainable on the continent and the Yukon's guides were world famous.

A second aspect of Yukon wildlife history is important for understanding relationships between Indians and Europeans elsewhere. In the Yukon during the same forty year period, Indians and whites were in nearly equal numbers. Since Indians were the main producers of fur and meat, the white component of the small, isolated society relied on the Indians' efforts to an unusual degree which does not seem to parallel exploitative modes described for other parts of the north.

The final point is almost a technical one. The Yukon's historical record is that of a Canadian province in miniature. It is extraordinarily condensed or compressed in archival materials and in the memory of the people living there. The Territory's isolation, particularly during the period of this study, becomes a historical virtue. Things seem to remain intact, uncluttered by the stimulation and change of the larger, outside society. A shift in emphasis, discernible only through shelves of documents in another, older jurisdiction, becomes concentrated into a manageable handful of papers; and if the historian or the merely curious wishes to obtain more details, he or she can quickly find someone with special knowledge and a long memory. This work is then a local history, but many parts of it may facilitate an analysis of wildlife management history in other areas.

Europeans who came to the Yukon during the Gold Rush or in the years after carried with them certain notions of wildlife use. These notions are very old, with roots in the English-speaking world at least, which can be traced back to the Norman conquest of England in the eleventh century, and even earlier. Yukon Indian people had their own attitudes stemming from centuries of use and trade of wildlife staples with peoples to the north and south. Their record is a verbal one, but that should not diminish its importance. One should remember that the history of contact between the two cultures is one of the briefest on the continent; the grandparents, even the parents of some elderly Indian people living there in 1980 spoke no English. Many of them never saw a white man until 1897. To provide a firm setting for the Yukon's history of wildlife use, the first two chapters discuss the two stems, European and Indian, supporting the Territory's attitudes to wildlife in the fifty years which followed the Gold Rush. Treatment of the English component is longer because the record is more complete and because it has a broad applicability to every other provincial or state jurisdiction in North America. Even before the Klondike discovery, game law was a subject of considerable interest. Thus it is possible to describe in general what those laws were and see if the changes in Yukon game laws kept in step with changes elsewhere. If the changes are not parallel, then we might expect that the difference is due to the large contribution made by Indian people in the use and management of wildlife. Putting it another way, the Yukon law would not be as wide in application as its counterparts in other jurisdictions because of the prominent role of Indians as wildlife users.

Any history of wildlife use in the north must combine two categories; big game hunting and trapping. A third category involving birds could be made, but this book will not consider them as they play a minor part in the Yukon's wildlife use. The hunting of big game species such as grizzly bears, moose, caribou, and Dall sheep by nonresidents continues in the Yukon today as it did in the early years of the century. Hunters from the United States and to a lesser extent from other countries continue to hunt there every year. They are trophy hunters. The meat of the animals killed is only partially salvaged, if at all. The Yukon Government balances license fees and trophy fees and the part-time employment offered to guides against the loss of the animals to local uses. This sort of hunting has been going on every year since the Gold Rush and its history is a colorful one.

Trapping has a longer history but no less colorful. The Yukon's abundance of fox, marten, mink, beaver, lynx, and wolf command top prices at southern auctions. But as subsistence or economic activities, trapping and guiding are quite different, being related only in that one law governs both. Trapping depends on external prices over which the trapper has no real control; guiding depends on the guide himself and the degree to which the wildlife is reserved for his use against other uses by residents. Consequently this work divides wildlife into these two parallel categories; a synthesis of their similar points will be reserved for the last chapter.

Chapter 1 introduces the origins and history of wildlife laws in England and North America which the Yukon's laws were later based on. Chapter 2 explains the evolution of game law in the Yukon. Chapters 3, 4, and 5 discuss big game guiding, while Chapters 6, 7, and 8 discuss the same fifty year period in the trapping industry. The book's final chapter, "Communications and Attitudes," reviews the Yukon's wildlife policies over the first half of this century and the influences that shaped these policies. The Appendix contains transcripts of verbal histories of three men, giving their observations and opinions about the events and personalities described in the previous chapters.

1

Old Laws — New Attitudes

In the English-speaking world, our laws about wild animals are as ancient as any in Common Law. At least nine hundred years of evolution lie behind the game laws of North American jurisdictions, and those of the Yukon Territory are no exception. A discussion of the Yukon's past and present game laws forms part of Chapter 2, while this chapter provides a brief overview of game laws from eleventh-century England until the late nineteenth century in North America, ending with the western Canadian situation in the years prior to the exploration and settlement of the Yukon Territory. To go back nine hundred years may seem to be a peculiar way to start a book about Yukon history, but only the longest view will help us to understand why Europeans, and English colonial administrators in particular, had some very definite and rigid ideas about game management at the time of the Gold Rush. Unfortunately, wildlife law is not a popular topic in historical writing, and the reader cannot be referred to other, single sources which will provide all the information compiled in this chapter.

Since the time of William the Conqueror a certain pattern in laws respecting wildlife seems to impress itself again and again— that the use of wild animals as objects of sporting pleasure has inevitably prevailed over the use of wild animals as meat. The pattern is first revealed in the laws themselves, in changes in diet for some peoples and not others caused by the decline in numbers of wild animals, and finally, in the evolution of a subculture preoccupied with wildlife sporting activities and immensely influential in the drafting of game laws. In North America there has been a reaction to older, European concepts of privilege in hunting rights, but as the numbers of wild animals declined, their use as objects of sporting pleasure came to prevail over their potential as sources of meat. This long background is needed to understand the core problem seen in the history of the Yukon Territory's game laws, game as trophies or game as meat.

Very little is known about the forests, wildlife, and hunting customs of England and Europe in the centuries after the Roman conquests, because the written records were not preserved. However, one Roman idea concerning game stayed behind and became part of the local attitude: wild animals belonged to no one until they were killed or captured.[1] In later centuries, one might have referred to "the King's deer," depending on where the animal was at the time it was taken. On common land it was fair game; in the King's Forests, it was not. "Forests" were designated areas of forested and open land not suitable for agriculture. Prior to the Norman Conquest of 1066 these tracts of land were owned by the regional Anglo-Saxon kings and administered as part of their realms. Within the Forests a distinct body of laws appeared. It was separate from the local courts and justice system known as the Hundreds, which heard minor civil and criminal matters. In fact there were several justice systems according to whose rights had been infringed upon, including those of the king, the church, lords, and the community members.[2] Within a given Forest another body of custom and law governed all activity, from hunting and fishing to timber cutting and grazing rights. Some of these forest courts were appallingly cruel; men proved guilty of some offences were hung, or lost limbs. The real importance of the

Forests and Forest Law as it was called, lay in the granting of franchises by the owner to others for grazing, timber cutting, and so forth. Abuses of these rights led King Canute in the year 1016 to proclaim new laws, and incidentally, to remove the worst penalties for offences, but hunting and hunting rights were never considered to be as important as timber.[3]

The whole legal system became centralized after the Conquest, bringing all the various courts under the king's authority, but the separation between the Forest Laws and Common Law was allowed to remain, probably because the Forests became William's most valuable possession. He enlarged these tracts by evicting tenants and destroying their homes and farms. His forest officers became infamous for their extortion.[4] The abuses became so intolerable under subsequent Norman kings that the lords demanded King John's assent to the Forest Charter in 1217. This document became the first "game law" in the English-speaking world, although its history has been much overshadowed by the Magna Charta, signed and sealed at the same place and time.

The Forest Charter and the administration of the Forest Laws for the next four hundred years used some distinct meanings of the word "property" which did not include ownership or free title in the modern sense. Before the Conquest, animals such as deer did not belong to anyone, but they only could be hunted by those having the king's permission. The king could grant his permission or sell those hunting rights to others. The timber, grazing rights, and all the other things of value were the king's monopolies, unless he chose to sell all or part of them as well. The king's principal source of income came through these franchises and rents. Ownership was by common assent, for which we might use the old legal axiom "possession is nine-tenths of the law." The forests were not held in tenure; there were no legal obligations on land users.[5] After 1066, William I claimed title by right of conquest to the whole of England and to all forested and unoccupied areas.[6] But he was bound by precedent to honor prior customs of management.

The principal source on the Forest Laws is a book written by an Elizabethan jurist named William Manwood.[7] His *Treatise on the Forest Laws* and another, more recent book called *Select Pleas of the Forest* reveal the way wildlife was managed in the medieval period.[8] This system of laws kept land uses such as agriculture or forestry in equilibrium with unoccupied lands. The word forest comes from Latin *fera statio*, or "abode of wild things." The preservation of wildlife in the forests was an important part of their administration. Each forest had any number of officers with titles meaningless today—foresters, rangers, regarders, verderors, and beadles of the Forest Court. Meaningless also are their ancient rights of agistment, assart, and turbary, which only the largest dictionaries tell us mean respectively, monopolies on herding cattle and pigs, cutting trees and brush for fuel and charcoal, and cutting peat. Manwood gives a long list of offences under the Forest Laws, some of which were: found in possession of a greyhound or other hunting breed, found in possession of arrows, baiting animals, witnessed deer stealing without raising a hue and cry, and other crimes not related to game such as opening a mine, building a town, a sheep house or a canal, collecting tolls or taxes, and so forth. Many of the offences heard in the courts concerned game, and poachers were fined or jailed for killing deer; but just as often, ordinary people resident in or adjacent to the forest brought complaint against forest officers for exceeding their authority.[9] Sometimes this involved the accused officers trying to keep all the game for themselves (in the absence of the king) while custom required the rabbits, game birds such as pheasants, and even the small roe deer to be available to those who lived in the forest and had taken them in the past. The forest officers were always trying to increase their authority, and since they were tax and franchise collection officers as well, their motives may not have been based on reasons of game conservation.

These laws hide a rich social tradition centered on hunting. For example, the Forest Charter included the curious clause (ch. 11) "Archbishops, Bishops, Earls or Barons may kill one or two deer when passing a king's forest if going to or coming from a Royal summons."[10] The clergy were avid hunters and this caused great debate within the church. The monasteries were important holders of forest lands, especially in Europe.[11] Some monks virtually worshipped wild animals as a means of return to Eden and to a state of innocence which might allow them to talk with wild beasts, as was the human condition before the Fall.[12] However, others thought that the timber in the monasteries' forests was very valuable, and the chasing of game on horseback one of the greatest of sports. Between these opposing views lay a more important concept, which American historian Clarence Glacken describes as "an awareness of desirable and undesirable changes being made in the natural environment, or an insistence on maintaining unchanged an environment that had been satisfying in the past."[13]

The natural forests were essential to medieval society. They provided food, fuel, and building materials. They may also have contained streams and fish, clay for pottery, and numerous other staples. Glacken shows it is an oversimplification to say that the forests were preserved for the animals within. Yet, when those forests had gone, by the time of the Renaissance, all the rituals and pleasures attending medieval hunts remained intact. Through the centuries hunting had become an exercise in privilege with a life of its own, even if the animals hunted were to become tame, fat, and slow.

Some of the earliest secular books described the rituals attending hunting, which suggests the importance of the hunt in the society of the day. Since the hunt seemed to be more than a pastime or a way of getting meat, it was likely tied into a demonstration of ownership, "beating the bounds" or "showing the flag" in today's terminology. The owner or steward of a patch of forested landscape seemed to gather in the surplus from it in the form of wildlife, and then distribute it to those of his and custom's choosing. The royal hunt included a highly ritualized process of sharing which at the same time established the rights of that person to the land. All sorts of other rationalizations for hunting were to emerge later, when the forests had ceased to be considered common land and the sharing aspects had been eliminated.

The oldest books in English about hunting are *The Master of Game* by Edward, Second Duke of York and written about 1413; and *The Art of Hunting* by William Twici, written in the same year.[14] It is possible that both books were translations of French works. During Elizabeth I's reign, George Turbervile wrote *Book on Falconrie or Hawking* and its second half, *Book on Hunting*.[15] For a modern source, the reader should see David C. Itzkowitz's *Peculiar Privilege: A Social History of English Foxhunting 1753-1885*, for this shows the final, evolutionary result four hundred years later of the customs to be described below, in all their bewildering and ultimately, absurd complexity.[16]

A royal hunt in the Middle Ages involved large numbers of people, horses, and dogs and many days of preparation. Retainers to the hunt assembled the provisions and the equipment, which included beautifully engraved spears for deer, boar and bear, axes, several kinds of knives and special tools for butchering game, and the medieval equivalents of picnic hampers and Thermos flasks. The equipment for a hunt, then as now, included many things of considerable investment and pride.

Dogs were indispensable to medieval hunting; nowhere was dog rearing carried on with more enthusiasm than in England. A book by Edward, Second Duke of York, lists five hunting breeds including the greyhound, the mastiff, and the wolfhound. A large part of his book is devoted to their care, training, and the treatment of their diseases. A huntsman began his training as a boy by looking after the kennels. A group of men which cared for the full hunting pack included the hound master, various grooms, the berner or kennelman, and the lymerer, who handled the lead dog or lymer. Manwood's book lists many offences of the Forest Laws involving dogs, for it seems that rank within a forest determined who could own them, including kind and number. To own a hunting breed was a privilege—but to be found in a forest with one was proof of intention to hunt. An old practice was the "lawing" of dogs, or mutilating a front paw so that it could not run deer, and forest officers could order this to be done.

Typically a royal hunt would be on a day sometime between Midsummers Day and Holy Rood Day (September 14). Attending the king or lord would be his Master of the Hunt; however he might well act in that capacity himself, if qualified or confident enough. Other officers attending would be the Yeoman of the Kings Bow, a hornblower, and all the motley officers of the forest; verderers, regarders, foresters, and rangers. The party would gather at a designated spot chosen by the foresters. This assembly was one of the most important parts of a hunt; Turbervile's book devotes pages to it. Engravings show the monarch—James I in the 1611 edition, Elizabeth I in the earlier one—sitting on a brushwood dias below a canopy while surrounded by attendants, platters of food, wine flasks, and nosing dogs. Here the actual hunt was planned in detail, for once mounted and in pursuit, the hunting party could be scattered in all directions. Grooms and lymerers came to the hunt master with any droppings of the quarry found nearby and everyone offered opinions as to the age and significance of the animal's *feumes* or *feumints* as they were called. Animal tracks or *slots* were also reported and included in the plan. The hunt master considered all these clues and his own knowledge of the terrain, which would be considerable, then announced the strategy for the hunt. The party would mount their horses and be off, close behind the dogs.

The hunted animal would be startled from its cover by the dogs and pursued until it was halted by exhaustion. Typically the dogs and their handlers would keep a larger animal at bay until the Master of the Hunt caught up to them. His was the prerogative of ordering the animal killed and he might assign the task to someone in the party as a test of nerve, for in the case of a large red deer or a wild boar, to kill it with a spear was often a dangerous thing to attempt. After the killing it was customary to "blow the death" with a specific horn call from everyone assembled, using one of the many calls known to experienced hunters. Then the animal was gutted or *gralloched*, a job left to the woodsmen present in the party because, according to Edward's account, the butchering was the art of a woodsman and not a hunter. Curiously the word gralloched is the only Gaelic word to survive in an essentially Norman French hunting vocabulary.[17] The "Breakeing up of the Deare" was also a very ceremonial occasion. Persons received cuts according to their status, so the chief huntsman received the muzzle, tongue, ears, sweet guts (sweet breads), and testicles, the foresters took the shoulders, the hound master the hide, and so forth, while the chief Huntsman or Master of the Hunt would apportion the remainder according to his own or custom's choosing. Even the ravens had a piece reserved for them, the *os corbin*, while the all-important dogs were fed the entrails with even more ceremony and horn blowing. The authors who gave us these descriptions wrote about the ideal, or kingly behavior on a hunt; the reality may have been quite different. However, the hunt was very ceremonial, that is clear, and it was connected with the exercise of prerogative over a patch of forest and countryside.

Such hunting customs have continued in some form or another right up to the present day in Europe. Periodically letters will appear in English newspapers or elsewhere complaining of the barbarous custom of hunting foxes by hounds and mounted men and women, and persons committed to those hunts might offer confirmation that they still do "blood" young hunters on their first hunt and kill. This bizarre custom should not distract the reader

from the fact that fox hunting preserves even today very strong
notions of rural privilege and status. The sport's survival cannot
be separated from the ownership of large tracts of private land,
kept in part for the exercise of that privilege. A second point should
be made in connection with the appearance of the "sportsman"
in Chapters 3, 4, and 5. Hunting traditions have lasted a very long
time. European hunters steeped in those traditions preserved them
and carried them to other countries. Guides in those countries
found a social niche for themselves in the old customs and preserved them in turn. The sportsman-hunter is not a creation of
the industrial age.

With this glimpse of the role of hunting in rural medieval society we can return to another aspect of the forest, as a supplier of
timber and meat. The old forest laws had requirements, for example, that foresters had to protect young valuable trees from cattle
by constructing brushwood fences, and that trees could be felled
only at certain times of the year.[18] The natural bounty of the
timber and brushwood had rules for its apportionment based in
the same application of custom and privilege as was the case for
game. Rights lay with the king, or with the lord, or monastery,
and they in turn allowed timber cutting for beams and lumber,
for charcoal burning, for firewood, and so on. The forest court
acted like the forestry department of a Canadian province in that
it managed the forests, collected fees and rents, and assigned
responsibilities; but it also acted as prosecutor and judge. The
system was open to abuse. In 1306, Edward I was aware that his
foresters were selling his timber without royal assent.[19] Later, the
forest courts became notoriously poor tax collectors—or at least
tax deliverers—to the royal treasury. By 1381, royal finances
reached such a low level that the advisors to the young King Richard
II instituted a poll tax, an extremely regressive measure. Abuses
in its collection led to the famous Peasant's Revolt and furious
vengeance was directed at the learned men, the lawyers, whom
they saw as the instruments of new, unpopular laws.[20] Among
the peasants' demands was a specific request to curb the power
of the forest officers and open access to the forests to everyone.[21]
Their demands failed and passed into history. By then, the decline
of the forests was well advanced through the ever-growing need
for wood. Europe was fast becoming an agricultural society. The
need for revenue caused the forests to be sold and cleared; only

in Germany did there seem to be the belief that the forests deserved preservation and management under a "sustained yield" system.[22] The final stage came in the sixteenth century when soaring populations and shipbuilding all but eliminated the old forests. Severe winters during that period must have been yet another reason, for wood was virtually the only fuel used.[23]

The extinction of the Forest Laws came in the seventeenth century. Overharvesting of the forests and lax or indifferent collections of franchises and fees severely weakened the income of English monarchs. Soon they could no longer sell trees without interfering with their hunting pleasure in the forests. Even though the king could clear the forests, and tax the new, emerging fields without the permission of Parliament, he could not rely on these lands as revenue sources because of inadequate harvests or pestilence. They were difficult to administer without harsh collection measures. The confrontation between a penniless sovereign and Parliament came in the reign of Charles I. He noted that huge amounts of money were due him from users of the ancient forests and demanded their retroactive payment.[24] These demands may have been quite legal, but they were not politically wise at a time when the King's authority was under challenge by Parliament. After the Revolution and Charles' execution, the Forest Laws fell into disuse.

As the forests of Europe diminished in the sixteenth century, so did the consumption of meat by Europeans. French historian Fernand Braudel has described a dramatic population increase in Europe, and presumably in England as well, in the period from the late sixteenth century to the beginning of the nineteenth century.[25] There was a corresponding decline in living standards during the same period, seen particularly in the meat consumption of the average person.

In the early sixteenth century, all major cities in Europe possessed markets where every variety of game meat and birds could be purchased, often at prices below butcher's meat.[26] Hunters brought game into markets at great distances from Europe's forests. Meals in the poorest houses contained meat; wealthy homes were characterized by excesses of it. The great occasions were feast days where platters and carcasses of meat of every variety melted away under the bare hands and personal knives of the guests. Between 1550 and 1600 material life changed greatly. The diet of all classes relied increasingly on corn and vegetables. The poorest classes ate only a gruel of cereals, the ancestor of today's oatmeal porridge. Not until the late nineteenth century would the diet of Europe's poor improve in meat consumption. After 1600 and most noticeably after 1700 "delicate" eating became the custom in wealthier homes, and we see the appearance for the first time of table forks and elaborate cookery using spices and vegetables brought from the newly-explored lands. The perceived needs of luxurious living had to be served from meats which became more costly—and more thinly sliced—as the abundance of the Middle Ages passed away.

As forested lands vanished for ship timbers and grazing lands so did the common man's opportunity to supplement his diet with wild meat. Within the forest, only the royal beasts of chase were forbidden to him; he could obtain rights to catch game birds, hares, and rabbits. Depending on his relationship to the "King's Hunt" or the vast body of men, horses, and dogs involved in it, he might have allotted to him a portion of the venison taken. He might have the right of grazing his pigs or his cattle in a portion of the forest, or a right to operate a fish trap on a good stream. On the forested lands and their fringes there was a zone wherein anyone could graze animals or catch small game. As the forests shrank, their owners increased the classes of protected animals meaning, for example, that commoners could no longer set rabbit snares at will. Opportunities for grazing, or for obtaining venison decreased. Risk of capture for deer stealing increased, as did the penalties. Hunting rights became closely tied to property qualifications. In the fourteenth century one needed forty shillings' worth of property to hunt deer; three hundred years later one had to show one hundred pounds a year.[27] Forests were broken up into successively smaller units called chases, parks, and warrens so that those forests became in effect, game farms, with their bounty available only to the propertied class. It seems likely that the shrinkage of the total area of forests had a cascade effect going far beyond the borders. When coupled with the population increases of the period 1550-1800 this shrinkage must have caused nearly an exponential decline in meat consumption by the poorer classes.

The late seventeenth century began a new period in game mangement in England. A deepening wall of privilege surrounded the sport. Fines and penalties for trespassing and poaching reached a severity not seen in hundreds of years. Before the Revolution, in the time of James I, killing a deer illegally would cost a man three months' imprisonment and triple the damages for the value of the deer. Cromwell's Protectorate did not change the Forest Laws or indeed alter the exercise of privilege, despite pressure to do so from the Levellers, perhaps because Cromwell himself enjoyed hawking and hunting.[28] After the Restoration, penalties increased to fines of twenty pounds and up to a year's imprisonment.[29] William and Mary added an hour in the pillory to the penalties, and caused the fines to be divided equally between the owner, the informer, and the poor.

The Hanoverian monarchs were very fond of hunting but their game laws came to reflect larger political issues than mere poaching. George I's Parliament raised the penalty to a fine of fifty pounds and a three year jail sentence, then added the option of transportation to the colonies for a period of seven years.[30] Then in 1723 came the infamous Black Acts, with their chilling warning that armed and disguised persons in the forests "shall suffer Death as a Felon without Benefit of Clergy."[31] Many since that time have interpreted this to mean that deer were more valuable than human life; but this is oversimplification. A recent book by E.P. Thompson, *Whigs and Hunters*, shows that the Blacks, the "armed and disguised persons," were defending their ancient privileges under the Forest Laws, which of course had become disused at that time.[32] The Blacks became allied with the Jacobites, implacable enemies of the Hanoverians, so the law was aimed at quelling a local but potentially dangerous insurrection and had little to do with deer. In any case as Thompson shows, a royal hunt by that time had become little more than a drunken farce.[33]

Thanks in part to the Black Act, poaching and poachers appear in English folklore as both heroes and villains: heroes because of their skill in woods lore and in avoiding detection, villains because of their callousness in killing game. Poaching is a word of comparatively recent origin. According to the *Oxford English Dictionary*, earliest references to the word appear first in the late seventeenth century and gain wider currency in the eighteenth. Poaching is a unique sort of crime with a confused relationship to Common Law. Wild animals on private lands are not owned by the landlord in the same way as his cattle or dogs are owned, so a poacher is not a thief. He is a trespasser first of all; if he then kills an animal, he steals the landlord's pleasure, but not his property. Only if he crosses the property line carrying the dead animal or game bird does he become a thief as well. These distinctions may seem absurd to the North American reader, who must look to the thoroughly modern crime of shoplifting to find the closest parallel.

These definitions aside, poachers, particularly if they were armed, were regarded as a menace. Landlords retaliated by using gamekeepers, and until they were outlawed in 1827, murderous devices such as set guns and iron man-traps.[34] Yet one should not think such enmity is a thing of the past, or regard it as a "cops and robbers" fantasy. In March 1978, a coroner's court in England found that gamekeepers in the employ of the Duke of Norfolk had no responsibility for the shooting death of an armed poacher on the Duke's North Yorkshire estates.[35]

Game laws as we know them today grew out of reforms to the old Forest Laws and acts of the eighteenth century during a time of reform under George III and William IV. Hunting licenses appeared for the first time in 1784, which helped to separate hunting rights from the ill-defined, artificial class owning one hundred pounds a year or more which had exercised the privilege for over one hundred years.[36] The 1829 Night Poaching Act replaced the old Black Acts, and in 1831, all property qualifications for hunting was abolished.[37] The changes in law continued during Victoria's reign. Constables gained powers to search the possessions, wagons, and so forth of persons suspected of concealing game, game birds, or eggs, and they could seize the effects of anyone found in commission of an offence under the acts. Another aspect of game law appeared as well. Animals and birds were to be taken only at particular times of the year, and limits were placed on the numbers which could be taken. By 1871, game laws had become such subjects of interest, that the British Home Secretary had cause to inquire into and publish the game and trespassing laws in all the other countries in the world.[38] This revealed that several jurisdictions in North America had game laws by this time, and while their origins may be due to very old principles in English law, they soon evolved a life and a momentum of their own.

The early immigrants to North America would have resisted any attempts by colonial administrators to deny them access to land and wildlife. The promise of abundant wild meat had wide appeal to those driven from the land by enclosures or the effects of the Industrial Revolution. An added inducement lay in the promise of economic gain based on wildlife such as the traffic in furs, hides, and meat. The immigrants hunted without restriction as to harvests and shooting seasons, for such restrictions would have conflicted with the expansionist philosophy of the age as well as with the economic activity. The European, used to English deer parks or European game preserves, must have seen the continent's game resources as limitless, especially in light of the European and English experiences with the extinction of some species and the depletion of game. Through the centuries Europe and England had their share of animal extinctions. Aurochs or wild cattle were last hunted in the time of Charlemagne, in the ninth century.[39] Bear vanished from England's forests in the eleventh century followed by boars or wild pigs in the twelfth or thirteenth centuries, in the same era that wolves were ordered to be destroyed by a royal warrant.[40] Within decades of landing on the eastern shore of North America, Europeans reduced populations of game and fur-bearing animals near their communities, while the Indians extended the same process in zones beyond the new settlements. Calvin Martin's book, *Keepers of the Game,* argues that Indians in the eastern half of the continent were active agents in these extinctions. His thesis is that at the time of contact between the cultures, something other than whitemen and their new economic notions upset the old "contractual" relationship between the inhabitants of the continent and the animals they depended upon.[41] If this is so, then those changes have their parallel in new philosophies in Europe, and in England in particular, which saw extinctions as natural consequences. A medieval nostalgia for Eden was replaced by a Nature that was hostile to man; the wilderness became an enemy.[42] Theorists like Darwin drew from the late eighteenth-century writings of Thomas Malthus and built upon such quotations as "there is a natural tendency and constant effort in population to increase beyond the means of subsistence."[43] Extinctions were perceived as due to God's will; man was not morally responsible and could forget the myth of Noah. Man could offend nature without offending God, since Nature had her own implacable laws and her own purposes.

Yet the fledgling states and colonies in North America made

some early efforts to manage wildlife populations. Pennsylvania had a game law in 1760 which required landlords to preserve wildlife on their property.[44] In New York, certain counties were closed to moose hunting in 1868 for five years to give depleted populations a chance to recover, while moose and deer could not be hunted anywhere else in the state between January and August. By 1870 both British Columbia and Newfoundland had closed seasons on deer as well, but the earliest law in Canada seems to have been one which protected grouse on Prince Edward Island in 1864.[45] To these obvious demonstrations of concern could be added the writings of Americans Henry David Thoreau, Ralph Waldo Emerson, and Walt Whitman, who urged a communion or empathy with Nature, in marked contrast to the "wilderness as enemy" idea. Given that men knew something about the need to manage wildlife and that articulate, influential writers urged the enjoyment of Nature, why then did the enormous slaughter of buffalo occur in the 1870s?

The buffalo problem had a distinctive influence on game law in North America. It is still a widely-held opinion that the disappearance of the North American plains buffalo from its historic range was caused by unrestricted market hunting; the subject continues to be one of wide interest and debate. The buffalo numbered in the millions in the 1850s and 1860s. Grouped into two vast herds, the north and the south, the animals ranged from Texas to northern Alberta, from the Rocky Mountains to Lake Erie. Historian F.G. Roe's book, *The North American Buffalo*, argues that the buffalo were already declining in numbers at the time of westward settlement and movement in the years before 1850.[46] He does not gloss over the staggering numbers destroyed after that time, nor does he attempt to diminish the role of men, both white and Indian, in driving the animals to the precipice of total extinction in less than a decade—and yet his evidence is that another process was at work as well. Market hunters accelerated a decline that Nature herself had started.

At the time of westward expansion and into the 1860s the buffalo were unknown as to their range and total numbers, especially in the light of past experience, so that by 1870 prevailing opinion held that it would be impossible to exterminate them.[47] The banality of facts hides what must be one of the most wasteful acts of mankind in his troubled history. The process of decline attributable to man accelerated slightly each year in the 1850s as more and more land became accessible to immigrants from the east. Settlers used the meat and hides locally, for there was no means of transport at any distance beyond the great rivers. Indians contributed to the decline in that they harvested more buffalo than their traditional subsistence needs would warrant in those years to exchange buffalo products for trade goods. As the Indian lands were traversed by the new railways and as whole populations succumbed to smallpox and starvation, the survivors had to expand their hunting efforts into new territory and on declining numbers of buffalo out of simple economic necessity, to obtain trade goods needed for their survival. Thus by 1870 Indians and non-Indians may have viewed the buffalo herds the same way, as objects of unrestricted economic exploitation. In the early 1870s the killing reached the levels of a frenzy—over two million were slaughtered in 1872-73.[48] Ten years later, the plains buffalo had all but vanished.

Technology explains much of this relatively sudden and massive killing. According to American historian Francis Hines, in 1870 or 1871 a German tanner perfected a method to turn the heavy, spongy buffalo hide into a hard, durable leather, making the hides much more valuable.[49] For the first time buffalo hides became commodities on a large scale, outstripping the animals' local worth as a source of hides and meat for markets along the new railways and rivers. A dramatic expansion of heavy industry following the American Civil War led to an ever-increasing need for strong leather belting in both Europe and the United States. Factories at the time used one central power source. Machines for boring, milling, and so forth typically took their power from a central, powered overhead shaft running the length of the shop floor. Views of factories in this period are dominated by these belts: it is reasonable to suppose that their leather could have been from North American buffalo. For whatever end use they were put, the demand for hides was such that a green, dried buffalo hide could be sold at the railhead or steamboat landing for the equivalent of a laborer's wages for a week. By 1872 up to twenty thousand men were buffalo hunting, according to Hines.[50] The demand for leather outlasted the buffalo.

Today we would be apt to assume that in 1874, it was obvious that the buffalo, and the larger southern herd in particular, were in danger of being eliminated. Yet few contemporary travellers or writers foresaw this happening. If they had tried to warn the continent they would not have found a particularly receptive audience. Western exaggerations were a way of life. No premium was given to fact at a time when print was cheap and getting cheaper. To limit the hunt would be to deprive buffalo hunters of their income and railways of a portion of their revenue, actions likely to be sensitive political issues in frontier areas. Besides, the buffalo were in conflict with possible land use by settlers and cattle. Even with a lucrative traffic in hides and meat, lands used as pasturage or cattle range could be shown to have a greater value than lands left for buffalo. Land was the valuable commodity, not wild meat. The government did not need to be hostile to the buffalo. If the U.S. Department of the Interior had any attitude at all in that decade it was one of benign neglect.

Trophy hunters led the last depredation against the buffalo. They had both time and money to pursue the animals into the remotest parts of the Rockies and shoot them all, destroying even the remnants by which the area could be restocked. Hines refers to the adventures of one of them in the Dakotas in the 1880s, who personally killed sixty-four and left others wounded, according to his own account in a sporting magazine of the day.[51] The same man complained about the inroads made by hide hunters in the buffalo populations. The irony is obvious today but one hundred years ago it was not. This change is not only in people's attitudes toward wildlife today, it is also in the perception of scale, of space itself. Sixty-four animals were insignificant when the popular culture of the day believed that the animals were dwindling, but still roamed, out there somewhere, in numbers that could not be counted. Legislation to protect the buffalo was out of the question in the United States until much later, but the Canadian situation was different.

The northern buffalo herd was international in its range, spending part of the year in present-day Manitoba and Saskatchewan. By 1870, the mixed community of Indians, Métis, and Scottish settlers in the Red River district had been hunting the buffalo for over fifty years. Each year parties rode far to the west to intercept the herd. In the 1860s American river steamboats conquered the Missouri as far upstream as Fort Benton and much of the river lay scarcely one hundred miles south of Canadian

Territory. Hide hunters working from that river and shipping south to St. Louis made serious inroads into the northern herd. In 1870 the North-West Territories emerged as a political entity when the two hundred year old Hudson's Bay Company grant of land was sold to Canada. When its residents became aware of the rapid decline in buffalo and the need to feed thousands of Sioux refugees from American territory, the fledgling local assembly enacted *An Ordinance for the Protection of the Buffalo* in 1877.[52] But this unique, home-grown conservation measure, which owed little to English or Canadian game laws, was too late to save the buffalo.

The Buffalo Ordinance shows the early use of game management concepts which were to be laws elsewhere a hundred years later. One section read:

> It shall be unlawful at any season, to hunt or kill buffalo from the sole motive of amusement, or wanton destruction, or solely to remove their tongues, choice cuts or peltries; and the proof in any case that less than one half of the flesh of a buffalo has been used or removed shall be sufficient evidence of the violation of this section.

This would not prevent the sale of animals legally taken, but would seem to limit hunting them for that purpose alone. Pounding or herding the animals over a cliff was prohibited because it wasted meat; the individual lost control over the number killed or taken and there were always a lot of cripples. A closed season on females and immature animals showed a concern for the animals during calving season and acknowledged the ability of the skilled hunter to distinguish the sexes. Exemptions were allowed to this "in situations of pressing necessity." Peace officers, which would be the North West Mounted Police in this case, obtained powers of arrest, search, and seizure similar to English antipoaching laws of the period. Penalties on conviction were to be up to $100, or three months in jail. But these points are germane only to the evolution of North American and western Canadian game law. Unfortunately, the buffalo respected no borders, and understood no laws. Each year fewer of them came north into Canada and by the time the Canadian Pacific Railway crossed the Prairies in 1882, they were gone.

The North American plains buffalo, the passenger pigeon, and the sea otter of the Pacific coast were casualties of the European settlements and exploitation of North America. The patterns of settlement, subjugation of the Indians, and altering the environment are well understood. Less known is the important, long-term effect that the problems posed by these extinctions had on the continent's perception of wildlife through its laws, its attitudes towards hunting—especially market hunting—and finally through awakening a conservation ethic in the countries' populations. The buffalo extinction did not initiate these ideas, for they had been known in some circles for nearly a century, but it helped to give them substance in the public consciousness. Earlier the Hudson's Bay Company learned the essentials of management of fur bearers in "ruined fur ground." In 1822 the company could limit the use of steel traps, close seasons for harvesting, refuse to purchase undersized animals, or even relocate its trading posts to give an area a chance to recover to its normal abundance.[53] But such management notions could hardly apply to the buffalo in the 1870s. After the buffalo vanished the way opened for their adoption. The conservation ethic has been the underlying philosophy or moral purpose behind the game laws of most jurisdictions since that time. Combining this ethos with the democratic system of universal access to game imposed on everyone that same degree or perception of conservation. This is a word loaded with cultural values. North American Indians did not share some of those values because, to them, the meat—not pleasure—was the reason for the hunt. Where necessary, game laws had to side-step cultural questions by granting what are styled "traditional hunting rights" to Indians. But even today when a species is recognized as being in danger of becoming extinct, Indians and Inuit are required to obey the law.

No sooner had the buffalo vanished than a political movement was born with the avowed purpose of conserving wildlife. By 1900 this movement installed the idea of the public interest in wilderness and its preservation into the political and administrative thought of the day. Wildlife was never a central theme, indeed for nearly two decades it was little more than a side issue to the effort devoted to land development and forest policy; and yet the buffalo became a symbol, almost a cult object to conservation advocates. In 1888 some members of the hunting fraternity formed the Boone and Crockett Club. This club put an official seal to an old idea, that hunting was a pleasurable activity, worth carrying on for its own sake without having any utilitarian values.[54] At much the same time, "outdoor" clubs appeared in the United States, particularly in California. Spokesmen such as John Muir, naturalist and mystic, made it fashionable to experience or more importantly, to express to others a sort of nostalgia for the wilderness. A continent newly spanned by railroads and telegraph lines concealed no more mysteries, no more secret, undiscovered places.

Americans not caught up in expansionist philosophies could be sorted into two classes; those who wanted islands of wilderness preserved as spiritual oases against all manner of development, and those who were forming notions of "wise use" of the wilderness which permitted only certain, restricted styles of exploitation. These differences were pronounced when focused on timber, water power, or land. On matters of wildlife they would be more likely to agree. Despite the recent buffalo extinction, wildlife conservation had not taken root as an issue. The new conservationists were of the same generation, so to speak, as the buffalo hunters. While they no longer saw nature and the wilderness as an enemy, the same perception did not apply to wild animals. They were dangerous and unpredictable. Killing something and making a trophy of its head was proof that one was more clever than the animal. After the Boone and Crockett Club started to record trophy measurements, a measure of respect, even pathos hung about the trophies. One revered an animal by killing it and nailing its head to the wall. It was permissible in those days to advertise oneself in this way, but regardless of the motives, by the end of the century one could be either a "conservationist" or a "preservationist" and still hunt animals for sport without appearing to be in contradiction.

Most jurisdictions had game laws by the 1890s. That part of western Canada which today includes the Yukon Territory had a law as early as 1894, at least in theory. The evolution of game law and policy there in the next fifty years forms part of the next chapter. Before closing this one, the situation in western Canada should be explained, in context with the evolution of wildlife law to this time. We can compare an Ontario *Game Protection Act of 1893* with the federal *Unorganized Territories' Game Preservation Act of 1894.*[55] There will be no discussion here about any discrepancies between the laws as written and the law as practiced or enforced. However, the laws do tell us something about the prevailing attitudes of the legislators. Both laws set closed seasons for birds, fur bearers, and big game species such as moose and caribou. Both exempted Indians and isolated settlers from many parts of the law. Both prohibited certain "unsportsmanlike" practices such as using poisons, letting dogs run deer, shooting waterfowl with large-calibered shotguns (punt guns), and using traps or snares to catch animals other than fur bearers. Both laws created game officers or wardens with certain unique powers of enforcement including seizure, arrest, and when granted a warrant, powers to search private homes. Ontario set a bag limit of two moose and two caribou per season; the Territories law had no limits. Ontario collected a license fee of $25 from nonresident hunters, the Territories did not. On June 2, 1894, Minister of the Interior T.M. Daly spoke in the House of Commons in Ottawa on the introduction of the *Unorganized Territories' Game Preservation Act*. He said,

> . . . the only thing we can do is prevent these animals from being shot by others than the inhabitants . . . It is impossible to make the bill more stringent [towards Indians] unless we are prepared to feed these people.[56]

He disagreed that bag limits should be included in the bill because he believed that the closed season was in itself sufficient to preserve game. If he was thinking about the vast unpopulated area of the northwest, or the "Great Lone Land," he may have been right. Two years later events along the Yukon River would prove the law to be inadequate.

This chapter gives only an outline of a subject which deserves book-length treatment. Compressing nine hundred years of history into a few pages must overlook many important topics which could contribute to the theme "game as trophies or game as meat," but some generalizations are possible. North Americans today believe that they have equal rights to kill animals for food or other uses, subject to certain laws, which in turn are subject to enforcement by those whose business it is to protect wild animals. These general rights are similar to those held by people living in or near the forests of Europe, and England in particular, nine hundred years ago. But as the centuries passed, these rights became defined to an extraordinary degree and closely tied to that place where the hunting was or was not to be carried on. Social rankings based on property determined who could hunt for certain animals. This ranking appeared also in ceremonies and rituals attending hunting. It survived while the forests declined and became agricultural land, then strengthened through the application of progressively more restrictive property qualifications and penalties on wildlife users. The ultimate effect of these changes was to grant to property owners certain rights over wild animals which were identical to outright ownership of them. Reforms made in the nineteenth century provided concepts of limited universal access; that is, all men (with a license) may hunt some of the time. This has been the principle behind North American game laws ever since. By selling licenses, the government acts both as gamekeeper and a vendor of hunting rights and makes no distinction between those who hunt for pleasure and those who hunt for meat. Each state or province also attempted to manage wildlife by limiting the numbers killed in designated places and confining killing to certain seasons. It imposed certain notions of wildlife use which discouraged or outlawed wasteful practices or unsporting behavior. Finally, jurisdictions having large numbers of Indians, granted them specific exemptions from licenses, seasons, and bag limits. All these principles would have been known to officers of the North West Mounted Police, Hudson's Bay Company traders, and others familiar with the workings of government in the open expanse of western Canada. To them, the greatest value of wild animals lay in their use as food by the Indians and prospectors, but even that use must be made subservient to the needs of national development and its relentless appetite for land.

2

The Law in the Yukon

At the turn of the twentieth century, the Yukon Territory was famous throughout the world. As the years passed, North Americans forgot about the Gold Rush and this triangular slice of the northwest, or confused its identity with that of Alaska or the Northwest Territories. Yet when the place is named, it is called *The* Yukon, and not "Yukon" standing as an isolated word, like Alberta or Alaska. The Yukon is a place which old, nostalgic echoes keep buoyed up in the collective memory of a continent. Its written history is scarcely a hundred years old, and easily dismissed as a pattern of mineral development followed by economic stagnation. Even today it has fewer people than it had during the Klondike Gold Rush. But the Yukon has a history which sets it apart from its northern neighbors, and that separation is seen in the way the Territory has managed its wildlife.

Canada's Yukon Territory lies hidden behind the vast icefields and mountains of the Coast Ranges which rim the Gulf of Alaska. For the most part it is a mountainous plateau containing the sources of the Yukon River, one of the continent's largest. Alaska is its neighbor to the west. Wide along its border with British Columbia, it narrows northward to a sliver of beach on the Beaufort Sea, while its eastern border is lost somewhere in the northern extensions of the Rocky Mountains. The Yukon Territory comprises some 536,000 square kilometers, most of it forested with spruce and pine, birch and aspen. This vast empty space is crossed here and there by gravel roads, and smudged in placed by the remains of mining, but otherwise it looks as it always has, more a home for moose, caribou, and bear than for people.

Recent archaeological work shows a continuous record of human habitation extending beyond thirty thousand years in the northern Yukon. To begin the Territory's history with the Gold Rush would be to tell only half the story. The oral history of the Indian people is just as important in understanding the development of the Yukon's wildlife policies and laws.

It is sometimes argued that North American Indian culture was altered fundamentally by the arrival of European fur traders. Canadian historian Harold Innis wrote:

> The rapid destruction of the food supply and the revolution in the methods of living accompanied by the increasing attention to the fur trade by which these products were secured, disturbed the balance which had grown up previous to the coming of the European.[1]

Under this interpretation, Indian people changed their perception of wildlife and land use to one more compatible with notions of commodity production or resource harvesting and export of the surplus. Stating it another way, trading products from one area for goods and tools far beyond a region's borders is explained as a foreign, European concept. This may be argued for other parts of Canada, but the Yukon's peculiar history, geography, and resources set it apart. Peoples adjacent to the Yukon had established trading links with the interior before Europeans became an influence. The introduction of European goods followed old routes and did not necessarily alter existing trading patterns. Interior and coastal peoples traded across deep linguistic and cultural

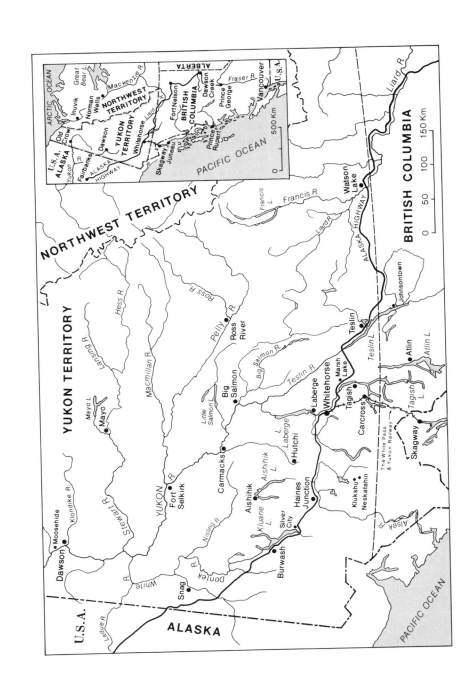

boundaries which separated them as effectively as did the mountain passes. In the 100 years between the founding of the Hudson's Bay Company post Fort Yukon and the collapse of the fur market in 1947, Yukon trappers had advantages not available to their counterparts in the Northwest Territories. They always had a choice of markets, even a choice in the kinds of trade goods available to them; they were never the victims of a monopoly of one company, or even of one country.

The history of northwestern Canada is in part, a history of the Hudson's Bay Company, just as the history of Alaska is tied to that of the Russian American Company. The Yukon has a bit of both influences, for the boundary between those empires after 1825 forms a part of the Yukon boundary today. However the dynamics of trade in furs, hides, copper, and other goods owed little or nothing to Europeans; in fact, their technology made its appearance long before Europeans themselves penetrated the region. Indian middlemen dealt with the traders, taking their tools such as steel knives, axes, guns, powder, and shot into the interior and returning with fine furs, moosehides, and other goods. Canadian and Russian traders in and adjacent to the Yukon basin knew their tenancy was a fragile one, entirely dependent on the goodwill of their neighbors and trading partners. Murder and pillage did occur; retaliation was impossible, or of dubious benefit. If the post failed, the regional administrators of the fur company would merely write off the cost of the post as a bad investment. Elsewhere in Canada, save in the farthest north, land was first acquired by the profits from fur. This historically relentless process did not operate in the Yukon because the old fur empires were stretched to their limits, and yielded only meagre profits. It was the discovery of gold and the technological marvel of its day, the river steamboat, which finally delivered the whole basin into Canadian and American hands.

For information on interior peoples' trading with the coast, historians must rely on verbal information given by descendants of those who lived there in the nineteenth century. Anthropologists Catherine McClellan and Fredrica de Laguna have published these stories, and they have been confirmed by the archaeological record given by William Workman.[2] Two other partial accounts given by Mr. John Joe and Mr. Johnny Taku Jack are in the Appendix of this book.

Copper was the most valuable trade commodity before the arrival of Russian iron. Interior Tutchone peoples found placer nuggets of native copper on the north side of the St. Elias mountains, in the headwaters of the White River. Copper use near this place has been dated back to the fifteenth century and may be older.[3] The second most valuable trade items were moose and caribou hides tanned in the unique interior manner which left the hides light, waterproof, and as soft as chamois. The hide from a big bull moose might yield nearly nine square meters of this leather. Neither the animals nor the tanning methods would have been known to coastal peoples, or to the Inuit to the north. Valuable furs such as beaver, marten, and fox moved along the same trade routes used for copper and hides, as did medicinal plants, stone tools, decorative shells, and so on, but the furs never received as much attention as other goods until after contact with European traders. The Tlingits on the coast used Yukon copper as a trade item in their dealings with people farther down the coast, the largest coppers being worth eight or ten slaves.[4] The Tlingits were middlemen in a sense, between two technological innovations, copper tools and ceremonial objects from the north and inland, and sea-going canoes from Haida territory farther south down the coast. They turned both ends of this trade to their advantage. Not surprisingly, Russian traders found the Tlingits to be stubborn adversaries, their equals in trading.

People living on the Yukon basin or plateau dealing directly with the Tlingits would then trade farther inland, ranging as far as the Pelly River basin, or north and west into the White River country. Friction along trading boundaries was intense. Warfare was a fact of life until late in the nineteenth century and still figures largely in legends and in the attitudes of some Yukon peoples toward their neighbors even today. The relative ease of communication between Tlingit-speaking peoples along the coast from Juneau north to Yakutat would have permitted them to be more than passive agents in the interior wars. Similar disputes occurred between interior peoples and the Inuit to the north.

The Russian presence in Alaska had a poor beginning. Two boats from the first Russian ship to make contact failed to return and their occupants were assumed to have been massacred. The other ship in Bering's expedition of 1741 encountered no Indians, but its crews discovered the rich potential of Aleutian sea otters and initiated the eastward expansion of the Russian companies down the Pacific coast. English expeditions later in the century by captains Cook and Vancouver did not encourage that country to challenge Russian trading supremacy in the Gulf of Alaska. Merchants back in London may have forseen the decline of the sea otter stocks on which the largest profits depended. England's interest remained in the interior of the continent. In negotiations with the Russians in 1825, England pressed for the adoption of the 141st Meridian as its westernmost boundary and conceded the Alaska coastline to the Russians as far south as their first, fatal landfall of 1741, or 54 degrees 40 minutes north.

The Anglo-Russian treaty of 1825 was negotiated with consultation between the Hudson's Bay Company and the Prime Minister George Canning.[5] Their diplomacy was complicated by lack of knowledge of the interior and an increasing American interest in the coastline. However the 1821 merger between the Hudson's Bay Company and its rival, the North West Company, had opened the whole western interior to uniform administration. The Pacific coast became less important. Ten years later, after a journey to the coast by the governor, George Simpson, the Company decided to explore westwards towards Russian territory, "for the extension of trade in that quarter . . . and with a view of opening communications with our posts and shipping on the coast," because by this time the Company was operating in southeastern Alaska under special license from the Russian company.[6] Efforts by James McLeod, John Hutchinson, and Robert Campbell to establish a toe-hold for the Company in the Liard-Dease lake area of northern British Columbia failed because the Tahltan Indians obtained higher prices by trading down the Stikine River to the sea. Westward exploration between 1839 and 1842 by Campbell, Alexander Isbister, and John Bell touched on lands drained by the Yukon River, though the river itself was not seen by them until Campbell proceeded down the Pelly River to its junction with the Yukon in 1843. In 1844, Bell crossed the divide from the Mackenzie River westward over the Richardson Mountains to the Porcupine River, and then followed it downstream, to its mouth on the vast river his Kutchin Indian guides called Youcon, or Yukon. That winter Simpson evidently concluded that the river Campbell saw from the Pelly and the one reported by Bell were the same; but since Campbell reported Indians there to be within the Russian-Tlingit trading sphere, he ordered a post built at the Porcupine junction. This was done by Alexander Murray in 1847, knowing he was within Russian territory under the 1825 treaty and expecting to be evicted by them at any moment.[7]

In his report to Governor Simpson, Murray noted:

> We are over the edge and that by a "long chalk" which I call six [sic] degrees across the Russian boundary . . . . I wish it was our own, I mean the Hudson's Bay Co.'s, at least for a term of years until we thinned it of its superabundance of Beavers and Martens.[8]

But the Russians gave Murray's post little attention. It continued to support a small but profitable business, mainly through the refusal of its traders to buy low value pelts such as muskrat, and the use of what H.A. Innis called "questionable methods of trade."[9] In 1848 Campbell was instructed to build a post at the junction of the Pelly River and the Yukon, which he later called Fort Selkirk. This post proved to be no more profitable than Campbell's Fort Frances on the Liard-Pelly height of land, because the transportation route back to Fort Simpson was too long and too difficult. At Fort Selkirk, Campbell found himself in direct competition with Tlingits who had journeyed inland from the coast. They offered a lower tariff than Campbell and soon bartered away all the fur held by the local Tutchone people.[10] In time both Campbell and Murray made their presence felt, but only Murray secured regular trade. In 1851 Governor Simpson ordered Campbell to travel downstream to confirm the belief that the large river at Fort Selkirk and Fort Yukon was the same, and to see if it was a more practical way to supply the upper Yukon post. That fall Campbell returned via Fort Yukon with a much larger outfit and prepared to increase his competition with the Tlingits. In the summer of 1852, the Tlingits returned as usual, saw Campbell was better supplied and promptly ransacked his fort. Thus the Company's efforts on the upper Yukon did not succeed. Trade remained in Tlingit hands for another twenty or more years.

Following the purchase of Alaska by the United States in 1867, Fort Yukon lived on borrowed time. Its transfer to American control came in 1869, when a steamboat operated by San Francisco successors of the Russian American Company made the thousand mile journey upstream from the Bering Sea. The Hudson's Bay

Company retreated up the Porcupine River to a point east of the 141st meridian and left the Yukon River trade to American interests. The next thirty years were a period of American commercial supremacy which was not broken until the construction of the White Pass and Yukon Railway in 1900.

Even before the important discovery of gold in the Klondike River basin, the emphasis in trade matters had changed from fur to placer gold; but the Territory's Indian people did not have to make substantial changes in their lifestyles or patterns of wildlife utilization. This period has not been well-documented; only meagre information is available about prospecting and virtually nothing about the fur trade. However it seems that by 1880 miners were working streams in the Yukon basin, having climbed the Chilkoot Pass on the old Tlingit trading route to the interior. An important gold discovery was made in 1886 on the Fortymile River. A year later George M. Dawson and William Ogilvie entered the district under instructions to make surveys for the government of Canada. Both men asked the American traders about the fur trade, but Ogilvie later explained their predicament: "It is a delicate question to ask a person who is selling foreign goods in Canadian territory to reveal to a Canadian employed by the government the amount of his trade. Very likely had I asked, I would have received a short answer."[11]

In 1894, Inspector Charles Constantine of the North West Mounted Police reached the district to report on its administrative needs. While at Fortymile, he met with several Indian men and heard their complaints about American fur traders. He quoted one as saying, ". . . there are plenty of furs in this country and I would like the English traders [Hudson's Bay Company] to come and trade with us, because their goods are better and they deal more fairly with us."[12] Here the man may have been referring to their confusion over the American practice of changing fur prices according to market conditions, for the Indians had little experience with that market and preferred the Hudson's Bay Company method of using fixed prices. The Americans introduced a cash system using gold dust, and they dealt with anyone, not just the senior, experienced trading men in the Indian family groups. The steamboat, and contact with the San Francisco fur market changed the ground rules for the trapper, but he could adjust his trapping effort or trap in a new district. He did not have to alter his old perceptions of trade which saw him as a commodity producer. But it was not the traders and their methods who changed things, it was the diseases and alcohol brought by the prospectors that made adjustment difficult, breaking apart many family groups.

Many Indian people adapted to new opportunities created by the mining activity. Constantine reported Indians acting as meat hunters for mining camps.[13] Others caught and sold salmon from the prolific Yukon and Klondike Rivers. There were opportunities as contractors—cutting firewood, or laboring, or packing for the mines. Indian people were not bystanders in the changes occurring in their country. The famous team of George Carmack, Skookum Jim, and Dawson Charlie showed that Indian people could participate in the tiny local economy in many different ways; they were not solely dependent on trapping and the traders' prices. Of course it was these three men who made the Klondike discovery in August, 1896, and made an unknown part of the continent into a household word.

On the eve of that discovery scarcely a thousand Americans, Canadians, and other nationalities had joined about three thousand Indian people in the Yukon Territory.[14] They took meat and fur without restriction by any laws then in practice. Since these four thousand people were scattered along the Yukon River for hundreds of miles and nowhere concentrated to more than a few hundred, the effects of their wildlife use must have been insignificant, except in the immediate vicinity of mining villages. This was the situation in 1894 when Inspector Constantine arrived. If he heard reports of scarcity or waste of the region's game resources, his report would have mentioned it. In theory, the new *Unorganized Territories Game Preservation Act* had application over the district and some effort could have been made to enforce it; but the largest concern to Constantine and his superiors was the risk of an American pre-emption of the Territory, for they far outnumbered the British subjects.[15] Collection of local taxes and gold royalties would take precedence over game laws by any system of priorities, especially given the cheerful anarchy of American mining communities and their resentment of any outside interference.[16]

It was the Klondike Gold Rush that made the Yukon famous in 1897. Millions of people heard about it; hundreds of thousands had their lives affected by it, and tens of thousands actually reached the Yukon Territory. The western half of the continent seized upon an idea of fabulous wealth available for the taking, and mobilized in a logistical equivalent of a small war. Several circumstances gave the Klondike its global fame. Its streams were incredibly rich in gold. North America was then suffering through an economic depression. New technology in newsprint and presses and their integration with telegraph and expanding telephone networks combined to make the Klondike stampede the world's first media event. The public seemed prepared for the news in some way through the pulp writings of Horatio Alger and many others and the burgeoning interest in the great outdoors. These made a persuasive combination out of a thirst for adventure in unexplored places and the virtuous example of self-reliance and pluck.

While the actual discovery of gold was in August, 1896, vast distances and the approach of winter kept the information bottled up. But when the new Minister of the Interior Clifford Sifton took up his appointment in Ottawa in November, a notice of the discovery was on his desk.[17] Otherwise, only rumors of the discovery flowed down the coast to the southern cities. It was not until a shipload of miners, with their bulging, heavy suitcases, reached San Francisco in July of 1897, that the continent began to take notice. Throughout that year thousands of people made their plans to go and started moving to the departure ports of Seattle and Victoria. Few actually reached the new town of Dawson City at the mouth of the Klondike before the arrival of winter. In the spring of 1898 the Stampeders poured into the Territory in an avalanche. By midsummer over thirty thousand crammed into Dawson City, and had they not been required to bring a year's worth of supplies with them, the food problem would have been acute. As it was, there was soon a thriving market for local game meat.

Given Dawson City's distance from major cities to the south, it was natural that it inhabitants relied on game for their fresh meat. Moose were then abundant in the valley bottoms in winter. Twice a year in its annual cycle a herd numbering thousands of barren ground caribou crossed the Yukon River close to Dawson City, passing only a few miles from the gold creeks. There were waterfowl every spring and fall, and grouse and ptarmigan year-round. There were occasional rabbits, mountain sheep, and goats and abundant salmon from the Yukon River. Some domestic meat could be purchased. Even before 1896, entrepreneurs drove numbers of cattle over passes from the coast and barged them down to mining camps, but this meat had to compete with game in the market place. In those days and in the following decades the sale of game meat was customary in the Yukon.

The invasion of the Yukon and its effects on wildlife became a concern to the North West Mounted Police. Writing from Dawson in January, 1899, Inspector Harper reported:

> A great many moose were brought to town during the past summer and sold from butcher shops in town, also lately, ptarmigan, grouse and rabbits have been abundantly exhibited in front of the various restaurants and butcher shops. The Game Ordinance was not enforced here last summer. This I think was a mistake as if the quantity of moose that was brought in last summer is brought in every year very few will shortly exist in the country.[18]

Other detachments reported that the Yukon River valley had been devastated by fires deliberately or carelessly set by the Stampeders. Indians complained that the game had been driven off and that they had to travel up to twenty miles to "catch" their meat. Harper thought there was a general, widespread decline in game and fur bearers.

The police concern was not necessarily motivated by some new conservation ethic; it was the worry of an administrator. Yukon Indians depended on game and fur for their maintenance and well-being. The police knew from long experience on the prairies that when Indian people had been deprived of their traditional sources of food and staples for trade such as the buffalo, their dependence on the government for goods, clothing, supplies, and medicines increased greatly. The government's policies towards Indians were entrusted to the police and each detachment carried them out using requisitioned supplies from its own stores and its own budget. If the Yukon's wildlife received no protection then the government could expect greatly increased costs in administration solely because of the Indian's destitute situation. Of course the administrative aspects were only one reason why they were concerned about game; it is reasonable to assume that policemen posted to the Yukon would have been appalled simply by overkilling of game. Memories of the plains buffalo lingered back at their

headquarters in Regina. Above all they appreciated the degree
to which a frontier settlement relied on wild animals, and that
settlement had to survive the vicissitudes and short life of a gold
rush. Despite Harper's report the Ottawa government did not order
the federal game act to be enforced or introduce a new one. It
ignored the matter for eighteen months, then handed the responsibility to the new government in the Yukon Territory.

In an amendment to the 1898 *Yukon Act* passed in July, 1900,
the Laurier administration at Ottawa granted the Yukon Territory
legislative powers over its wildlife resources.[19] The same amendment permitted Yukon residents to elect two representatives to
the Territorial Council and exercise this limited measure of self-
government. The election was held in the fall and the new
members took their oath of office in December, 1900. One of the
first items of business to be considered by the new council was
An Ordinance for the Preservation of Game in the Yukon Territory,
enacted in January, 1901.[20] It received no comment in the local
press. Less than a year later it was up for revisions. In fact, the
Territorial Council or Legislature has revised or amended the
Yukon's game laws at virtually every session of the Territorial
Council or Legislature since that date. In the Yukon, the game
laws serve as a weather vane of attitudes towards wildlife.

This first game law was a close copy of the *Unorganized Territories' Game Preservation Act* of 1984. This resemblance soon
disappeared. Constant revisions beginning in the fall of 1901
reflected changing attitudes, changing economics, and a stubborn
defense of the Territorial Council's jurisdiction. Sometimes the
amendments seemed reckless and frivolous, other times far-
sighted; but for fifty years the changes were frequently at odds
with the opinions about the Yukon's wildlife held by nonresidents.
Their concerns were the prevention of wastage of a valuable
resource and the recognition and protection of the economic value
of wildlife through trophy hunting, fur farming, and trapping. The
law reflected the imposition of changed attitudes which were
essentially cultural in origin. These included restrictions on
shooting female big game, making only selected parts of the Ordinance apply to Indian people while exempting them from others,
imposing licensing requirements, and changing the law in response
to cycles of "wolf hating." The analysis which follows cannot be
more than a subjective treatment because animal populations and

harvests were generally unknown at the time the amendments were made, nor can it be a study in the effectiveness of game management methods; however the law does reveal something about Yukon society and the role of wildlife.

The 1901 Ordinance set annual limits of six caribou, two moose, two sheep, and two goats per hunter, with penalties of up to $500 for exceeding those limits, or killing out of season. Later in the same year Council raised the limit for moose to six, lowered the penalty, but added another of $500 for wasting meat. That amount was the equivalent to a hundred days' wages.[21] Over the next decade the amendments recognized the appearance of big game hunting and a significant "outside" attitude towards big game. Nonresident hunters required a license at $100 each. The bag limit for moose returned to two per year where it was to remain for decades. Most significant was the year-round prohibition on shooting female big game, based on the assumption—a dubious one for moose—that one male will impregnate several females.[22] Such a provision had been in the game laws of other jurisdictions for many years, for example since 1894 in Nova Scotia.[23] However it caused bewilderment among Yukon Indians hunters and was largely ignored.[24] Another amendment at this time was a constitutional oddity: no trophies could leave the Yukon without a permit. This seems clearly *ultra vires* or beyond the Yukon's powers as a government, yet it was a common law in the provinces, designed to prevent trafficking in heads and horns. In the rest of the country, wildlife had become a subject of some interest at long last, and the demand for animal heads reflected their status as objects of a new cult.

Outside the Yukon, interest in wildlife matters gained momentum. The last wild passenger pigeon fell victim to an American hunter in 1900; a survivor languished in a zoo until 1914. During that interval birds held the attention of conservationists while a more general interest in nature and "the great out-of-doors" made the climate for legal changes much more favorable to conservation measures. An important but short-lived conservation issue brought these changes about. Women's fashions in the 1880s and 1890s favored birds' wings, feathers, and indeed whole carcasses on hats and other garments. A movement to stop traffic in the feathers and plumes of endangered birds increased its efforts, even while writers like Ernest Thompson Seton and others exerted an enormous influence on children using anthropomorphic (animals-as-people) stories. Conservationists used photographs of bird kill-ings as devastatingly effective propaganda, and shrugged off gibes from the milliners and feather importers who showed that many of the same class fighting the issue killed enormous numbers of birds while sport hunting.[25] Clearly the emotional nature of the debate was exploited by the conservationists: an air of righteous-ness surrounded them. The Victorian sense of fatalism about nature and animal extinctions had been broken by a public interest taking precedence over market forces. With bird protec-tion legislation assured, attention passed to the problems of migratory waterfowl and insectivorous birds. In 1916, the United States, Mexico, and Great Britain, acting for Canada, enacted a treaty protecting these birds and setting hunting seasons in each country.

This treaty had been anticipated by Canada for several years. In 1910 the government created the Committee on Conservation under the chairmanship of the former Interior Minister Clifford Sifton.[26] Its terms of reference were "to take into consideration all questions which may be brought to its notice relating to the conservation and better utilization of the natural resources of Canada." It had a seven member subcommittee on fisheries, game, and fur-bearing animals, but the full committee's interests were more with water and land use decisions than with animals and birds, and the subcommittee did not meet in the first year.[27]

A sudden increase in fur prices in 1912 made the subcommit-tee take an interest in fur farms, but not until the American in-itiative in its Federal Migratory Bird Law of 1913 did wildlife mat-ters become an important concern as a political issue in Canada.[28] After the 1916 bird treaty was signed, Canada formed an Advisory Board on Wildlife Protection, with a mandate to ad-vise the government on treaty matters and to suggest changes in the *Northwest Game Act* of 1906, the new title of the amended federal game act of 1894.[29] Five years later, its secretary, C. Gor-don Hewitt, announced in a speech that the Dominion Government, through its Advisory Board on Wildlife Protection, was responsible for game in the Northwest Territories, the Domi-nion Parks, and in the Yukon.[30] Had this been known in Yukon, it might have raised eyebrows. As it was, the only concern peo-ple in the Yukon had about wildlife that they cared to tell others about was that the Migratory Birds Treaty and federal legislation which followed, prevented them from hunting waterfowl in the spring and late summer. Even while the rest of the continent became enthusiastic about preserving birds and animals, and opposed to market hunting, the Yukon took more interest in the economic possibilities of its wildlife.

In 1920 the Yukon Territorial Council approved a number of significant changes in the Game Ordinance. The degree to which these changes were influence by the Advisory Board on Wildlife Protection is not clear today, as the archival record examined is incomplete; but for the next two decades the Board was to be a close, even meddlesome observer of Yukon wildlife matters. The new Ordinance encompassed the fur industry for the first time and set closed season on the animals. It extended year-round protection to little brown cranes, sandhill cranes, whooping cranes, swans, and curlews. It granted to the commissioner, or "governor" of the Territory powers to license guides, assistant guides, and camp helpers for the increasingly important big game industry, and to license game market hunters and meat dealers as well. Until 1920, Yukon Indians were exempt from game laws. The Ordinance changed this by making prohibitions against selling meat without a license, using poison, exporting hides, and killing females apply to Indians, including the penalty provisions. Enforcement of the law continued with the federal police.

One might believe that such extensive changes would have provided wide public discussion. In fact, the game laws are scarcely mentioned in the Territory's two newspapers until the 1940s. The few thousand adults living in the Yukon virtually ignored the game laws. Bag limits, seasons, and restrictions on killing females were forgotten by Indians and non-Indians because they could avoid detection. If individual officers of the North West Mounted Police—later named the Royal Canadian Mounted Police—had decided to enforce the law, they could have done so only by extensive travelling and surveillance, and at the risk of losing whatever esteem they held in those communities. Officers and their families at the many small communities along the Yukon River remained at their posts for many years and they knew the game conditions there as well as anyone. If current practices, even if contrary to law, had no effect on game populations, there was no need to enforce that law, particularly with Indians. The only exception to this might be the restriction on killing of females, which the police often enforced, sometimes harshly.

The police had another role at the time which reveals something of their role in the district around their detachment. The 1920 Ordinance required "Game Guardian Returns" to be completed quarterly with the hunter's name, the kind, number, and sex of animal taken and the place and date of killing. After 1921 the number of completed forms diminished as officers went from quarterly to annual returns. Numbers of animals reported killed seemed to decline and become more vague as the 1920s wore on; finally the reporting stopped. The Yukon's small population and small government budget when set in a vast, unpopulated area full of game led to a haphazard and finally, nonexistent system of record keeping. Only the license fees mattered: after all, the police obtained a commission on their collection. The Game Ordinance of 1920 and the amendments which followed in the next decade reflected not so much a desire to preserve the Yukon's wildlife, but that community's response to requests from others to bring those laws into line with the attitudes of the rest of the continent. The senior government held powers to disallow any Yukon ordinance—indeed it abolished the Yukon Council at one point. By 1920, the Yukon's commissioner and Council had learned the necessity of cooperation with Ottawa in order to ensure their very survival as a political entity.

Requests, comments, and criticisms about wildlife matters came into the Yukon from three directions; from the senior officials in the Department of the Interior in Ottawa, from "sister" jurisdictions in Alaska and British Columbia, and from individuals appealing directly to the Yukon commissioner. A word about this man and his role may clarify the chain of authority. The commissioner was the one-man executive of the Yukon with much the same powers as a provincial premier or state governor. He sought the advice and consent of the elected council for approval of his budget, tax measures, and so forth; but the Yukon was not a "province" in the full Canadian sense any more than it is today. Its council or legislature could not introduce money bills, or pass any laws concerning land use, forests, fish, or minerals; but it did control local issues such as wildlife. Consequently it was more than a little possessive about these powers. The result was that the commissioner had a very difficult role as mediator between the elected council and the senior bureaucrats in the Department of the Interior. The commissioner was an appointee of the minister and therefore his employee, but he had to live with local political realities and bear the brunt of all differences in perceptions and attitudes between Yukon residents and the outside world.

An example of each kind of influence could illustrate the reactions of the commissioner and Council. In 1928, RCMP officers, acting on direct instructions from the commissioner, began collecting $100 per year license fees from "non-resident" Indians normally living in central Alaska or in the Mackenzie valley, who by long tradition hunted and trapped in the Yukon.[31] For the first time, Alaskan Indians from Fort Yukon, who normally travelled upriver to the great muskrat areas in Old Crow Flats, were made aware that the Alaska-Yukon boundary had real significance. The reason why this policy change came about is not evident, but people in Old Crow may have complained about others coming in and taking what they saw as their own game and fur. The collections soon met with dispute. Indians at Fort McPherson on the Mackenzie side complained about paying for hunting and trapping licenses. The RCMP detachment at Fort McPherson reported this to the Commissioner George I. McLean. He consulted with members of the Territorial Council, then instructed the police to enforce the law. The reaction of the Department of the Interior is illuminating. The superintendent general of Indian Affairs acted on complaints from the Anglican Church and his own field staff and wrote a long letter to the director for the Yukon and Northwest Territories. The deputy minister added his concerns to a growing file of letters and telegrams on the subject received by Commissioner McLean. The director for Yukon Affairs, O.S. Finnie, was nominally McLean's superior. In September 1929, he made a charter flight by float plane to Aklavik, Fort McPherson, Dawson City, Whitehorse, and Carcross. Considering the aircraft of the day, such a trip must have constituted high adventure. Finnie interviewed Commissioner McLean and visited with each of the Yukon Territorial councillors in their constituencies, specifically to discuss the Peel River Indians and the licensing provision of the law. By the time he left he had general agreement that the law would not be enforced against Northwest Territories Indian peoples. Perhaps Finnie used some veiled threat of withdrawal of federal funding or disallowance of the Yukon ordinance to obtain agreement, but the Yukon's authority to pass game laws was not weakened.[32]

Alaska was another influence on Yukon wildlife policy. The governor of Alaska was a frequent correspondent with the Yukon on wildlife matters because of similar geography and shared borders. It could be noted here that relations between the two territories were much closer in those decades immediately after the Gold Rush than they are today. In June 1919, Governor Thomas Riggs asked Yukon Commissioner George F. Henderson to assist Alaska in enforcing its closed seasons on beaver. He was concerned about Alaskan beaver being bootlegged into the Yukon and sold as Canadian beaver, but he also raised the matter of the Migratory Birds Treaty and its unfair treatment for northern residents. He proposed that some joint licensing system be used for areas near their mutual borders so that the big game kill would not be duplicated and therefore doubled in its effects on game populations.[33] The Yukon responded by maintaining its closed season on beaver in 1920 and by agreeing with the Alaskans' objections to the bird treaty, but the Yukon Council did not cooperate on the matter of hunting licenses. Later though, in 1939, cooperation between the two territories was to result in a joint patrol of the border area on a search for violators of wolf bounty regulations.[34] The third outside influence on the Yukon's game laws came from the many hunters who came to the Territory each summer and found something wanting in the way the wildlife was managed.

The Territorial Council made a number of changes to the Game Ordinance between 1920 and 1947, the year of its next major revision. These twenty-seven years included a time when trapping made the largest single contribution to the Territory's economy after gold mining. In fact, because the federal government regulated Yukon mining and collected all royalties, trapping could be said to be the major source of locally-generated earnings for the Yukon administration in those years. The value of production averaged about $300,000 per year from 1920 to 1947, with peaks in 1928, 1945, and 1946 of over $600,000 per year.[35] Yukon furs were more valuable relative to those of other jurisdictions; less than one percent of Canada's fur production in wild skins came from the Yukon, but their cash value represented over three percent of the Canadian total during the twenties. The

Territorial Government increased its regulation of both the fur trade and the activities of trappers. With a decline in fur prices which came in the late forties, the government's interest in wildlife passed to big game hunting where it was to remain for another thirty years.

The Second World War ended nearly forty years of isolation in the Yukon Territory. The Alaska Highway brought technological changes, an irrevocable population increase and an end to the Yukon's cultural equilibrium between Indians and non-Indians and its unique attitudes to wildlife. In the twenty years between 1921 and 1941 the population increased by merely ten percent. A continous labor shortage allowed Indians to participate as much or as little as they liked in the wage economy, and they had the alternatives of trapping, big game guiding, or even market hunting and fishing to earn cash. While in practice there may have been some discrimination between Indians and non-Indians, there were no incidents to foster ill-will; in fact, both halves of the Yukon community depended upon each other in a sort of cultural symbiosis—separate, distinct, and interdependent. Both the Indian and non-Indian communities regarded the wildlife resources as virtually without limit and drew from the resource with a confidence borne from decades of use. The overall attitude was complacent. It was to be a poor one for the coming decade.

The Alaska Highway brought literally tens of thousands of men to the Yukon between 1942 and 1943. The roads they built made a permanent change in the Yukon's culture and landscape, starting with the displacement of river traffic and immigration to Whitehorse and new, smaller communities along the highway. The roads placed severe hunting pressure on wildlife adjacent to the right-of-way, despite later efforts to enforce no shooting zones on either side. The Alaska Highway had another more lasting effect on the Yukon. Alberta and Edmonton replaced the Yukon's traditional links with British Columbia merchants and professional associations. The new Alberta hegemony carried with it attitudes towards wildlife which were quite different from Yukon custom. A group of recent arrivals organized the Yukon Fish and Game Association in 1945. In two years they were literally drafting the new game laws. A general antipathy towards Indians and traditional game use appeared. New attitudes included a seemingly irrational hatred of wolves, a desire to import Alberta animals such as elk and bison into the Yukon, reductions in bag limits, increased enforcement, and finally, endorsing for a licensing system for big game hunting which prevented Indians from participating as managers. New attitudes and new laws appeared exactly at a time when fur prices suffered a greater decline than had ever been experienced, even including the period of the Depression of 1929-32. In the space of merely two to three years, Yukon Indians lost both their economic mainstay and their influence on wildlife policy. The change was permanent: the days of equilibrium were over.

For forty years, the Yukon's stagnant economy, small population, and abundant wildlife allowed it to go its own way in making and enforcing its game laws. Wildlife formed an essential part of its economy. In this respect, it was unlike any other provincial jurisdiction in Canada. Similarly, the isolation of the Yukon protected its citizens from the changing attitudes towards wildlife. Practices or manners of wildlife use continued to be followed decades after they had been made illegal elsewhere for reasons of game conservation. Even so, the Territory's administration showed a continuing interest in the way other jurisdictions managed their game. Those who had reason to question the Yukon way of doing things seemed to be unaware of the importance of wildlife in the society as a livelihood, as a source of government revenues and as a local staple. Outsiders had the expectation that Yukon laws would be uniform with those of other jurisdictions. This difference in attitude persisted for over forty years, until the completion of the Alaska Highway. Improved communications ended the isolation and therefore the distinct attitude towards game.

3

Big Game: Heroes and Losers

The big game hunter poses an interesting problem for the would-be social historian. He is regarded with equivocal attitudes by both local residents and conservationists; they rely on his wealth and influence and value his friendship, yet they are uncomfortable with his enjoyment of killing and his frequent wastage of meat and hides. Despite the residents' objections to trophy hunters, they do obtain the short term benefits of wages and expenditures in the economy. They learn to rely on the hunter's money. Conservationists have a similar, uncomfortable choice. Those who would object to the wasteful destruction of the animals might find themselves in an uneasy alliance with hunters because of similarities in their desires to protect wildlife, for the hunters usually have money, political power, and hold a lively interest in conservation matters. The hunter is a twentieth century phenomenon, born out of the Edwardian fascination with the great outdoors; and yet his roots are ancient, his motivations almost mystical in their intensity.

One way of understanding these big game hunters is through what they wrote about their experiences. It may be that the hunters, or sportsmen as they styled themselves, experienced changes in the way they regarded the sport and that those changes ultimately came to bear on the animals. In the nineteenth century, the moralist and historian Lord Acton wrote:

> The exercise of the chase is, in truth, so noble in itself that the greatest monarchs of the earth have authorized it by their example, in all ages it hath occupied the leisure of heroes themselves; with them the pleasures of the chase succeeded the toils of war; it is the proper school for the soldier, it accustoms him to fatigue, it prepares him for assault, it sustains and seconds the courage of the man, in it is found the best relaxation from the cares and business of life.[1]

Perhaps his thoughts about hunting reflect the beginning of a heroic and romantic perception of the contrasts posed by "civilized" man in the wilderness which was to bloom about the time of the Klondike stampede and find expression in the writings of Jack London, Robert Service, and others. This ideal man could indeed conquer the wilderness, but there was no shame in admitting that it was far from easy. Theodore Roosevelt wrote in his introduction to the 1904 edition of *The Master of Game*:

> The chase is the best of all national pastimes and this is none the less because, like every other pastime it is a mere source of weakness if carried on in an unhealthy manner or to an excessive degree or under artificial conditions. . . . It is a good thing for a man to be forced to show self-reliance, resourcefulness in an emergency, willingness to endure fatigue and hunger and at need to face risk.[2]

All sentiments of the Klondike experience are expressed and they include the strong appeal of camaraderie, which was to be one of the greatest pleasures of the hunting party for the next few decades. As for the hunting itself, it became a display of exactness, of control, in which the animal's life was unimportant. English writer and hunter Nevill A.D. Armstrong wrote in 1937:

> But apart from the fact that unnecessary killing tends to eliminate these splendid animals, slaughter is not sport. It is the stalking of a particularly fine head and bringing it down, perhaps with a difficult shot, that provides the thrill which makes the long arduous and sometimes dangerous excursions into the wilderness so well worth while.[3]

Finally an end point is reached in the hunter who has mastered the wilderness and fallen victim to his own vaulting ambition and need for self-expression. This last quotation is from a book by James Bond, written in 1947. Bond was to play a prominent role in Yukon wildlife politics after that time.

> I was delighted with the thought of killing two maybe three grizzlies in one day. It was apparent to me that there were too many grizzlies here for any good. The country would be better off with few of them.[4]

In contrast with the changing attitudes suggested by the above quotations, Yukon residents maintained quite a different one. For over forty years they saw wildlife as a convenience, a utility. There were several reasons for this. Moose and caribou were abundant. Their meat was nearly a substitute for bread in both Indian and non-Indian homes. Of course Yukon residents were isolated from the rest of the continent and therefore were relatively indifferent to the spread of the conservation ethic. Even though the Yukon community was a small one, it had full legislative control over wildlife from the beginning of its administration. The community was half Indian, half non-Indian. Because many families of mixed marriage acted as catalysts, the community was a culturally stable one with no deep economic disparity between its parts. Scarcely anything happened to alter the relationship between the community and the land.

In the twenties and thirties, Yukon Indians as a group were virtually on an equal footing with non-Indians. Trapping, abundant opportunities for wage employment on the Yukon River steamboats or cutting cordwood fuel for them, commercial fishing on the lakes, fox farming, and work as guides and wranglers were among the choices of livelihood available to the Indian man. The mixed marriages had a distinct role in building a homogeneous community. People related to these marriages became guides or agents for the expanded big game business, or served as fur buyers or traders. But ties to the Indian culture weakened through the policy of the Indian Affairs branch of the federal government to place Indian children in residential schools where use of their parents' language was discouraged. The government, the Anglican Church, and white society in Dawson City and Whitehorse fostered a dual perception of the Indian person. Ideally, either he or she became closely associated with European or white society by learning to read, becoming an entrepreneur, and so forth, or he remained a "bush Indian." Yet life in the small communities and along the river, as well as the mixed marriages, constantly broke down that class separation, and pulled the community together. Beyond this view of things one should not form an idyllic picture of this isolated, stable society. Aged or ill Indian people were destitute and utterly dependent upon the RCMP and the Indian Agents for food and medical supplies. Tuberculosis was endemic; influenza destroyed whole families. Intense feuds between families were common, and while they stopped short of violence and murder, the feuds crossed Indian-white cultural lines and had important effects on wildlife matters. These were some of the features of Yukon society into which came dozens of sports hunters before 1942.

The big game or trophy hunter believed he was entitled to kill his limit of each kind of animal as set under the Game Ordinance because he had paid for an expensive license to do just that. "Ownership" of the animals and traditional hunting rights to a given area were not his concern; the government had guaranteed his rights with his license. It fell to the guides themselves to deal with these matters and to act as go-betweens. The guides hired local men to help them and often the assistant guides, camp helpers, and wranglers were related to them by marriage or other kinship ties. The hunters did shoot a large number of animals; but the meat might not necessarily be wasted. Often it was dried and cached on the spot for winter trapline used by those same men. Thus the hunting party could serve several purposes, trophies for the hunter, license revenues for the government, wages for the guides, and meat for a winter's trapping. Under these conditions the big game hunting party might not necessarily disrupt the meat and trapping economy of an area; in fact, it might even enhance it by providing the capital needed to start and maintain a trapline. The hunters themselves were wealthy men and free with their money. Typically they often were intensely interested in the region's natural features apart from the size and abundance of its trophy animals. Guides and hunters became friends and often kept up a correspondence for years, or the hunter returned again and again. These roles for the guides and hunters were to persist until the building of the Alaska Highway. They show that the hunter was not an intruder, but a guest who paid his way.

The second important factor in shaping the Yukon attitude towards big game hunting was the thriving traffic in game meat. The numerous butcher shops which sold game meat in Dawson City have been mentioned. At first the police were concerned over the effect market hunting might have on the game resource, but since the town's population declined rapidly, such concerns were not expressed in later years. Butchers sold every variety of wild meat: caribou, moose, sheep, goat, rabbits, and birds such as ptarmigan, grouse, ducks, geese, and swans. Game meat was freely available from 1897 to 1947, decades after the practice had been made illegal elsewhere on the continent. Market hunters received nearly all the blame for the extinction of the passenger pigeon and the buffalo. The idea took root early in the 1900s that to sell wild animal or bird products such as meat, horns, hides, or feathers would lead to the extinction of those animals through man's insatiable greediness for money. Few attitudes about game, with the possible exception of the prohibition on shooting female animals, have been as deeply ingrained in the continent's thinking as the belief that sale of game meat leads to extermination. Yukon people would have considered that idea to be absurd, yet they had difficulty in explaining that confidence about animal populations to outsiders, who continued to see the matter in their own, continental perspective.

From the beginning of the Gold Rush, game had to compete with cattle, hogs, and domestic sheep in a *laissez-faire* market. Before 1900, beef came to Dawson City in two ways, either driven overland and barged down to Dawson for slaughter, or carried frozen in special refrigerated steamboats on a long voyage upriver from St. Michael on the Bering Sea. After 1900, the new White

Pass and Yukon Route lowered freight rates substantially. In 1906, prices were 40 cents per pound for pork and 50 cents for beef-steak.[5] By contrast, moose or caribou sold for an average of 30 cents per pound. In a report for 1904, the North West Mounted Police listed Dawson City's meat imports as 2428 cattle, 3154 sheep, and 245 hogs.[6] The same report did not reveal the town's fast-dwindling population, for such information had been kept un-published since 1901.[7] However it did reveal that 3437 people left the Yukon in that year. Since the Territory's population was published as 27,200 in 1901, those who took the trouble to ex-trapolate that rate of emigration might have predicted the Yukon to be empty of people in 1909; in fact, the 1911 population was 8500. With these qualifications on population data and meat im-ports, one can estimate how much moose and caribou meat was consumed in the town of Dawson City in 1904, and gauge the impact of market hunting on local game populations.

The unknown factor is Dawson City's population in 1904. It can be approached through meat consumption, however, and com-pared with an estimate from the known census data. According to the *Canada Year Book* for 1974, this meat-eating country con-sumed 140 pounds per person, per year, carcass weight.[8] Given the adult nature of Dawson's population in the mining camps, a reasonable figure might have been 200 pounds per year. Now the meat imports of 1904 can be calculated to equal approximately 1,200,000 pounds of meat.[9] Dividing that by 200 pounds per per-son per year gives a population of 6000; but by interpolating be-tween known population figures and applying the rate of decline reported by the police, the Dawson population would be closer to 9000 and not 6000, in 1904. Either those 3000-odd "extra" peo-ple ate no meat, or they ate game. If we assume the latter, then 3000 people eating 200 pounds of meat each, or 600,000 pounds of game meat for the year, can be translated into moose and caribou carcasses taken into Dawson or the mining camps.

One more questionable assumption has to be made; that the meat taken was half caribou and half moose. A dressed moose can yield 500 pounds of meat, a caribou 130. By splitting that figure of 6000 pounds and applying those weights per animal one can conclude that in Dawson City, in 1904, some 600 moose and 2300 caribou were used as local food. That seems to be a large number of animals; and yet it is likely a *low* estimate of the total kill. If the population was more than 9000, or if the people there used more than 200 pounds of meat each per year, the estimate would have to rise. But the greatest uncertainty lies in the interval between the animals in the wild and their delivery to the cookhouses and meat markets, and the woodsheds of those who shot their own meat. If the hunters shot more than they killed, or killed more than they hauled out, or hauled out something less than 500 pounds per moose or 130 pounds per caribou—if these and the previous uncertainties were all to apply, then the estimate of 600 moose and 2300 caribou in 1904 could well be doubled.

Some things are clear by this estimate. The number of animals is very large indicating that a vast area had to be hunted, with the carcasses being freighted into Dawson City. Caribou might have been taken closer to the town, because the Fortymile caribou herd passed close by on its annual migration, so the numbers taken may have been larger than the above estimate implies. Yet police reports make no special mention of market hunters in the years after the Gold Rush, nor were they concerned about their take. License records of market hunters during the twenties show that a majority of them were Indian men: obviously non-Indian hunters found the work unrewarding. The sale of game meat was very much a part of the Yukon scene.

The prevailing opinion, which saw market hunting as necessary and desirable and posing no risk to game populations, was at odds with the opinions of big game hunters who came into the Territory every summer. Local people not involved with the guiding industry may have felt a lingering dislike or contempt for sportsmen, much as any isolated, provincial populace might feel contempt for the well-travelled, better educated, or more "civilized"— the typical sportsman of the early decades was all of these things. Outsiders had no influence over Yukon opinion on the matter of market hunting.

The description and quotations which opened this chapter provide a glimpse of the sportsman-hunter between 1900 and the 1940s, while the information on market hunting and the Yukon's society in that period conveys something of the situation the hunters found when they arrived there. The balance of the chapter can now explore some of the personalities and events surrounding perhaps the best years of the Yukon guiding industry. Sources for this account rely on several books written by the hunters about their Yukon experiences and on the verbal history of those who remember them.

F.C. Selous was one of the first men to hunt in the Yukon and write about his experiences.[10] He was an Englishman who had travelled and hunted in Africa for many years before coming to the Yukon in 1904. In August of that year he joined a party in Dawson City consisting of J.B. Tyrrell, the well-known Canadian geologist, F.T. Congdon, lawyer and Yukon commissioner, Judge Dugas of the Yukon Supreme Court, and two other local businessmen. Later this party joined forces with three Americans famous in the "outdoors" world, Charles Sheldon, hunter and author, Wilfred Osgood, biologist and naturalist, and Carl Rungius, then becoming established as a wildlife artist.

Selous's party spent the hunting season on the upper Macmillan River, a large tributary of the Pelly. Reading his narrative one soon becomes uncomfortable with the numbers of animals killed. What is significant are his comments on market hunting. He complained that 1500 caribou were shot by market hunters in the Klondike River basin in the winter of 1903-04 and that the same hunters took moose from the Macmillan district down four hundred miles of river by raft to supply the Dawson market. That number of caribou does not appear to be an exaggeration when compared to the earlier estimate. Selous believed that sportsmen and prospectors posed no threat to game, unlike the market hunters and Indians, whom he regarded as a menace. On this trip he renewed his acquaintance with Nevill A.D. Armstrong, who was gold mining in the area and later had similar things to say about market hunting in the Yukon. Charles Sheldon wrote his own book about his Yukon adventures.[11] He candidly admitted killing seven Dall mountain sheep in a week while on other pages wrote about market hunting in the same manner as Selous. Both men describe leaving a kill "taking as much meat as we could carry" or words to that effect: the usage or abandonment of game meat is an issue skated over with deceptive speed in these kinds of books.

Sheldon and Selous's party evidently attracted some local interest and scrutiny. RNWMP Superintendent Snyder in Dawson City wrote in his annual report for 1904:

I would strongly recommend the imposition of a heavy tax on sportsmen from other countries, coming into the Yukon and hunting moose, sheep and like game, there having been an enormous slaughter of both moose and sheep in the upper Yukon this past year, and I feel sure that both moose and sheep will become extinct unless the Game Ordinance is framed more closely to protect them.[12]

Changes to the Game Ordinance did not include big game hunting until 1908. Selous's book implied that Alaska was closed altogether to big game hunting by nonresidents in 1904.[13] In 1908, however, Alaska licensed nonresidents for the first time.[14] The Yukon followed Alaska's lead when it instituted licenses for nonresidents at $100 each—an important sum of money in those days—for it changed its law in the same year. The intent may well have been to prevent competition between the two regions which had similiar game resources and a need for cash. Neither Selous nor Sheldon hired guides, and both did their own "out-fitting," assembling all the supplies and equipment that were necessary for several months' stay in the bush. The business potential of guiding began to be appreciated after these initial hunts, but guides did not need to be licensed until 1920, and nonresidents were not put under any obligation to hire those licensed guides before 1933. The early years of the industry were quite unregulated; the later years, as we shall see, were characterized by an excess of regulation.

Beginning before the First World War, sportsmen began to take notice of the area adjacent to the White River in the southwestern Yukon. Prospectors moved into the district first, by travelling up through the mountainous region north and east of the fabulous Kennicott copper mine near McCarthy, Alaska. They crossed the passes and glaciers dividing that region from the Chisana, Tanana, and White Rivers of the Yukon watershed. On the Canadian side, Burwash Creek on Kluane Lake had been worked for its placer gold since 1904 and settlements sprang up there and at Silver City, on the shore of Kluane Lake. The Territorial Government built a one hundred and twenty-mile wagon road from Whitehorse to Silver City as the mining region developed. A major discovery in the Chisana district started a miniature gold rush to the headwaters of that river. The Whitehorse-Silver City road carried some of the freight to the district, as the only other route was over a dangerous pack trail through the ice fields separating it from McCarthy.

Miners and packers returning to the towns reported on the abundance of Dall sheep, the pure white, thin-horn mountain sheep peculiar to the mountains of Alaska and the Yukon. It soon became—and remains today—the continent's most sought-after trophy animal.

An American hunter and writer named Thomas Martindale travelled into the Kluane Lake area in the summer of 1912. According to his account, he learned about the hunting possibilities from Wilson Potter, a fellow member of the Poor Richard's Club of Philadelphia, who had hunted there in 1909.[15] Martindale hired Burwash men Thomas A. Dickson and the Jacquot brothers, Eugene and Louis, to serve as his guides. This is the earliest mention of these men who were to play such a large role in the Yukon's guiding business in coming decades. Martindale tended to depreciate efforts made by Dickson and the Jacquots in their long journey from Whitehorse to the Burwash area, as though he was used to better or more refined service from his guides. Seemingly, the men were just getting started in the guiding business and had not learned the guide's necessary arts of entertaining, catering, and flattering the vanities of big-city clients. Guiding was only a sideline to the men's usual livelihood of placer mining and trapping, but this changed in the next few years.

Dickson was a former member of the North West Mounted Police. He married an Indian woman and started a large family, some of whom maintained his interests in the guiding business for many years after his retirement. Louis and Eugene Jacquot were immigrants from Alsace, France, first to the United States, then to the Yukon and Burwash area. According to his son, Joe Jacquot, who stayed in the guiding business, Eugene learned his trade as a cook on American transcontinental trains. In fact, the quality of the cooking and skillful butchering and cooking of game meat in the camp was to become a point of pride with Yukon guides.

To those names can be added, A.R. (Shorty) Auston of Carcross, first mentioned as a guide in 1907 and according to some, the first Yukon guide; Morley Bones, an eccentric miner and fox farmer whose guiding efforts were dogged with near-disasters; Shorty Chambers, a fur buyer who may have grubstaked guides, especially the Dicksons; Jack Hayden, an American veteran of the Gold

Rush, who guided with Dickson; and Charlie Baxter, who was the best known of them all for many years, thanks to his advertising efforts. All these men were white men. Auston, Chambers, and Hayden had Indian wives and like Dickson, founded large families. To the same list can be added the names of the Indian men Johnnie Fraser, Paddy Smith, Albert Isaac, Frank Stick, Jimmy Kane, Bobby Kane, Jake Fred—all well-known men from the Southern Yukon. Other Indian men were undoubtedly involved at various times, but the writers never recorded the men's full names, and the verbal record today is often contradictory.

Seven years after the Martindale hunt, the White River district had become known as the best place to hunt Dall sheep on the continent. In July, 1919, Yukon Commissioner George P. Mackenzie received several letters introducing one B.B. Comer, manufacturer in Birmingham, Alabama, who was to be hunting in that district. Alabama senators Bankhead and Underwood thought it necessary to write to Mackenzie with their wish that he would extend to Comer "advice or courtesy" at need. Even President Woodrow Wilson's Interior Secretary Frank K. Lane saw fit to write on behalf of his good friend Comer, saying "I know you will be very happy to make his stay as pleasant and interesting as possible."[16] Such endorsements were common when nonresidents made license applications, as though it was necessary to show that the hunter could be trusted to behave in a sportsmanlike manner. However, many American politicians, museum curators, officers of hunting clubs, and others with such introductions made special requests to the commissioner to allow more animals to be taken than was permitted under the Game Ordinance; usually they were given this permission.

Comer's party shared the White River district that summer with at least two other parties, one outfitted by Charlie Baxter in Whitehorse, another by Morley Bones and the Jacquot brothers. West Virginia pharmacist and state senator G.O. Young described the Bones-Jacquot hunt in his book *Alaska Trophies Won and Lost.*[17] This book is easily the best account of a Yukon big game hunt, as Young had a keen eye for the details that can make such a book timeless and memorable. The three hunters in his party had an experience that they probably remembered for the rest of their lives; but they killed an enormous number of animals. Their total bag, taken on both sides of the Alaska-Yukon border, included seven moose, sixteen caribou, nineteen Dall sheep, nine goats and two grizzly bears. Comer's party and the third one likely killed equal numbers of animals, so quite possibly one hundred and fifty animals were killed in the six hundred square miles of mountainous country centered on the White River.

No one in the Yukon seemed alarmed by the growing number of animals taken each year because they were just becoming aware of the benefits the hunters could bring. In 1918, three nonresidents took out licenses. In 1919 there was a substantial jump to twenty-three then thirty in 1920. The number stayed at that level until the thirties, when it declined to less than ten for four years, before recovering.[18] Some possible consequences of loosely-regulated hunting were recognized by officers in the Department of the Interior in Ottawa three years before the first good year for guides, in 1919. The 1916 edition of the official Yukon guidebook contained the passage:

Of late years however game of all kinds has been very scarce in some localities, owing to the extensive killing carried on by those who hunt for the market offered by the mining camps. The Indians, having lately acquired high-powered magazine guns are responsible for a great deal of the slaughter as the average Indian who gets into a band of big game shoots as long as his cartridges hold out, whether he can use the meat or not. Head hunters who come into the country in search of fine specimens do a great deal of damage as they have been known after a day's hunting to leave enough meat to spoil on a hillside to supply a prospector with provisions for a whole winter.[19]

This quotation illustrates the metropolitan view of the Yukon's wildlife resources with its worries over market hunting and the actions of Indians, as well as the comments on big game hunters. Perhaps the guidebook was designed to embarrass the Yukon into changing its laws; however, no one there seemed alarmed, even when the big game kill took on alarming proportions. The attitude of Yukon politicians was clear. They wanted the business expanded.

The biggest obstacle to this new and lucrative business was outside the Yukon's jurisdiction. As early as 1906, Canada's customs laws prevented the export of deer and game birds, except as authorized by regulations.[20] The regulations allowed export of fewer animals than a hunter could legally take under Yukon law. A second matter was pointed out in a letter from the commissioner to the Yukon's member of Parliament in 1911, in which the commissioner explained that Yukon Indians had sold the heads of animals they killed for food.[21] Neither of these points could win any arguments in the conservation-conscious outside world. Territorial Council then sent a memorandum to the Governor-General in November, 1919 asking him to change the regulations and allow more trophies per hunter for export. The preamble to their petition said in part,

> AND WHEREAS there are vast quantities of game in the Yukon Territory, more than will ever be depleted by the present population or visiting hunters,

> AND WHEREAS the hunting of big game by nonresident hunters in the said territory is a source of considerable indirect revenue through monies spent locally in outfitting hunting expeditions, each party spending from $2000 to $3000 locally for supplies etc. in proportion to the size of the party . . .[22]

This petition failed, but Council solved the problem themselves three years later. They lowered the nonresident bag limit to coincide with the customs regulations.

In due course their petition would have passed to the new Dominion Advisory Board on Wildlife Protection.[23] The secretary must have taken more interest in the Yukon wildlife situation, for in May, 1920, he asked the commissioner to comment on two letters to the editor printed by the American magazine *Outdoor Life*, in February and May.[24] The February letter had been written by Charlie Baxter. It was similar to a letter he wrote the commissioner a month later, complaining about the game laws and the lack of enforcement. He charged that Indians had been killing animals only for the hides, then made the rather startling assertion that Indians had left piles of caribou and moose hair twenty to twenty-five feet high. Tom Dickson wrote the other letter, which sparked the interest of the Board secretary. Dickson made a similar complaint about Indians killing and wasting too much game. The commissioner's reply to the Board indicated that he did not take their letters seriously. Baxter was a frequent writer of rambling letters of complaint to the commissioner, while Dickson, smarting from a minor game ordinance conviction, bore a grudge against some Indians in his area. However the Advisory Board continued to keep a watchful eye on the Yukon's efforts to manage its wildlife.

The year 1920 marked a turning point in the Yukon attitude towards its big game animals. Instead of indifference, the attitude became protective, especially after reports of the 1920 season started to come in. Whitehorse Mining Recorder and Agent Frank G. Berton wrote to Commissioner Mackenzie in October, "I believe that the nonresident big game hunters have left between $50,000 and $75,000 in the Territory this season."[25] While this figure may be exaggerated, it shows something of the excitement the new business must have caused in Whitehorse, for it was money never before received by the small river community. A month after Berton's letter, Governor Thomas Riggs, Jr. of Alaska suggested a joint management scheme to protect the animals in the White River district which straddled the border between the two territories. He wrote:

> I shall be glad to request the Secretary of Agriculture to limit the bag of sheep in the White River to two sheep instead of three to conform with your law and suggest that it might be well to limit your caribou in this district to three instead of six. If you think better, I should be glad to refuse to issue a license to anyone holding a Yukon Territorial license provided this agreement too could be made reciprocal.

He concluded by noting that the animals crossed the borders freely and could not be considered as solely Canadian or American but were common property, therefore needing common laws.[26] Council later refused this quite reasonable request. Perhaps they thought that any curtailment of the hunting would limit business expansion in Whitehorse. A second reason would be that they believed the game to be so numerous it needed no extra protection. Commissioner Mackenzie offered to send to Riggs the names of hunters in the boundary area on the Yukon side, so that at least the Alaskans would know the situation. In the meantime, Council raised the nonresident license fee to $200, perhaps in an attempt to raise more government revenue.

In 1921, the Yukon's game laws and policies came under criticism from two different sources, both big game hunters and capable of wielding influence. First of these was Nevill A.D. Armstrong, an Englishman who divided his time between England, eastern Canada, and the Yukon Territory. Armstrong was held in little esteem in the Yukon, where he was known as the sort of miner who bought his gold from others before he left the country in the fall. He made a presentation to the Advisory Board on Wildlife Protection in Ottawa in November, 1920. Armstrong painted a bleak picture of wildlife conditions along the upper Macmillan River, on the basis of his third visit there in 1920. He said he saw no game in the area in marked contrast to what he saw on his 1914 trip. He blamed trappers, both Indian and non-Indian, based at a point called Russel Creek on the Macmillan, for shooting all the caribou and moose to feed their dog teams. Identifying himself as a prospector, he said,

> the question now arises: are the game laws in this country to be legislated in favour of the alien trapper, big game hunters and the Indians or in favour of the *bona fide* prospector?

Warming to his subject he said that two trappers and ten dogs consumed between ninety and one hundred moose in two and one half years, or about thirty moose per season. He concluded with the statement "One trapper in one year will exterminate more game than fifty wolves in five years."[27] In 1921 the Board sent a copy of the minutes of the meeting to Commissioner Mackenzie for his comments. RNWMP Superintendent R.E. Tucker in Dawson City wrote the Yukon's rebuttal to Armstrong's brief. As senior police officer in the Territory, he would have been better informed on the game situation than most. He disagreed with Armstrong's observations, saying that many fires had occurred during the summer of 1920 close to the area where Armstrong was camped. Those fires would have disturbed the game and driven the animals elsewhere. While he did not specifically disagree with Armstrong's assertion about trappers and the moose they killed, he took great exception to the remark about wolves. He said, "Armstrong's statement that one trapper in one year will exterminate more game than fifty wolves in five years is ridiculous and not worthy of serious consideration."

Some months after the Advisory Board received Tucker's memorandum, it wrote to Commissioner Mackenzie again, asking his opinion on establishing a game sanctuary on the Macmillan, close to the place described by Armstrong.[28] Game sanctuaries were being established in other parts of Canada at the time, particularly in the Northwest Territories, so this interest and perhaps Armstrong's continued lobbying prompted the federal agencies responsible to continue their scrutiny of the Yukon situation. The Yukon's new commissioner, George Henderson, replied that such a proposal needed the approval of Territorial Council, and that in any case he thought no sanctuary was needed.[29] Complaints and suggestions from outside government could not be handled with the same finesse.

Council's decision to raise the nonresident license fee to $200 caused at least one hunter to complain. William N. Beach of New York wrote letters of protest in the late fall of 1921 to the commissioner and members of Council. He wrote,

> The law you passed this year made a man feel he was going to kill the limit. . . . I had intended to do but little shooting as my trip was planned largely for photography, but when we found the cheap political trick that had been played on us it resulted in the game suffering and we ended in bringing out a full bag. The spirit of the time is conservation and if it is not practiced it is not going to be many more years before you won't have any more game.
>
> I happen to be a member of the Conservation Committee of the Campfire Club of America and I know it is the feeling of this committee that the laws of the Yukon are not very strong for game conservation. This is not told you in a spirit of criticism, but just for your information.[30]

Commissioner Henderson considered the letters from Beach "discourteous" in tone, but he and the councillors took them seriously enough to amend the Game Ordinance at the next session. Acting on advice from guide Charlie Baxter, they lowered the bag limit for nonresidents to one moose, one sheep, one goat, two caribou, and two deer.[31] Hunters wanting to kill more than this had to pay an additional $25 per trophy; and the nonresident license went back to $100 where it was to remain for another sixty years.

The big game industry had good years during the twenties, but the Depression which followed had its effect. The average number of hunters coming to the Yukon in the thirties was half the average for the twenties. The guides at that time were Charlie Baxter, Eugene Jacquot, and Tom Dickson in the White River-Kluane area, Alex Coward and Ira Van Bibber in the Pelly-Macmillan district, and Shorty Auston and Johnny Johns in the Carcross area, south of Whitehorse. Following the slow years in the thirties, only Johnny Johns and Eugene Jacquot remained in business and kept their outfits. But the early thirties were not difficult years for the Yukon, however. Gold mining in the Klondike area supported the transportation system, which provided many jobs, and all the opportunities for contract and wage employment continued as they had in the past. The Yukon's distance from Vancouver and other large cities and the cost of travel to it kept many men away. They were still years of labor shortage. Those men who might have worked as guides and helpers had no problem finding other ways of supporting themselves, although they would have preferred to stay guiding. It was the most interesting and sought-after job available to Indian men and it payed well.

The success of the Yukon's big game industry depended, finally, on the Indian men employed in it. They maintained the requisite intimate knowledge of the terrain and of the animals' habits. They were available to work at times when white men were most deeply involved in gold mining, transportation, or prospecting, and the working season was perfectly complimentary with the trapping season. Beyond these reasons, many of the big game hunters preferred to go with Indian guides. They welcomed the opportunity to learn "woodslore" from the expert, the North American Indian. The books the hunters wrote about their Yukon experiences offer snippets of information on the country and its history that they learned from their guides. Of course the guides themselves encouraged this curiosity once they learned of the hunters' interests, in a desire to please them which could be reflected later in the customary tips at the conclusion of the hunt. One hunter recounted how he and Albert Isaac stalked a moose by going through six inches of fresh snow in their bare feet. Isaac had insisted on this as the only quiet way of approaching the moose.[32] Isaac may well have been making the most of the hunter's gullibility for his own entertainment and that of the other guides, even though he shared the ordeal, but there is no doubt that the experience left a deep impression on the hunter. He killed the moose, but best of all he had a good story to tell about it. The big game hunter in the years before World War Two wanted a memorable wilderness experience above all else. Yukon Indians provided an essential part of that experience. One would think then, that the administration would have maintained or initiated policies which would preserve or enhance the role of Indians. In fact, they did the reverse.

In 1923, the Territorial Council amended the Game Ordinance to specifically bar Indians from becoming chief guides, while not preventing them from applying to be guides, assistant guides, and helpers.[33] Thus Indians could be employees, but they could not become contractors, soliciting their own business and hiring their own men. This was the first appearance in the game law of a provision which discriminated against Indians; prior to 1923, they had been exempt from the Ordinance.

An example explains the effect of the 1923 law. Johnny Johns is an Indian man. He became the most famous and successful Yukon guide by simply surrendering his Indian status, under a procedure in the Indian Act. By doing this he obtained the rights of ordinary Canadian citizens, that is, to vote, buy liquor, and in this case, to enter into business contracts, but he lost his Indian rights, rights which were available irregularly in Canada and included treaty benefits (although not in the Yukon), medical care, education costs, and so forth. His children also lost their Indian status. The labyrinthine nature of politics of the Indian Act goes far beyond this treatment, but Johns had to make a decision which in some ways is more permanent than a marriage in order to become a chief guide.

Johnny Johns was born in 1898, at the height of the Gold Rush. His family was of Tlingit-Tagish people of the southern Yukon, and he maintains kinship ties with people in southeastern Alaska. He started in the guiding business in 1917 with Shorty Auston of Carcross and obtained an assistant guide's license in 1923. By 1925 he was applying to become a chief guide, as was Billy Smith, another Indian man of Carcross and Whitehorse. Johns said that he realized he could become a chief guide when he found an outdoors magazine thrown away by a tourist. He saw the advertisements for guides elsewhere and concluded he could do the same thing. When he applied for a chief guide's license in 1926, Whitehorse government agent Larry Higgins listed his camp equipment as "16 horses, 20 saddles, 6 tents, 6 chairs and tables, 4 stoves and 6 axes"—an impressive display of wealth for a twenty-eight year old Yukon man.[34] A year passed before Johns was successful and during that time he had to surrender his Indian status and become enfranchised as an ordinary citizen. He never looked back. Johns went on to become one of the continent's most famous guides. A list of his hunters' names through his fifty years in the business would read like a *Who's Who* of the sporting world. His personal contribution to the territorial economy through the years from 1917 to 1967 would have to be reckoned in the millions.

Soon after Johns obtained his chief guide's papers, Whitehorse Government Agent Higgins complained to the commissioner "It really means the taking away of the livelihood of guiding from the white man if any more Indians are granted the privilege of acting as Chief Guides."[35] Higgins was the man who handled most of the inquiries to government concerning hunting and issued virtually all the licenses, since the hunting parties invariably started from Whitehorse. His remark likely reflected an antipathy felt by the Jacquots, Dickson, and Baxter towards Indian competitors, but since that season and the next two which followed were the busiest ever for guides, none of them bothered to lobby for changes to the law. On the other hand, Indians did have allies in the Indian Affairs branch in Ottawa, who could intervene in those cases when prejudice against Indians by the Territorial Government became apparent. One other example reveals how the licensing system for guides worked against Indian men.

George Johnson was a ranking person among the Teslin Lake Indian community who had become quite wealthy from his trapping efforts.[36] In fact in 1928, he bought a Ford Model A from Taylor and Drury's in Whitehorse, and carried it three hundred miles in his own gas boat by lake and river to Teslin Lake. There was no road, but he had hundreds of miles of lake and river ice to drive on at the height of the trapping season in the spring. The car allowed him to speed up the servicing of his neighbor's traplines along the lake. He applied for a chief guides' license in 1933 but after a year's delay, he was turned down because he had no horses.[37] Johnson probably reasoned that if he were given the license, he would buy the horses in Whitehorse and take them to Teslin, since there were none there and he was a man of some considerable means. There was little point in him purchasing the horses on speculation of obtaining a license. Such a circuitous situation could be turned in any direction by the commissioner, and he chose to turn it against Johnson, despite a favorable recommendation by the Teslin RCMP officer on Johnson's behalf. With the appointment of George A. Jeckell as commissioner some years previously, the administrative attitude had hardened, for about the time Johnson made his application, Jeckell was replying to an inquiry about hunting, "every nonresident hunter must be accompanied by a licensed White Chief Guide."[38] Some superior reality may have operated in that decade which could blunt the force of what appears to be prejudiced behavior fifty years later, but there is no clue in the commissioner's files as to what that reality could have been.

Market hunting of big game also continued in the Yukon during the period before 1942, long after it had been outlawed everywhere else. In 1921, the Dominion census reported Dawson City with a population of 975 persons, while returns under the revised Game Ordinance of meat dealers showed some 7100 pounds of moose meat and 3600 pounds of caribou had been purchased. Records from the White Pass and Yukon Route steamboats show they landed about 50 cattle per year in Dawson, with only minor numbers of sheep and hogs.[39] If 50 cattle at 450 pounds dressed weight are added to the meat sold, dividing that total weight by the population gives a very small per capita meat consumption of only 33 pounds. Putting it another way, some 33,000 pounds of meat would feed only 236 people for a year at 140 pounds of meat each. The only other way Dawson people could get meat would be to shoot it themselves or buy it privately. Using a calculation similar to the one described for 1905, one would have to conclude that in 1921, Dawson City people used some 120 moose and 460 caribou in addition to those killed and sold by market hunters. While that may seem like a great many animals, the harvest continued at that level for another thirty years at the least. Clearly, the Yukon's game population was so abundant it could absorb levels of killing outsiders would find unacceptable.

In the period from 1900 to the beginning of the Second World War, the Yukon big game hunter's perception of the trophy hunt changed in its purpose. At first it was a slightly affected exercise in self-reliance in which only one's personal standards mattered in the way one killed game. The true sportsman would never waste the animals, but there was a world of difference between the local view and the changing sportsman's view of what constituted waste. In the next few decades the perception of a hunt changed to become the ultimate wilderness experience in which killing the perfect animal was an essential part. This newer attitude coincided with the phenomenon of the tourist, for the twenties was the decade in which people said "See America First," and they had the money to do just that. The thirties' wilderness adventure became too costly for everyone except the small group that could afford the expense of travel and the hiring of guides in addition to the thirty or sixty days needed for a hunt. Hunting expeditions became expressions of nostalgia towards golden Edwardian days before the horrors of the First World War, and away from the confusing and frightening politics of the decade. The big game hunter mirrored some of the attitudes of his age and carried them into the Yukon, but few of those attitudes took root.

. The same forty-year period saw the Yukon's administrators make a substantial change in their perception of the Territory's game resources. At first, trophy hunters seemed to be a nuisance and a threat to game. Following Alaska's lead, the Yukon began to license these hunters for a fee which was close to a Yukon tradesman's wages for a month; clearly a deterrent tax. However, as sportsmen came in increasing numbers, more men began to earn a living as guides. In 1919, the nuisance became the big game industry and an important source of government and local revenue. Most of the institutional concepts created then were to persist in the Yukon's management of its wildlife for another forty years.

The big game industry was well suited to the Yukon's peculiar society and geography. It had a stable population with economically dependent Indian and non-Indian components. The chief guides were usually related by marriage to Indian families and their work fitted in well with the annual round of activities and use of resources. The administration, however, discouraged Indians from participating in the business beyond being employees of non-Indian chief guides, reflecting an institutional attitude of the day which sought to keep the "traditional" Indian existence separate and distinct from the modern. At the same time, the administration had to defend the Yukon's game laws particularly with respect to market hunting, from pressures to change them coming from outside the Territory. Underlying the administration's attitude was the sincerely-held belief that the game resources were without limit. Every year in Dawson City, council members at the spring budget session had only to look up on the surrounding hills to see the Fortymile caribou herd in their numberless, ceaseless migration. With so much abundance the Yukon attitude during those years should not be surprising.

4

The Alaska Highway

It was a pleasing sight when about one hundred and thirty men of the Corps of Engineers, United States Army, arrived at the local depot on Friday [April 3, 1942] although it must be admitted that the weatherman was not at all considerate on that auspicious occasion ... It is understood that a complement of between three and four thousand men will be engaged on the project which is one of the greatest of its kind ever undertaken on this continent.[1]

The editor of the four-page *Whitehorse Star* predicted that his dusty riverside town would soon replace Dawson City as the Yukon's commercial capital and that the new highway would have a lasting effect on the Yukon. His predictions were correct, for Whitehorse became the capital ten years later. During those ten years the Yukon's population doubled, and its character was transformed. The highway brought about many changes that affected the Yukon's wildlife.

In the eight months between April and November of 1942, a pioneer road was cleared between Dawson Creek, British Columbia and Fairbanks, Alaska. Several years passed before the road was improved enough to warrant the term "highway," but that should not diminish the achievement of the U.S. Army in planning and executing the project. They had the advantage of wartime controls and an open budget, but they also had much older plans to work with, for the idea of a highway to Alaska was an old one. Forty years after the event similar construction projects in the north are planned with consideration given to protecting the natural environment and wildlife. One might think that in 1942, especially under the pressures of a war the Allies were unsure they could win, government planners gave no thought to wildlife. In fact, they did, and the difference between the responses of the Canadian and American governments requires some emphasis. Even though they had over a decade to plan for a highway, the Canadians were unprepared.

In 1929, interest in the proposal to link Alaska, the Yukon Territory, and British Columbia by road was so great in Dawson City that the inevitable committee, the International Highway Association of Dawson City Incorporated, was organized to lobby for needed legislation and funding. In those years there was a busy commercial exchange between Alaskan and Yukon points and a correspondingly close political relationship. The origin of the idea is not clear, for it had been discussed in British Columbia at about the same time. Word of the interest in Dawson City reached Deputy Minister of the Interior W.W. Cory, who wrote Yukon Commissioner G.I. MacLean asking his opinion. MacLean replied,

> Such a road would be of inestimable value to the north country not only from a tourist standpoint, but also in opening up the Territory and assisting in its development. I shall keep you advised from time to time as to what further steps may be taken in connection with the matter.[2]

By the fall of 1929 it became clear that an American plan for the highway intended to bypass Dawson City and the Yukon interior in favor of a shorter route to Fairbanks through the southern Yukon. The administration became alarmed at this and started surveys of its own, to try and influence the route. The Yukon's member of Parliament, George Black, was appointed to a Canadian commission of inquiry, which was intended to work in concert with an American committee. Ottawa's reaction was not motivated to ease Yukon concerns, but to safeguard Canadian interests in the region and prevent their falling under an American hegemony. Beyond this, Ottawa was indifferent and only British Columbia's Premier Tolmie seemed to be actively promoting the scheme. Maclean's worries in Dawson City about being bypassed were a low priority.

The American International Highway Commission of the U.S. Congress made public their report in 1933. The report caused a storm of protest in Canada.[3] It suggested that American costs would be two million dollars while Canadians could expect costs six times as great, all for a road which would benefit largely American interests. There were important questions of Canadian neutrality at stake, for the road had military significance. Money shortages caused by the Depression were another reason why the idea was not taken up. In any case, in the long period from July 1931 to January 1939, no one wrote to the Yukon government on the topic. The Commissioner's Alaska Highway file gathered dust.

British Columbia Premier T.D. Pattullo helped to revive the highway idea in early 1938. Proposals to develop the northwestern part of the province have always been a singular preoccupation of its premiers, but Pattullo had lived in the Yukon decades before and he took a novel approach. He travelled to Washington to interview influential American politicians and bypassed the Cabinet in Ottawa. This resulted in the idea being revived again. Two parallel committees were struck, one American, one Canadian, to review plans for the highway. The Canadian International Highway Commission, formed by Prime Minister Mackenzie King in December, 1938, was comprised of the Hon. Charles Stewart, a former premier of Alberta, General T.L. Tremblay of the Canadian Army, J.M. Wardle of the Department of Mines and Resources, Arthur Dixon of the Department of Public Works, and J.W. Spencer, a Vancouver merchant. It would seem that a nice balance had been struck between British Columbian and Albertan interests, to counterbalance the federal presence; Canada was at last prepared to take the issue seriously.

Meanwhile, it was time to ask for the Yukon opinion again. R.A. Gibson, director of the Lands, Parks and Forests Branch of the Department of Mines and Resources at Ottawa was the civil servant responsible for Yukon affairs. In reply to his inquiry, Yukon Commissioner G.A. Jeckell wrote,

The greatest agitation in the north for this highway as in the past, and also at the present time is in the interior of Alaska centering around the town of Fairbanks.

The residents of the Yukon Territory have never at any time become very excited or enthusiastic about the project. The laboring classes are in favor of the project from the spending standpoint.

The mining operators and business interests are not much concerned, for they do not see where much benefit will accrue to the Territory after the construction period is passed, when possible they will be saddled with the cost of a very large part of the highway maintenance expense.

So far as the direct development of the Territory is concerned the opinion is that a highway through the Territory to the nearest tide water would be of much more value.[4]

The Highway Commission travelled to the Yukon a few months later, in July 1939, to sample local opinions first hand. The community hearings were absurdly brief: an afternoon hearing in Whitehorse was followed by one at Atlin, B.C. the same night and another at Carcross in the Southern Yukon the following morning. Not everyone who spoke was in favor of the idea of a road link to the "Outside."[5] There and elsewhere the Commission came to realize that the main problem facing the scheme was the choice of route, for each had its political adherents and opponents.

There were three land routes through British Columbia to the Yukon, usually designated the A, B, and C routes. The first was touted by Seattle and Alaskan interests, and it lay close in to the rugged Coast Mountains of the Pacific shoreline. The second route, the B route was the one eventually chosen by the Canadian commission. It followed the striking geographical feature called the Rocky Mountain trench northwards from the railhead at Prince George, and it was planned to pass through Dawson City. Neither the American or Canadian commissions gave attention to the C route as a compromise and they stayed deadlocked until the outbreak of the war. The Canadians went ahead with their plans for the Northwest Staging route, a system of isolated airports along the direct air passage from Edmonton to Fairbanks. This construction eventually precipitated the choice of the C route for the Alaska Highway. Shortly after the Pearl Harbor attack of December 1941, and the entry of the United States into the war, the road became an American priority. Yet even while the road was being pushed through, Seattle businessmen resented the commercial bonanza won by Edmonton with the choice of the C route. Everything became subordinate to the needs of the U.S. Army's logistical planners and the speed with which the engineers mobilized and started work astonished everyone. Certainly no Yukoner believed that the road could be built so quickly.

The speed of events from the arrival of American troops in the early spring, to the initial opening of the road in the late fall was so rapid and the changes brought by the road were so profound that Yukon residents were simply bowled over. One used to the isolation and stability of the Territory since the Gold Rush could not perceive either the scale of the project or the consequences. The Yukon's tiny government was overwhelmed. Whitehorse in particular had no time to prepare for the arriving troops. Prime Minister Mackenzie King announced the Canada-United States agreement about the highway's route on March 6, 1942. Scarcely four days later a small contingent of Army engineers came to Whitehorse to begin aerial surveys a month ahead of the vanguard of troops. Mail began to pour onto Commissioner Jeckell's desk concerning the Yukon government's role in the project.

George Jeckell had been a Yukon resident since 1902 and commissioner (controller) since 1930.[6] He was approaching retirement age after having served as the head of Yukon government for the longest period of any of its many commissioners before or since. His reputation for hard work, attention to detail, and administrative vigilance was well deserved. However he was to be denied additional help (or he did not seek it) to cope with the added work load, and a certain rigidity plagued his administrative methods. Jeckell's superior in Ottawa, Lands, Forests and Parks Director R.A. Gibson, was another long-serving mandarin with a similar reputation for hard work. Unfortunately both men found it difficult to delegate authority and exercise control where it was needed, in establishing a plan for the Yukon which was to emerge after the Alaska Highway was completed and opened to civilian travel. They were not imaginative men, so rather than try to change their methods, they simply increased their work loads; consequently new or unfamiliar problems received old, tried solutions. For the problems concerned with Yukon wildlife, the old solutions were no less than a mistake.

To Jeckell's credit, he did think about the consequences of the highway on the wildlife. On March 18, 1942 he received a copy of the Canada-United States agreement on the highway, which covered details such as funding, lands needed for the right-of-way, protection of U.S. nationals from Canadian taxes and excise duties, and the supplying of timber, gravel, and rock along the planned route. Asked by Gibson to comment on his government's role, Jeckell replied that no changes to Yukon laws seemed to be needed to accommodate the terms of the agreement. After reviewing four taxation ordinances he mentioned the Game Ordinance, of which he said, "I believe that this ordinance should remain operative from the standpoint of conservation of wildlife."[7] By this remark he proposed that it would be enforced and that there would be no unregulated hunting. This was the earliest official expression of concern over the impact the highway might have on wildlife. George Black, the Yukon's member of Parliament and a long-time resident wrote to Jeckell scarcely a week later,

It occurs to me, as it probably has to you, that the question of protection of Yukon game along the route of that road is worth considering. There will be many men on the job.

The country traversed is the habitat of moose, caribou, sheep and small game such as grouse and ptarmigan. Unless proper protection is made they might soon be exterminated. I think you could have the cooperation of the RCMP in this matter. A man or two in uniform, travelling through the construction camps unannounced, would have good influence.[8]

This would have reinforced Jeckell's idea that the soldiers and construction personnel would simply comply with the Game Ordinance regarding license fees, residency requirements, seasons and bag limits, that the solution to a problem he could see was already at hand, in existing law.

Meanwhile, Whitehorse was taking on the appearance of an armed camp. By mid-April, over one thousand men of the U.S. Army Engineer Corps and one hundred civilians of the Public Roads Administration were quartered in and around Whitehorse. According to an RCMP report, all were armed with rifles or pistols and many were interested in hunting while they were stationed in the Yukon. Under the Game Ordinance they could not, unless they paid the one hundred dollar nonresident's license fee and hired a licensed guide. One senior officer asked for a special exemption for his men, especially the officers, from RCMP Corporal Allan in Whitehorse. Allan appealed to Jeckell for instructions, since this was a Yukon law and not a federal matter. Police Superintendent W. Grennan in Dawson City, head of the Yukon police division, asked Jeckell to grant "special consideration" to the U.S. Army men, when he handed over Corporal Allan's report. Jeckell replied that he could not, "in the interests of conservation" and advised Superintendent Grennan "You will, therefore, instruct Corporal Allan that the Game Ordinance is to remain operative and that no special privileges are to be granted."

Jeckell communicated his decision widely. British Columbia's Game Commissioner F.R. Butler asked what the Yukon was going to do about the matter of hunting licenses, and later did follow the same policy throughout the war of preventing highway personnel from hunting along B.C. sections of the Alaska Highway. The same matter had been raised in meetings between Dr. Hugh Keenleyside, Canada's External Affairs deputy minister and J. Pierrepont Moffat, the American ambassador in Ottawa. As one account has it,

Mr. Moffat at once agreed with the viewpoint expressed by Mr. Keenleyside and said he was quite sure that there would be no tendency on the part of the United States to feel aggrieved if the Canadian regulations in regard to hunting were fully maintained.[9]

Letters from the deputy minister of Mines and Resources and from R.A. Gibson supported Jeckell's nondecision, but they arrived too late to be of use to him in his meeting with the U.S. Army commander, General Hoge, at his headquarters in Whitehorse. Jeckell was caught in the tyranny of distance, which caused sometimes two weeks to pass while a letter reached Dawson City from Ottawa. Then too, there was bureaucratic reluctance to use the telegraph, even assuming such a delicate matter could be discussed in that way. Gibson had earlier asked Jeckell to go to Whitehorse to see the situation at first hand, so while he made this journey, a few hours by air now, and not the week on a steamboat of former years, he did not know that others also kept a worried eye on Yukon wildlife.

For decades Whitehorse had been a small town of a few hundred people, with log and frame buildings, dusty streets, and board sidewalks. The biggest event each year was the arrival of the steamboat crews and carpenters to ready the boats for the busy navigation seasons on the Yukon River. It has been said that spring arrived with the knocking of caulking hammers down at the shipyards. Those yards, the small fleet of steamers and the narrow-gauge White Pass and Yukon Railway were virtually the only reasons for the town's existence. It was transformed, however, in April, 1942, by hundreds of troops, who soon became thousands. Vacant lots sprouted conical, olive-drab tents. Army vehicles crowded the streets, and just as quickly, Army graders filled in the blossoming potholes. Long time residents found themselves isolated in a sea of new faces—for many of the troops were Blacks. Residents began to lock the doors to their homes, something they had never done before. They were alarmed and apprehensive, yet at the same time they were caught up in the excitement of the events and the peculiar euphoria brought by the war. Enormous line-ups at the post office, and worse, at the liquor store were annoyances easily borne when there was work at high wages for anyone who wanted a job. The continent's attention was caught by the idea of the highway and the old romance of the Yukon experience. The Yukon was rediscovered. Its residents were bathed in attention and money; and yet there was no doubt as to who was in charge.

Yukon Commissioner Jeckell arrived in Whitehorse on May 5, 1942. He was deeply shaken by the changes that had taken place in the old Whitehorse he was familiar with, but he pressed on with his official duties as the Yukon's senior administrator. Two days passed before he was able to meet with General Hoge, days in which he was shown over the army establishment and had the plans for the road camps and buildings explained to him. Construction was well under way by this time and construction was proceeding in three directions, including the steamboat-supplied heading from Teslin Lake towards the Northwest Staging Route airport at Watson Lake. Jeckell had only an afternoon to meet with General Hoge. After other business had been covered, the matter of hunting privileges came up again. Hoge asked for special hunting rights for his men and Jeckell acquiesced. He agreed to ask Territorial Council to grant an amendment to the Game Ordinance.

Seemingly, Jeckell saw the problem the same way as Hoge, that the request originated more with the officers than the men, for they would not have been ignorant of the Yukon's reputation as a leading trophy hunting area. They did not forsee handing out licenses by the hundreds to all comers. On his return to Dawson City Jeckell found the letters from Gibson, Keenleyside, and other senior officials waiting on his desk. Those letters must have caused him anguish in view of his agreement with General Hoge, but he carried on with his intentions to submit an amendment to the Ordinance at the spring session of Council. He wrote to R.A. Gibson on his meeting with Hoge and said,

I propose in trusting the issue of a certain number of hunting licences to the United States Army Command officers. General Hoge stated that licences in that case would be issued by them only in limited numbers and to trusted officers and men, and be given as a reward for application to duty ... He considered that if there was total prohibition it would be like the enforcement of liquor prohibition, where no one could be trusted.[10]

But the mails and his reluctance to use the telegraph kept Jeckell out of touch.

British Columbia did not change its laws, and its game commissioner posted game wardens at both Fort Nelson and Watson Lake and kept them on frequent patrols along the highway route. West of the Yukon in Alaska there was an even stronger response to the perceived threat. Because it had merely advisory powers, the Alaska Game Commission could only recommend to the U.S. Interior secretary that the bag limits should be reduced, the seasons shortened and that the season on Dall sheep should be completely closed. These changes were in force by May 1942; in addition President Roosevelt proclaimed a number of new wildlife refuges throughout Alaska. A few months later the United States government closed the highway corridor to virtually all activity from the Yukon border to Fairbanks. Letters telling Jeckell these facts crossed in the mails with his own report on his conversation with General Hoge. In ignorance of this meeting Gibson had written,

It is the feeling of the administration that we should deal as generously as possible with the United States Army personnel giving due consideration to the interest of preventing extermination of our wildlife resources. However it is only reasonable that we should not extend them any greater concessions than their own government is prepared to give them in Alaska.[11]

Gibson may have anticipated the difficulty of Jeckell's position and was offering the commissioner an excuse to refuse permission to issue licenses. But Gibson was also aware that game management was solely a Yukon matter, not a federal one, and he had no authority to direct Jeckell to do anything; he could only advise or warn. He may have been hoping that Jeckell and the Territorial Council would use the Alaskan devices of shortened seasons or game refuges. Unfortunately this was not done. No one inside the Yukon or without objected to Jeckell's solution either. On July 23, 1942, the Territorial Council approved an amendment to the Game Ordinance which authorized the Commissioner to issue residents' hunting licenses at a dollar each to United States Army personnel. There was no comment in the press in either Whitehorse or Dawson City.

This act of the Territorial Council created a legacy of bitterness that was to last for many years. For example in 1949, George Black,

M.P., would write to the new commissioner (controller) J.E. Gibben,

> During the last American invasion of the southern Yukon the invaders practically exterminated the game, fish, animals and birds. Unless checked and watched it will be repeated. Your predecessor [Jeckell] treated them as residents. They fished and killed and left their victims to rot.[12]

The reasons behind this baffling decision can be understood at least in part by setting them in the context of the events of the Second World War at that time. In the months from May to July, 1942, the war was not going well for the Allies. Hitler was pushing back the Russians along a huge front. Tobruk had fallen to Rommell. Closer at hand, Japanese troops were landing in the Aleutian Islands and bombing Dutch Harbor. A Japanese submarine surfaced off the west coast of Vancouver Island to shell the lighthouse and meteorological station at Estevan Point. The *Whitehorse Star* featured front page stories on how to seek shelter during air raids and how to snuff out incendiary bombs. Although the town was crowded to overflowing with American troops, they were a reassuring presence. The easy familiarity and the "can-do" philosophy of the officers reflected itself in many ways; ball diamonds, sidewalks, and new buildings appeared. Men, materials, and labor were freely loaned for civic projects and Whitehorse residents were frequently guests in the American messes. Those residents, and their Territorial Councillor W.L. Phelps not least, would have been anxious to treat the Americans in a fair and civil manner. In short, there had to be an accommodation of the troops and good feeling between the two groups, Besides, the RCMP detachment was so small, the community was defenseless.

A second reason may lie in the Yukon community's perception of itself as a political and geographical entity. Whitehorse and Dawson City and the smaller settlements were like an archipelago in a small sea, where the physical separation was more of a reality than the actual distance, a perception unique to settlements served by ship. There were no road or telephone links between them. Two decades of economic stagnation and this isolation from the outside world prevented the formation of a vision which saw the Yukon as a political entity. Everything was subordinate to distance, to separation. Nobody worried about the game because nobody could grasp the totality of the problem, and there as everywhere, the war obliterated the long term view of things.

The outside world likely had two different views of the highway. One would have resembled the colorful propaganda written in the earliest books about the highway. Godsell's *Alaska Highway* is a good example. He wrote of the highway being built to counter "bright instruments flickering in dark, dangerous movement" in the Aleutians, repeating all the stories, so common during the war, of Japanese fishermen making quasi-military surveys along the coast years before the Pearl Harbor attack. Godsell found great satisfaction in the fact that it was the army that was building the road; his metaphors quite carried him away:

> As they hacked through black-massed battalions of spruce and serrated rows of collonaded pines still others rose in a seemingly impenetrable sage-green barrier ahead, parading in mass formation like an inanimate army determined by the very weight of numbers to resist and wear down the threatening forces of invasion.[13]

But Godsell gave little credit to the role of new technology in explaining the road's rapid progress. Aerial photographic interpretation, the bulldozer, and the DC-3 aircraft were inventions of the thirties, but it took the war years to move them into the public consciousness. After the war these and other tools became associated with the "man of action" in the same way that self-reliance and endurance were associated with the man of action in the Klondike stampede days. Thus the building of the Alaska Highway was in a sense a repeat of the old gold rush mythology with a modern, technological twist. Many books and magazine articles took delight in showing the contrasts between the bulldozer operator and the dog team driver, between the airplane and the steamboat. One would think that the U.S. Army engineers had discovered a northern Shangri-La where time had stood still.

But far behind those bulldozer blades were men who could appreciate the consequences the highway could have on Yukon wildlife. Some of those men were in Ottawa, but it took an

American initiative to prod them into action. United States Interior Secretary Harold Ickes had the wildlife in mind when he wrote to his Canadian counterpart T.A. Crerar in July, 1942. Ickes had just signed an order withdrawing over eight million acres of Alaska land "from all forms of appropriation under the public land law, including the mining laws, pending definite location and construction of the Canadian-Alaskan Military Highway."[14] He wrote,

> I am informed that the Canadian-Alaskan Highway will touch, or make fairly accessible, several fine areas within the British Columbia—Yukon wilderness. You of course are familiar with them. The Tuchodi Lakes—Toad River region is highly scenic and has exceptional game resources, including grizzlies, Osborne caribou, Stone sheep and the most northerly herd of elk. In the same general region are the Liard Hot Springs and the Liard canyon. West of Whitehorse, from Kluane Lake to the Alaska boundary are the highest mountains in Canada and some of its most famous wildlife.

> Many trumpeter swans are presumed to nest in the wilds of northeastern British Columbia and adjoining territories. Our own United States trumpeters were practically exterminated by unregulated human intrusion on their wilderness. Now we are endeavoring to rescue and restore the species by strenuous, costly work.

Ickes explained that the Alaskan closure was merely a provisional device to prevent wasteful and destructive exploitation and property speculation that might hinder the highway's construction or add to its cost. It was a step to creating development zones along the corridor. He concluded his letter with this appeal:

> The Canadian-Alaskan military highway is a joint enterprise that will help secure our countries against a common enemy. With such modifications as our respective laws and traditions demand, I wonder if we cannot establish a uniform policy of conservation along the Highway now and for the future.

The Canadians responded with alacrity. Scarcely a month later, Crerar and his comptroller of Parks, James Smart, started the bureaucratic process that would lead to the creation of Kluane National Park thirty-five years later. The delay can be explained by government indecision and bungling in the decades after the end of the war, but the Order in Council setting the land aside for that purpose was secured in merely four months. The letter from Ickes must have precipitated a storm in the Department of Mines and Resources, then responsible for Yukon land matters. R.A. Gibson sent a copy of Ickes' letter to Jeckell and suggested some possible solutions in his covering letter: a game sanctuary such as the Thelon Sanctuary in the Northwest Territories; a national park closed to mining, forestry, hunting, and trapping, and a game preserve, where Indians alone could hunt and trap.[15] Above his signature Gibson had scrawled, "Please let me have your views as soon as you can." But Gibson also asked Jeckell to go to Whitehorse to meet with Charles K. LeCapelain, who was "Liaison Officer between the Dominion Government Departments and the United States Army Officers." This must have rankled Jeckell considerably, to be pressured into making a decision on something so important and secondly, to have to consult with a man who had been a constant irritant to him for the past two months. Yet it was LeCapelain who found the eventual solution.

Charles LeCapelain came to the Yukon in late June of 1942 bearing letters of introduction from the long-time Parks Comptroller James Smart and Jeckell's superior, R.A. Gibson. LeCapelain was a highway engineer and formerly superintendent of Waterton Lakes National Park in Alberta. Since both Jeckell and LeCapelain reported to Gibson, they were nominal equals, yet the contrasts between them were great. Jeckell had lived in the Yukon for forty years, half of that as commissioner. Le Capelain was an outsider, a "cheechako" or newcomer, and worse, he was younger and educated. He started off on the wrong foot by meeting with army engineers to discuss timber cutting along the right-of-way and granting permission to them to burn their slash, even though no permit had been issued and the crews had no fire fighting equipment. Jeckell heard about this in Dawson City and was soon complaining to Gibson in Ottawa that LeCapelain had usurped powers vested in the commissioner by the Forest Fire Protection Ordinance, a Yukon law; moreover he had violated protocol by not contacting Jeckell upon his arrival in the Territory. LeCapelain operated out of his hotel room or borrowed office space and made all his reports in longhand, but he soon learned the necessity of sending smudged carbons to Dawson City to keep Jeckell involved. He made all the "line" decisions about federal resource matters— land, forests, water, gravel, and so forth—that were affected by the highway's construction. It is possible that he extended towards these resources the same philosophies and attitudes held by the national parks bureaucracy; whatever they were, they certainly did not mesh with the Yukon way of doing things. The needs of the war clearly outweighed ordinary diplomacy, however; the decisions had to be made, and made quickly.

LeCapelain's arrival marked the beginning of the expansion of the federal government's presence in the Yukon to a degree not seen since the Gold Rush. This was initiated by the inability, or the refusal, of the Territorial Government and in particular, its Commissioner George Jeckell, to exercise or expand its jurisdiction at the time of the building of the Alaska Highway. Within five years LeCapelain's successor, F.H.R. Jackson, would be making all the decisions respecting the location of highway road houses, sawmills, camp sites, and indirectly, liquor licenses and other commercial activity. It was as though the Yukon became divided in two, in both space and time. Jeckell hung onto the old Yukon at Dawson City and handed over the new Yukon—the Alaska Highway Yukon—to virtually total federal control. When the capital moved to Whitehorse in 1952, the process was completed.

This was the situation in August, 1942, when the letter from United States Interior Secretary Harold Ickes arrived in the Yukon. Prompted by Gibson's covering letter, Jeckell flew south to Whitehorse and discussed the matter with LeCapelain. On his return he wrote that they had agreed, that "certain large areas should be reserved for National Park purposes, or as game sanctuaries." The greater part of Jeckell's letter shows that he fully expected mining rights to be withdrawn or frozen, following the Alaska example. He suggested that part of the sprawling Dawson Mining District along with affected parts of the Whitehorse Mining District would have to be withdrawn from mining location or staking rights so as to give complete protection to the corridor. Clearly he had no ideas on what the governments should do. However on the same day that Jeckell was writing his letter, LeCapelain was also writing to Gibson, saying he had found the answer. His handwritten letter is historic; it deserves to be quoted at length.

That stretch of the road running from ... the Dezadeash River to the White River in the southwestern Yukon offers something that you cannot get anywhere else in Canada; a view of the St. Elias Mountains containing the largest glaciers and mountain peaks in Canada. Therefore I respectfully suggest that the area indicated in green on the attached map ... [generally, the present day park] ... be reserved for consideration as a National Park.

Concerning the matter of Game Sanctuaries and Preserves I feel that at the moment I do not have assembled sufficient accurate information to be able to make a worthwhile recommendation. This work will likely take some time. However, in the meantime I do not feel that the game will suffer adversely to a great extent on account of the road construction.

Without having come to a final conclusion due to incomplete information, I seem to be coming to the point of recommending no sanctuaries or preserves in the Yukon other than the possible National Park ...[16]

Scarcely two weeks after LeCapelain mailed his recommendations to Ottawa, Jeckell was asked to comment. He replied to Gibson: "During my visit to Whitehorse in August this matter was discussed very fully with Mr. LeCapelain and we were unanimous that the area should be reserved for a National Park." He was obviously relieved that somebody else had made the decision for him. LeCapelain's idea quickly gained momentum. In October, Parks Commissioner James Smart forwarded a memorandum to the Privy Council about the Kluane area. The Dominion Advisory Board on Wildlife Protection discussed the matter in the same month. Meanwhile the U.S. Army Engineers were pushing the road through. On November 20, 1942, Canadian and American dignitaries opened the Alaska Highway in a brief ceremony in snow and extreme cold, on a bluff overlooking Kluane Lake. Two weeks after this event, the Privy Council put all the lands around Kluane under an administrative freeze, the first legal step in making the area a park.[17]

From the time of Ickes' original suggestion in July to the Privy Council order in December, less than five months had elapsed.

Two things might explain this speedy decision-making. First, Canada was responding to an "outside" influence; indecision arising from administrative caution would have appeared weakness on the part of the Canadian government. Many in Ottawa were more keenly worried than ever about the spectre of American domination in the Northwest arising from the Alaska Highway. Second and most significant was the government's complete disregard for local interests and opinions under the impetus of a wartime emergency. But less than a year later, it was the Yukon's turn; an amendment to the Game Ordinance in the spring 1943 session declared the area a game sanctuary, closed to all hunting and trapping, a ban which applied to Indians as well.

Beyond these factors, the creation of a National Park—or at least the beginnings of one—offered the government a neat solution to the problem of wildlife conservation. It was politically conspicuous, but it did not close the Highway corridor to mineral prospecting as was done in Alaska. An equivalent order on the Canadian side would have loosened a strong protest from the Edmonton-based mining fraternity. These men had enough clout with R.A. Gibson of the Department of Mines and Resources in Ottawa and with U.S. Army headquarters in Edmonton to secure special passes to use the new highway a year after it was opened. As for the wildlife, those animals inside the boundaries of the new park were saved, if indeed they were in any great danger, but the rest of the highway was left wide open. Starting in the fall of 1942, U.S. Army personnel and employees of the road contractors that came later began to put relentless pressure on the game resources, using their newly-acquired, one dollar residents' hunting licenses. This then was the result of the weakness of George Jeckell, the impatience of Charles LeCapelain, and the thoughtlessness of R.A. Gibson and James Smart.

One of the most persistent themes in Yukon folklore since the war is that the Alaska Highway builders—U.S. Army soldiers in particular—killed or wasted an enormous amount of game. The stories seem to be tied to features of the highway's route or to local people in ways that give them the ring of authenticity. Yet proof that this did occur is hard to obtain. Johnny Johns, the big game guide, recalled the war years in his testimony to the Mackenzie Valley Pipe Line Inquiry in May, 1976:

During the time they were building, construction crews worked six days a week and got one day recreation. On their day off they generally wanted to hunt so they'd head off into the bush. I know for sure that there were 200 moose shot between Whitehorse and Fort St. John. A lot of times they would go hunting three or four miles off the road, pack a bit of meat out and either go on shift right away and leave the meat to rot or get some friends to help them go out and pack it in. Of course, they didn't know the country and usually they couldn't find it again, so the meat rotted.

Fishing was the same. Many times I saw strings of fish pulled up on the side of a lake full of rotting fish. Once I counted 60 trout pulled up on a string at Little Atlin Lake, left to rot.[18]

At the same inquiry, another Yukon resident testified about the effects of the highway on wildlife. Joe Jacquot, son of Eugene Jacquot, spoke of rumors that fighter planes had fired on moose and caribou. Referring to the licensing of the soldiers and civilians, he said "someone in Dawson goofed and we along the highway had to suffer the consequences."[19] A year after these men gave their evidence, another pipeline-related inquiry in the Yukon travelled to all the Alaska Highway communities. Many of the Indian people who spoke before the commissioner of the hearing gave similar stories to support their concern about the proposed Alaska Highway Natural Gas Pipeline. Such evidence as this cannot be called proof, particularly in the light of the Indian Land Claims which was the most important sub-issue surrounding the pipeline hearings. And yet they show that the issuance of licenses and the lack of a wildlife protection policy was a political blunder which echoed down thirty-five years.

The all-important letter from Interior Secretary Harold Ickes marked the beginning of a time of intense interest and concern about the wildlife in the Yukon and Alaska. Ira N. Gabrielson, director of the U.S. Fish and Wildlife Service at Chicago, wrote to his Canadian counterpart in November, 1942, worrying about rumors of U.S. soldiers killing game unlawfully and dynamiting fish. J.E. Gibben, acting as commissioner in George Jeckell's absence, simply dismissed the charge: "I would place little stock in the complaints made to Mr. Gabrielson."[20] When R.A. Gibson wrote to the U.S. authorities, Albert M. Day, assistant director of the U.S. Fish and Wildlife Service replied with a long letter describing the situation along all of Alaska's highways. The worst single incident was the discovery in the fall of 1942 of eight caribou carcasses, shot and abandoned on the road from Fairbanks to Circle. Other reports from deputy wildlife agents told of isolated cases of illegal or wasteful killing, though the largest number of incidents by far concerned small game, grouse, and ptarmigan. Day's report concluded with a reassuring note, however: "When so many tens of thousands of men are transported to new areas which abound in game it is only natural to expect some unlawful killing of wildlife. At the present time there appears to be no need for alarm."[21]

One other view of the game situation came indirectly, but it speaks volumes about the vigilance of the Canadian and American authorities. A letter sent home by a U.S. Army private of the 74th Engineers Co. had been intercepted by military censors, copied and forwarded on to Canadian authorities. After it landed on Gibson's desk in Ottawa, he wrote a reply and sent copies on to Jeckell in Dawson. The private had written,

> We get a lot of fresh meat up here. The fellows shot two moose and a mountain goat here last week. We ate all of it. The meat tastes pretty good. The Canadian Government has put out orders that we are not supposed to do any hunting or fishing up here. But who are they?[22]

Gibson replied to the office which sent him the letter by describing the Yukon game laws and said "it is quite likely fresh meat such as referred to would be obtained legally." Gibson's memorandum gave no hint as to his own feelings on the matter; either he did not share the concern of the Americans or he trusted the judgement of the Yukon administration. Outside concern about Yukon and Alaskan wildlife boiled down to a local enforcement problem. Given the liberal hunting laws—on the Yukon side of the border at least—was the enforcement adequate?

Since 1901 the RCMP had enforced the Yukon's game laws in an apparently impartial and thorough manner. Their duties were increased enormously by the Alaska Highway situation, yet they were chronically understaffed. U.S. Army soldiers and Public Roads Administration employees were policed by the U.S. military police; even incidents like drunken fights and stabbings were handled by them, not the RCMP. However Canadian law and Canadian enforcement applied to everyone else and with the population increase, high wages, and the isolation, the RCMP had plenty to do. In the small highway communities the RCMP also acted as government agents, consequently their increased work load prevented them from making more than cursory attempts at patrols to look for game offences. They had to rely on information given by others. Stories about large numbers of animals being left to rot assumed the helplessness or the indifference of the RCMP to deal with the situation. This may not have been true. Police informants could have included the many Canadians among the highway crews, particularly in 1943 and later, who would not necessarily conceal incidents of Americans killing game illegally. Friction between the two national groups existed, particularly over the differences in the wages paid to each. This friction did not exist in any organized or overt way, but it was strong enough to have sought expression through complaints to the police about illegal acts concerning game. Then too, it was the RCMP who asked that special consideration on game licenses be given to U.S. nationals. Perhaps they reasoned that the soldiers and civilians who were always subject to U.S. military law were exempt from Canadian law, and the Game Ordinance in particular, unless they purchased hunting licenses.

The RCMP regularly sent copies of their investigations of game offences to the Yukon Commissioner. Significantly there were no investigations of these in 1942. In the spring of 1943, two men at Teslin, one a highway employee, the other a priest, were convicted of shooting a cow moose, which was both illegal and out of season. The same investigating officer later found nine muskrat pelts obviously taken illegally, hanging behind a highway construction camp building, but he could not determine their owner. A similar case near Whitehorse saw an American citizen convicted of shooting a muskrat with a .22 calibre rifle. These incidents contributed to a decision in May 1943 of the Northwest Service Command at Whitehorse to order all privately-owned firearms to be collected and kept in locked cupboards, an order which applied to both civilian and military personnel.[23] At the same time, Territorial Council passed an amendment to the Game Ordinance which placed a mile-wide no-shooting zone along the length of the Alaska Highway in the Yukon. Probably there was confusion about the game law. Not everyone working on the road could obtain a resident's hunting license, so it fell to the police to make the distinction between who was eligible and who was not.

One farcical episode can put the game situation along the highway into a 1943 perspective. A sergeant of the U.S. 134th Quartermaster Company (Truck) based near Whitehorse wrote to the commissioner in June, requesting permission to keep a bear cub as the camp's mascot. Jeckell replied that he had no objection. In a memorandum to the RCMP he agreed that keeping a bear was technically illegal under the Criminal Code, but no one had ever been prosecuted for this before. Later in June, Constable G.F. Cunnings of the RCMP detachment in Whitehorse received a telephone complaint that a pet bear belonging to one of the camps had been illegally shot and that the evidence might be found in a certain car. He later found the car and discovered the carcass of a small bear in the trunk. The driver was a U.S. Army captain who later admitted shooting the bear with his service revolver. Cunnings' report should speak for itself:

> The captionally-named stated that he was a Captain and had not intentionally broken any laws and that he was under the impression that a hunting licence was not required ... It is not the opinion of the writer that anyone could reside in this area for any length of time and not know that a licence was required to hunt.

> In the late PM of 15-6-43 a telephone call was received from the informant in this case to the effect that the captionally-named had returned to McRae [near Whitehorse] to find out who the informant was and the informant admitted he was the one who let this officer know about the shooting of the bear. The informant stated further that the captionally-named had displayed conduct unbecoming to an officer and a gentleman, he had used expressions such as yellow, stool pigeon and had even threatened bodily harm to the informant.[24]

Aside from its value as entertainment, this report shows that the RCMP had informants within the U.S. Army as well. Cunnings could have dismissed the incident with a shrug; the fact that he acted on the complaint likely enhanced the reputation of the RCMP along the highway and made their task easier.

The building of the Alaska Highway and the enormous short-term population increase ultimately reduced the abundance of game along the highway corridor. Yet it is quite impossible to determine the degree of reduction, or the places where it occurred. Some of the causes may have been more natural, that is, not caused by hunting, but by fires, drainage changes, and traffic noises. But the Territorial Government made a serious management error—although then it may not have been a political error—in permitting U.S. Army and Public Roads Administration personnel to hunt as residents. Probably Jeckell did not properly estimate how many licenses would be issued, or the number of animals that would be taken. In 1942, such resident licenses showed an almost negligible increase over the normal number of three hundred to three hundred and fifty; in the spring of 1943, however, government budget figures show the number jumped to over one thousand and stayed at that level for the next two years.[25] Not all the new hunters would have taken game, but nevertheless it is reasonable to suppose that the Territory-wide moose kill, and certainly the sheep kill, would have doubled in those years.

The cause of this management blunder lay in the Yukon's long isolation from the rest of the continent. Since the beginning of the Yukon's administration, Dawson City had been the center of things. With 1942, the center abruptly shifted south to Whitehorse. Yukon Commissioner George Jeckell was trapped in Dawson City by a communication barrier which compressed day-to-day decisions into a single telegraph line, an infrequent and costly air service, or a slow steamboat trip up four hundred and sixty miles of river. Time after time the correspondence shows that it was faster for government agents at Whitehorse such as Charles LeCapelain to receive advice from Ottawa, three thousand miles away, than to obtain it from Dawson City. During the war years, such communications delays could not be tolerated. Jeckell's loss of personal control was caused by his own reluctance to travel to Whitehorse more frequently and exercise authority there. He could not overcome the habits ingrained by forty years' living in Dawson City. The inhabitants of the Yukon were unceremoniously dumped from the twenties into the forties, without ever passing through the thirties decade. They had never learned to rely on broadcast radio, the telephone, and mass-circulation newspapers carrying sophisticated political analysis. The war was baffling to both Indians and non-Indians alike. The old bureaucratic methods were unable to adapt and the Yukon's old communications archipelago dissolved in the warm sea of modern communications.

The total effect of the Alaska Highway on the Yukon's wildlife has probably been exaggerated. People who had always relied on wildlife for their daily bread and their income needs would have been shocked by the waste and rightly so; yet evidence of waste is hard to find. The soldiers ate what they shot; they had little or no fresh meat. One might wonder whether U.S. Army General Hoge had asked for hunting rights in order to save transport costs for fresh meat from Edmonton. However there undoubtedly was killing along the highway where none had occurred before, and the game populations declined correspondingly. One example can show how this came about. Johnny Johns has said that along the east shore of Teslin Lake the highway passed close to a number of salt licks. Because moose and caribou tend to cluster at such licks, wholesale killing there, legal or otherwise, would reduce moose and caribou populations over a far larger area than a crude animal-per-square-mile ratio could possibly predict. Johns's local knowledge supplies the evidence needed for game depletions in that particular section of road; elsewhere the road may have crossed country new or unfamiliar to him, so his estimates of changes elsewhere in say, moose populations, would be little better than anyone else's opinion.

The Alaska Highway's most important effect was an intangible one; it changed people's perception of the land. Local concern about the killings began after the highway was built and used for a number of years, not while construction was going on. The highway opened new territory to easy hunting, and effectively closed the old hunting grounds because it was no longer as convenient to go to them. The new territory held unfamiliar quantities of game; who was to say whether this was more or less than before? Finally, the highway meant speed. Journeys made by foot, or boat, or on horseback allowed slow and detailed examination of the meadows, lakes, and rivers encountered. The same journey made by car or truck at forty or fifty miles per hour shrank the time for examining those places down to a brief instant, so that he land itself would seem to shrink as well. A new perception of familiar landscapes required a new perception of game populations; again, who was to say if those populations were greater or less than before? But for those people who had always lived at the old settlements of Teslin, Watson Lake, Champagne, Burwash, or Carcross, the highway changed everything. The noise, the dust, and ultimately, the shooting chased the game away. The prosperous old order was ended after 1942 and a new, grimmer order had begun.

5

The Invasion of New Attitudes

The Alaska Highway changed everything. People were now free to come and go at times of their own choosing, the telephone allowed them to talk with their families or their supervisors at long distances from the Yukon, and most importantly, the road allowed hundreds of people to drive their own cars to the Territory and to make their homes there. The Yukon's attraction lay in its image as a northern Shangri-La, with game and fish in abundance. Whatever their motives, the newcomers had a profound and lasting effect on the Yukon's wildlife, not because they shot everything in sight but because they imported a different perception of wilderness and wild animals. In the five years between 1945 and 1950 this new perception took root and flourished, with the result that forty years of stability between Indians and non-Indians, between men and wild animals, faded into a memory of "the old Yukon."

It is worth repeating that in the long years from 1911 to 1941 the Territory hardly increased in population; the surge of westward expansion seemed to pass it by. Before the highway opened to unrestricted travel in 1947, few people came to the Yukon with intentions of settling there. A large number of men came every spring for gold mining or to man the steamboats, but they always left in the fall, and the Indians and old-timers had the place to themselves. Local people regarded newcomers with indifference or suspicion bordering on hostility. By long tradition in the Yukon and Alaska, the "cheechako" was one whose characteristic ignorance forced him to depend on others to survive, especially in winter. Before the war their numbers were insignificant and could have no effect on government policy. However, a stream started during the war became a flood after 1947. Whitehorse acquired a boom town society which had few links to the old Yukon, and the issue which this society seized upon for political action was the Game Ordinance.

The Yukon Fish and Game Association became the catalyst for the process of change in attitudes towards wildlife. It was organized in Whitehorse in February, 1945, even before the war had ended.[1] Less than two years later it included two hundred and seven members in a Whitehorse population of a few thousand, and from 1945 to 1950 was easily the Yukon's most influential public interest group. Even fifteen years after its founding, the dances, barbecues, and field days the Association organized were major social events of the year. It gained its energy from newcomers to Whitehorse who tended to socialize with each other rather than attempt to gain acceptance in the stuffy circles of old Whitehorse. However, long-time residents dominated the early executives of the Association, but their role was one of control more than it was of energy. Their traditional views were soon diluted by the press of new ideas, just as they themselves were drawn to the growing political and social nucleus provided by the Fish and Game Association.

The first president of the Fish and Game Association was Geoff Bidlake, a well-known and popular Yukon resident of many years. He had been a purser on the White Pass and Yukon Route steamboats and then an agent for Pan American Airlines before becoming a Territorial Government Agent and liquor vendor in Whitehorse. The secretary of the Association was W.D. MacBride, a publicity agent for the White Pass trains and a local writer and historian of some note. The vice-president was F.H.R. (Rex) Jackson, a forest engineer with the federal Department of Mines and Resources. He replaced Charles LeCapelain as the ranking federal officer in the southern Yukon and was responsible for the increasing federal involvement in local affairs. These three men were elected at a well-attended founding meeting in Whitehorse in late January, 1945. They began their activities with enthusiasm. MacBride wrote to Yukon Commissioner George Jeckell in Dawson City,

> We believe that this organization will meet with popular approval and that the membership will be considerable. Should this be the case, the organization should be of value and of assistance to the Yukon government in the enforcement of game laws and the study of wild life problems.[2]

Two months after the founding meeting members of the Association travelled to Dawson City to make a presentation to the Territorial Council about their concerns. One of the earliest intentions of the group was to influence government policy. They were to have remarkable success.

The Fish and Game Association had three ambitions in 1945. Its members wanted trapline locations to be plotted on government maps and registered to their individual users, following the practice already in use in Alberta and British Columbia. Their second objective was to have buffalo, elk, and mule deer introduced into the Territory. Finally, they wanted sports and commercial fresh water fisheries transferred to territorial jurisdiction from the federal government, which had maintained control over this resource since the earliest days. The Territorial Council endorsed these ideas in a memorandum to the Department of Mines and Resources.[3] However, these objectives were never fully realized. Five bison and nineteen elk were introduced to the Yukon in 1951 and in the same year the new trapline registration system came into force. Fisheries has remained under federal control to this day with the exception that the Yukon government obtained authority to collect sports fishing license fees. The inertia of the federal government on these three recommendations during the years 1945-1950 had no effect on the Association, however. It continued its efforts as a special interest group and won an important role in the management of game, the only resource under Yukon control.

From the beginning the Yukon Fish and Game Association drew many of its ideas and its support from Alberta. It was affiliated with the Alberta Fish and Game Association. Secretary MacBride sent copies of nearly all letters and memoranda to G.M. Spargo of Calgary, the secretary of the Western Fish and Game Council. A member of the Alberta group, also representing the international organization, Ducks Unlimited, helped to form the Yukon association. In turn, MacBride represented the Yukon at the annual general meeting of the Alberta Fish and Game Association. In 1949, the Yukon's first director of Game, Them Kjar [pronounced "tem care"] was recruited from Alberta through links established between the two organizations. However the greatest influence wielded by the group and its Alberta connections lay in the realm of ideas.

One of the most persistent myths about wild animals in Alberta soon established itself in the Yukon. This was the myth of the "wolf menace." Alberta stockmen, in common with American cattlemen far to the south, regarded wolves and coyotes as something more than a nuisance. This was natural enough, for predatory wolves sometimes define the boundary between wild lands and lands suitable for grazing. It was a conflict in land use that the cattlemen resolved by poisoning wolves and coyotes with strychnine-doped baits, or with spring guns loaded with cyanide. In 1946 the Association became determined that the Territorial Government should take steps to reduce the wolf population. They saw wolves as a general problem unrelated to any specific locale. They were townspeople, most of them strangers to the Territory. Their perception of the ecological system comprising wildlife and wolves was not attached to the actual land, but to their notion of the land; consequently they saw themselves as hunters simply replacing wolves in the system. Thus if there were fewer wolves there would be more moose or caribou for men to hunt. Association members who supported this idea may not have known that the use of poison for wolves had been illegal in the Yukon for decades and that there was a deeply ingrained fear of poison, especially among the Indians. However by the middle fifties, the Fish and Game Association, federal wildlife officers and the Yukon Game Branch were involved in poisoning programs all over the Territory. It was ultimately abandoned for economic reasons.

A second idea which took root in Whitehorse was the notion that the Yukon's variety and abundance of game animals were somehow inadequate or insufficient as compared to equal areas to the south, for example in Alberta. The Association believed that the addition of buffalo, elk, and mule deer would improve the game potential. On their own initiative members imported many pairs of ring-necked pheasant and released them near Whitehorse in 1945. This was an ill-conceived and ultimately cruel experiment. Pheasants lack the insulating layer of feathers on their legs possessed by grouse and ptarmigan. They do not roost in deep snow like northern birds, nor are they capable of browsing on the same trees and shrubs. Some pairs survived the first winter, but after that there are no further reports; the birds must either have frozen or starved. The bison and elk introduced in 1951 were a somewhat similar mistake. However, both species have reproduced and survived in the Yukon. Bison were last reported in 1973, while the elk, nearly thirty years later, had increased to something less than one hundred in total, showing only a marginal adaptation to Yukon conditions. Evidently members of the Fish and Game Association could not accept the fact that the Yukon was a complete, functioning ecological system not readily capable of improvement or even comparison to any other system, such as the Alberta Foothills. The Territory simply would not fit an imported view of its landscape and its potential.

The attitude of the Fish and Game Association regarding the rights traditionally exercised by Indians was also significant. The members of the Association were not particularly prejudiced against Indians. At least there is no direct evidence for this in the files or in the memories of those who belonged to the Association in those days. If any members held negative feelings towards Indians they certainly would not have been encouraged to express them to long-time Yukon residents. However the cultural equilibrium at all levels was disturbed by the weight of numbers.

Prevailing attitudes would have described the Indian culture as inadequate, and encouraged its assimilation to the larger, continental culture. An essential part of this assimilation process came through the imposition of new laws and new attitudes. Trapline registration requirements comprise the best example. Even as late as 1950, virtually all the trappers were Indian. They never expressed any desire to have their trapping areas recorded, or to obtain tenure for them, because such a concept was alien to their cultural notions about land. Also, it was against their interests to limit their potential trapping areas in this way. However, in both Alberta and British Columbia a greater proportion of the traplines was held by non-Indians. These trappers insisted on some degree of security for their areas and made it government policy. In the Yukon the system was clearly imposed from outside with the aid of the Fish and Game Association. A second example concerns market hunting; throughout the twenties and thirties, market hunters were nearly all Indian men. When the Yukon caught the continent's eye in 1942, the fact that market hunting was still permitted there caused much comment.[4] In the early forties the practice fell into disuse because of the many new opportunities for employment. The privilege was abolished in the 1947 amendment to the Game Ordinance on the recommendation of the Fish and Game Association. Interestingly, Indian Agent R.J. Meek was an executive member at the time.[5]

Three events in Whitehorse involving game laws and the Fish and Game Association can show the change in that community's attitudes towards wildlife and the Indians. These events were the new laws respecting big game guiding, the arrival of James H. Bond, both in 1947, and the appointment of Them Kjar as the first director of Game in 1949. These years began a process of separation, both social and economic, between the Indian and non-Indian cultures. In addition, these years saw a substantial decline in fur prices as well, so the net effect was total disruption for the Yukon Indian communities. Only with the rise of Indian political organizations and Land Claims' negotiations in the seventies has this situation shown some signs of reversal. The Alaska Highway created the situation in the first place, the Yukon Fish and Game Association acted as the catalyst, and the weakness and isolation of the Territorial Government acted as the medium for the changes. The Yukon's decades-old wildlife policies transformed themselves. The wildlife became detached from the landscape, from any local, site-specific understanding of varieties and abundance, only to become a free-floating, Territory-wide system providing trophies and other cult objects for export out of the Yukon. Its use as sustenance and a livelihood became less important.

An American entrepreneur was the principal cause of the Game Ordinance amendments of 1947. During the later years of the Second World War, U.S. Air Force Lieutenant Carson Shade was a frequent visitor to the Yukon while flying to Fairbanks, Alaska, with war cargoes.[6] He liked what he saw. Being possessed of a good business sense, he conceived the idea of bringing hunters to the Yukon by charter aircraft. Together with five brothers and sisters, he formed an ambitious enterprise. They advertised in the Los Angeles area for clients, chartered a DC-3, and flew in a load of hunters directly from California to an Alaska Highway airstrip at Teslin, Yukon. From there the hunters were taken by bus up the Canol Road to one of three hunting camps. After two weeks of hunting and fishing they returned to California by plane while another party came into the country. It was an ingenious system. Its appeal lay in the novelty of chartering an aircraft, curiosity about the north, modern advertising techniques, and the lure of hunting trophy animals in a world famous area.

The Shade brothers caused a local uproar. They operated within the terms of the 1938 Game Ordinance, but they hired Indian guides when the law contemplated guides being contractors, not employees. Hence the high profits earned by the guiding fell to the Shade partnership, and not to Yukon residents. Their parties kept the hunters in the field for merely two weeks when a traditional Yukon hunt was thirty days and frequently sixty. With the shorter hunting period, more hunters could be accommodated and more animals taken in a season, without correspondingly increasing the earnings to the guides and local businesses. There also would be greater likelihood of wasting meat. Clearly the Shade operation, or any like it, could not be allowed to continue. The law had to be changed to protect the livelihoods that depended on the big game business.

In 1946 the Shade brothers took in thirty-eight hunters, virtually all from the Los Angeles area, in the three flights that they made to the Yukon. Not all the men were successful in their hunts: together they took twelve caribou, sixteen moose, twelve sheep, nine grizzly bears, and four black bears. As Territorial Agent Larry Higgins at Whitehorse wrote to Acting Commissioner Gibben, "To most of the hunters it was a disappointing outing and proved to be a fantastic advertising scheme conceived by Shade brothers."[7] They had guided over half of the seventy hunters that came to the Yukon in the fall of 1946, but they accounted for far less than half the caribou, moose, and grizzly bears taken. By traditional standards it was a poor hunt. Besides its harm to a Yukon monopoly, the low quality of the Shade operation threatened to give all Yukon hunting a bad reputation.

By the time the facts were in it was December, 1946. The problem was taken up by the Yukon Fish and Game Association. The executive met with Commissioner Gibben (George Jeckell had retired earlier that year), Yukon Member of Parliament George Black, and RCMP Inspector Cronkhite to discuss the problem of the nonresident hunters. Gibben invited the Association to propose amendments to the Game Ordinance for submission to the spring session of Territorial Council.[8] The executive met several times a week throughout January, 1947, the meetings including Rex Jackson, the federal timber and lands supervisor, R.J. Meek, the Indian agent, and Territorial Councillor R.G. Lee. They prepared a list of changes which was discussed, amended, and approved at a well-attended public meeting on February 11, 1947.

The correspondence which followed the meeting is very illuminating. The executive wrote to Commissioner Gibben asking the government to move quickly in drafting the needed amendments, using a tone that revealed a less than deferential attitude towards the Yukon administration.[9] They wanted Gibben to issue a notice several months prior to the Council session to the effect that the administration would be proposing substantial changes to the Ordinance. Gibben agreed, drafted the form, and left the Fish and Game Association to fill in the blanks. The Commissioner's surrender was complete, if indeed he had any misgivings over the group's intent. The Shade partnership was notified in this way months in advance that they would not be allowed to repeat their 1946 hunting scheme.

Two items in Bidlake's letter to Gibben of early February reveal the full extent of the group's influence. First, they obtained a letter written to Territorial Agent Larry Higgins, the senior government employee in Whitehorse, from Carson Shade. Shade's letter was written on the same day as the Whitehorse public meeting, February 11. He had written,

We have quite a number of reservations for next Fall's hunting season and quite a few of the fellows who were up last year are planning to return and the word has spread and has brought a fine bunch of new inquiries. If there is any information you could give us that would affect our operation as compared to last year we would greatly appreciate it.[10]

Higgins gave the letter to the Fish and Game Association weeks before he forwarded it to his supervisor, Commissioner Gibben in Dawson City. Shade probably never received a reply. At much the same time the Association received a second, even more privileged piece of information. The manager of the local Bank of Commerce, A.E. Hardy, informed the group early in February that an American industrialist planned to finance the efforts of two Indian men to become chief guides. As a matter of government policy, such licenses had always been reserved for non-Indians, with the notable exception of Johnny Johns, who after all had to surrender his Indian status for the purpose. This second incident requires some elaboration for it suggests what was uppermost in the minds of those drafting the amendments to the game law.

The American industrialist was Edwin P. Hurd, of the Hurd Lock and Manufacturing Company of Detroit. In company with several other men, he had hunted in the 1946 season in a party "outfitted" by Mike Nolan, who owned a highway lodge at Marsh Lake, south of Whitehorse. This party had been guided by Frank Slim and John Joe, two Indian men who were well-known in the southern Yukon. Hurd wrote to the bank in January, 1947, enclosing a draft for a thousand dollars. Frank Slim and John Joe were to use this money to equip themselves for a hunt in the fall, not as employees of Mike Nolan, but as a contracting partnership. Evidently Hurd did not want to do further business with Nolan. Once bank manager Hardy told them this, the executive of the Fish and Game wrote an amendment to the Game Ordinance which effectively prevented Frank Slim and John Joe from becoming chief guides. The amendment, which was approved by Territorial Council and given assent by the commissioner in early July, required all applicants for chief guides' licenses to be completely equipped with horses, camping equipment, and so forth to care for six hunters at a time. This would have cost much more than a thousand dollars. Clearly no Indian man could afford to invest this amount of capital, particularly when just starting out in the business. Similarly, only those holding chief guides' licenses could contract to provide a hunt.

In fact, John Joe was able to take the Hurd party out on a hunt, but only after Hurd himself arrived in Whitehorse, and used his influence and powers of persuasion on Indian Agent Meek and Territorial Agent Larry Higgins. Higgins sent a wire to Commissioner Gibben, who delegated all authority to Higgins to issue a license, using a long-standing section of the Game Ordinance which allowed the commissioner to waive parts of the law at his discretion.[11]

The intention of the Fish and Game Association was to limit competition in the Yukon big game industry. They imported the concept of "outfitter" from Alberta and applied it to a person who normally provides the equipment and who does all the organizing that is necessary. Before 1947 these things had been done by holders of a chief guide's license; but after the changes in the law, chief guides became "outfitters" provided they could meet the equipment requirements. No residency requirement had been imposed; all a prospective "outfitter" needed was money. The motives behind the Association's intentions are elusive. Everyone was aware that the Yukon had been rediscovered. There was a great interest in hunting throughout the continent in the late forties and it was a time of rapid growth in industries and magazines devoted to fish and game. Keeping out foreign competition was one valid reason for the new law, but the severe restrictions imposed on those who wished to join the Yukon outfitting fraternity have only one explanation: the established guides did not want any more Indians in the business as independent operators.

A further example should make this obvious. An American hunter named James H. Bond wrote to the commissioner in December, 1946, inquiring whether he knew of anyone in the Mayo area who would be able to guide him on a hunting trip into the Ogilvie Mountains. The name of Mayo trapper Louis Brown was mentioned. Following the traditional procedure, Gibben wired Ivor Mast, the Mayo RCMP officer, inquiring about his suitability. Mast in his reply noted that Brown had been convicted of poisoning wolves in 1941, but concluded that he should be licensed, probably because there was no one else available to do the guiding.[12] Brown had never been a guide before and Gibben did not ask, nor did Mast volunteer to tell him, whether or not Brown was

properly equipped with horses and camp supplies. It is significant that Brown was licensed as a guide and outfitter with no experience, a dubious record, and having no proof of the necessary
capital, at exactly the same time that John Joe had so much trouble
gaining the same licenses. The inescapable conclusion is that
Brown received every consideration because he was not an Indian.

Louis Brown took James H. Bond into the Ogilvies in August
of 1947. Bond was a writer and publicist from Portland, Oregon
who made 16 mm films of his hunting expeditions and sold them
to firms engaged in the expanding tourist industry. Canadian
Pacific Airlines was one of these companies; after filming a sheep
hunt in the Alberta Rockies for them, Bond was asked to do a
feature on the Yukon, for Canadian Pacific had just obtained
lucrative airline routes from Edmonton and Vancouver. The company was in communication on the matter with W.D. MacBride,
the White Pass Railway publicity agent in Whitehorse, and it was
MacBride who directed Bond's inquiries.

Bond arrived in Whitehorse in June, 1947. He spent part of his
first week talking to Geoff Bidlake and W.D. MacBride, absorb-
ing some of their notions of game management. Less than two
weeks later he wrote to Commissioner Gibben,

> I have known it to be a fact that a number of Indians in the
> fall of the year, coming upon game, will kill every one, shooting
> until the last animal is down or until they run out of ammuni-
> tion. Indians will kill game of either sex and at any time of year.
> Most Indians have ten or fifteen dogs and they do not go without
> meat. I am well advised that the Indians will not catch fish for
> drying in the summer or fall months, thus facing the winter
> without food for either themselves or their dogs.[13]

It was somewhat presumptuous of him to pass on the fatuous
generalizations of Bidlake and MacBride, but since those men were
central in the Fish and Game Association, Bond saw no reason
to doubt their word. After this letter, Commissioner Gibben's
replies to Bond's correspondence were always polite, but tangibly
cool in tone. It made an inauspicious beginning for his involvement in the Yukon Territory over the next three years, for Bond's
1947 hunt was to cast a long shadow over the Yukon's game policy.

The story of Bond's hunt appeared a year later in his book *From*

Out of the Yukon.[14] It is quite an engrossing account of a hunting expedition, reminiscent of G.O. Young's book about hunting in the White River district in 1919. Bond, Louis Brown, and Norman Mervyn, the assistant guide, made a long, arduous journey through a rarely-travelled district. The book was larded with the author's opinions on game management and his criticisms of the Yukon situation. In addition to a bizarre comment on grizzly bears in which he contemplated killing three in one day, he made continual allusions to Indians and wolves as being the main causes of a decline in the numbers of big game. He believed that wolf poisoning and rigid game law enforcement were required. However, he continually made errors in his facts, showing that his knowledge of the Territory was either cursory or invented. Most curious of all the statements made in his book are the facts that Bond shot three caribou when the new, 1947 limit was one, and that both Brown and Mervyn shot moose and caribou while actually guiding, which was also illegal. This information appeared also on a handwritten, unsigned, and undated note tucked into the commissioner's game file.[15]

James Bond was clearly the P.T. Barnum of Yukon big game hunting. He was actually more of a publicist than a hunter, or naturalist, or "conservationist"—the terms he used in his promotional tours throughout the United States in 1948. He spliced the films of his Ogilvie Mountains hunt into a 5000 foot adventure film. That film and his book took him from city to city, to appearances in sporting goods departments of large stores during the day and in hired halls in the evening. He faithfully clipped all his advertisements and reviews and sent them north to Commissioner Gibben. In both Dawson City and Whitehorse, people had mixed feelings about him; his playing to the media and glossing of facts made Yukoners wary, or even embarrassed; yet they recognized the value of his publicity in bringing tourists into the country. One long-time resident, the late Miss Victoria Faulkner, saw all Bond's letters and clippings as they arrived. She strongly defended the man, thirty years later, as though he was still a controversial figure. She said he did a great deal for the Yukon. Mr. G.I. Cameron, a Yukon resident since 1930 who knew Bond well, could not be prompted to volunteer anything more about the man beyond saying "He was a businessman."

Bond returned to the Yukon in 1949 after writing to Gibben in

March, enclosing yet another wad of newspaper clippings. These ads for his film said "He made the picture while studying wildlife for the Yukon Territorial Government and hunting in the Yukon."[16] In an effort to retain his cultivated image of respectability and authority, he sought an assignment from Gibben, while making it clear he was not asking for either a salary or expenses. He wrote "Enclosed is a form-like letter indicating what you might say in the way of an 'official appointment' for me." The attached "letter" said in part,

> You say you are in a working mood. Well, that's good. We have much for you to do. There is a tremendous section ... of mountainous country we would like you to look over .... We would like you to spend about three months in a general study of the wildlife of that section, counting, enumerating and photographing what you find .... We would like you to make recommendations for the future of that area. It will be a tough trip but you won't mind that ...

Gibben did not respond to this illuminating, finally pathetic request. But another side of Bond's character emerges from his later correspondence. He changed his opinion about the Indians and condemned the endemic local prejudice against them. He also was very generous, and staunchly loyal to his friends. No wonder that this larger-than-life personality dominated most discussions about Yukon wildlife from 1948 to the middle fifties.

In the same year, 1949, the Yukon Territorial Government appointed Them Kjar as its first director of Game and Publicity. He was another controversial figure in recent Yukon history for he was of an energetic, intense, authoritarian nature and did not observe all the courtesies of the old, pre-war Yukon. He brought with him from Alberta the methods and philosophies of the province's game authorities with whom he had worked. Until their relationship soured, he worked very closely with the Yukon Fish and Game Association. He was the first—and last—conservation officer to introduce road blocks and automobile searches for game ordinance violations during hunting seasons. Within weeks of his appointment he was chafing at his lack of power to issue wolf poison permits and experiment with the Coyote Getter, a dangerous spring-loaded cyanide pellet gun widely used on the prairies. Patterned on an Alberta idea, Kjar introduced the spring bear hunt to recruit more nonresident hunters. In 1951, he was instrumental in making an older idea a reality when he supervised the release of imported elk and buffalo from a corral near Whitehorse.

Them Kjar had been only a few weeks in his new job when James Bond's activities came to his attention. He complained to Gibben that Bond had abandoned game during his 1949 hunt in the Macmillan district, so Kjar proposed some restrictions on the use of aircraft during big game hunting. Something must have happened to change Kjar's impression of Bond during the year that followed. Surprisingly, Them Kjar and James Bond became close friends. In the fall of 1950, Kjar was only too pleased to be able to attend "James Bond Week" in Portland, Oregon. Bond's publicity efforts and his constant criticism of Yukon guides made him very unpopular later in the fifties with the Fish and Game Association and the outfitters, who by then had their own organizations. But Kjar always defended Bond because he recognized the value of good publicity. In the end, however, the ill-will against Bond made Kjar's own position in the Yukon untenable, and he resigned in 1958 and returned to Alberta.

A period of great change in Yukon game policy was initiated by the Fish and Game Association and carried on by the new director of Game and Publicity, Them Kjar. The big game industry grew at a rapid pace, while the fur industry, crippled by low fur prices, dwindled to its lowest level in a century. The Indian Affairs Branch and the Territorial Government imposed trapline registrations, depriving Indians of any measure of control over the boundaries of their trapping areas, while low prices for furs made those areas of uncertain value and extent. Kjar obtained amendments to the Game Ordinance that enabled him to carry on a vicious program of wolf poisoning all over the Yukon that was to continue for nearly twenty years, and that has recently reappeared in the 1980s.

The growth of the trophy hunting business partially offset losses in trapping for Indian men, for many of them worked as guides, but the control of nonresident hunting lay with the Territorial Government and with the outfitters. At the end of Kjar's tenure as director of Game, the transition was completed. The new director, Geoff Bidlake, made an agreement between the government and the outfitters which was similar to that created for the traplines. Outfitters obtained monopolies in particular areas, in that a nonresident could hunt in a particular area only if he was a client of the outfitter which "owned" the area, a system which survives to the present day. Thus the common resource comprising all the moose, caribou, sheep, and bear in a district became "owned" by an outfitter and managed for his benefit by the Territorial Government. Of course the law did not forbid residents and status Indians from hunting in the outfitting areas, but the new policies valued the resource more for the export of trophies than for local use. These policies placed wildlife in a huge preserve which was more responsive to foreign dollars than local needs. Despite Them Kjar's idiosyncracies and maybe because of them, he saw this happening in the early fifties. He resigned because he could not prevent it.

The management of big game will prove to be an important test of the maturity of the Yukon Territorial Government. Outfitters regularly buy and sell their outfitting areas for sums into the hundreds of thousands of dollars as though those areas are real estate, and yet they have no legal tenure of the lands or of the wildlife within them. The government could abolish nonresident hunting by an amendment as simple as that passed in 1942 which allowed American soldiers to buy resident licenses—and it would not need to compensate the "owners." A license is not property. Similarly the government could license market hunting once again and make big game of greater direct and indirect benefit to Yukon residents in this way. The prospects of this occurring are remote when one considers the long history of game management through the centuries and in the Yukon since 1901. The government had to decide between game as trophies and game as meat, letting alone nonconsumptive uses such as photography and tourism. It is apparent after considering all the events surrounding big game from 1900 to 1950, that trophies had become more important.

6

Yukon Furs: The Early Decades

Fur has held a unique place in the clothing industry because of its
scarcity and cost, its long wearing qualities, and its obvious and
unique function: warmth with light weight. The Yukon Territory
has long been the home of some of the world's most valuable furs.
In the years when prices were strong and steady, Yukon trappers
earned a good livelihood without having to consider the international marketing factors lying far beyond their borders. Pound for
pound, skin for skin, Yukon furs were among the best available.
The trappers provided a staple to the fashion industry under conditions of little or no competition and with only minor government
regulation or outside marketing control. The Territory's small
harvest was always in strong demand in eastern and European fur
centers, just as clothing made from those furs always found buyers.
Within the fifty year period described by this book, the fur market
had many fluctuations, following shifts in buying. The next three
chapters will describe the Yukon's fur industry from 1900 to 1950,

separated into three distinct periods; the early decades when the Territorial government made its first efforts to regulate it, the years between the wars when trapping made its greatest contribution to the economy, and the years after the Second World War when the fur market collapsed. In each period it will be necessary to examine clothing fashions and the fur market as well as the lives of individual Yukon trappers to provide a broad base for the history of this distinct wildlife industry, and the Territorial government's efforts to manage it.

It may seem that some of the history described in previous chapters will be repeated, that since both big game and fur bearers are described by the term wildlife, their histories will be the same. In fact, they are not. Trapping provided the main source of income for Indian people for decades, while big game guiding affected a much smaller number of people and was concentrated in the southern Yukon. The industries overlapped only in the sense that they were complementary in their seasons, guiding in the summer and fall, trapping in the winter and spring, so the same individuals often participated in both industries. But the perception of the wildlife resources in the two industries was quite different. From the earliest times, the trapper was the owner, prime user, and manager of the animals along his trapline. In comparison, big game guiding was a free-for-all.

For the first twenty years of the century, neither the Canadian government nor the Yukon administration paid much attention to the fur harvest. There are very few sources which even mention fur, and the task of reading twenty years of Dawson newspapers is probably fruitless. In 1904, the administration compiled a huge file of statistics about the Territory and its resources. But despite pages of detailed and interesting reports on agriculture, timber, fisheries, and of course, gold, there is absolutely nothing on fur.[1] Consequently, this analysis must rely on a paper written in 1910 by Fredrick Congdon, M.P., who had been Yukon commissioner for several years, and given to the newly-established Committee on Conservation.[2] A shortage of original data and correspondence before 1920, however, does not prevent a picture of the Yukon fur trade from emerging from a mosaic of sources.

Congdon's paper was entitled *Fur Bearing Animals and How to Prevent Their Extinction* and was written at the request of Clifford Sifton, chairman of the Committee on Conservation, and a former minister of the Interior. Congdon and Sifton were old political allies.

Being something of a liberal visionary, Congdon saw the Yukon as a distinct political entity, an "instant province," capable of managing its own affairs and its own natural resources. He wrote,

> One difference between hunting by trappers and by Indians is that, while the Indian always leaves a stock of all the fur bearing animals in a district to continue the species, the white man does not. He goes into a "creek" and absolutely extinguishes all the individuals in it and therefore makes it impossible that it should be restocked from any animals left in the district.[3]

Generalizations such as this have their risks, but Congdon's years in the Yukon would make him sure of his facts. By 1910, the Yukon had experienced over-trapping in at least one area, the Pelly River valley, and was beginning to wake up to the economic possibilities offered by a viable fur industry. He wanted to draw the Committee's attention to the fur industry, and to the important role of Indian people as suppliers, at a time when wildlife conservation was becoming a national political issue.

Congdon's paper complained that various levels of government were indifferent to the fur trade, and that as a consequence the industry was of little benefit to the nation. It reported that Canada collected very little statistical information; trade goods entered the country and furs were exported without proper records being kept. The available data, however, showed that Canada imported almost as great a value of dressed furs as it exported in raw furs. The biology of fur-bearing animals, their ecology and the economics of the fur trade had not received any serious study.

Congdon quoted government records which reported that the Territory produced only $19,500 worth of furs in the year ending in March 1909; yet he knew a man who had personally taken $25,000 worth out of the Territory in the same period. It was commonplace, he said, for Yukon residents to take raw furs with them when travelling to the United States, and since no customs declarations were necessary, reliable figures on Canada's fur trade were impossible to obtain. He believed that the greatest dangers to the survival and growth of the industry lay in the use of poison, followed by risks of overharvesting, and finally, an increase in the number of wolves. Poison, he alleged, could kill through seven "removes," for the carcass of the poisoned animal would kill the scavenger which fed on it, and so on, for seven times. He referred to overharvesting by describing events in the Yukon during the winter of 1904-5, when high prices for marten fur resulted in an excessive harvest in the Pelly River valley. His concern about wolves was a common sentiment, but he opposed the use of poison to control their numbers.

The Committee on Conservation must have given Congdon's presentation polite attention, but their thoughts were elsewhere. The national government had no real interest in wildlife at that time. The committee's work lay in water, forest, and soil conservation, and to iron out jurisdictional disputes between Ottawa and the provinces: until the national parks became established, wildlife remained only a provincial matter. Concepts of resource "preservation" and "wise use" originated in the United States and came to Canada as a result of a joint U.S.-Canada meeting in 1909, under the personal sponsorship of President Theodore Roosevelt.[4] There soon emerged a separation in attitudes towards wilderness between those who sought to preserve it from human exploitation of any kind, and those who wished to control the manner of its development and exploitation. Both viewpoints were opposed to unregulated exploitation, which had been the manner of development in both countries until that time. Conservation became a hot political property in 1909, but unfortunately for Congdon, the Committee on Conservation was more interested in fish than fur and it did not seem to perceive wildlife as a renewable resource. The federal government remained indifferent to the fur trade until the silver fox boom, prior to the First World War.

New technologies and cultural modes lay behind increased demands for furs in the pre-World War One era. The expansion of printing caused by cheaper paper encouraged artists to design and publicize new clothing fashions. The late Victorian fashions originated with couturiers sewing for small exclusive groups of upper-class buyers. When these craftsmen and women became influenced by the imagery of Art Nouveau, the fashionable decorative style of those years, they displayed their designs in small, limited circulation magazines and started the close association between clothing fashions and visual arts that exists to this day.

Clothing of the Edwardian era used fur extensively. Large fur stoles and muffs were essential accessories for day and evening wear, and dark furs such as marten and later, silver fox, had pride of place. They needed longer, light furs of uniform color. Dyeing of cheaper furs and trimming of guard hair, which made them resemble more costly furs, became a common practice in Europe. This new industry owed its growth to German technology with coal tar derivative dyes. Fortunately for the Yukon, marten was the fur in greatest demand. It was cheaper than fox, easier to match, and darker and more attractive than beaver. Other fine peltries such as mink and muskrat found their uses as linings or borders on fabric coats and jackets. The fur coat as it is known today was not common, for it would have been seen as a too-conspicuous display of wealth. Yet it was the appearance of the automobiles which caused long, variegated furs like lynx, wolf, coyote, and raccoon to be used for automobile coats for both men and women. In the Belle Epoque one needed a change of dress for every occasion. The centuries old fur market started to bloom.

Naturally enough the Yukon felt this market growth. In 1903, RNWMP Superintendent A.E.R. Cuthbert at Dawson City reported;

> Every season the number of men employed in trapping increases and the output of furs from this district is an important item.... Last winter about 125 men were trapping on the Pelly and brought down to Selkirk in the spring over one hundred thousand dollars worth.[5]

He said that most of this fur went out to San Francisco, while about $15,000 was bought by a Victoria firm, and that "marten was the principal fur obtained." Other sources refer to this harvest. The official guide book for the Yukon Territory, issued by the minister of the Interior in 1906, said "In 1902 - 1903, two trappers caught 446 marten and a large number of otter, beaver and mink, which they sold at Fort Selkirk."[6] Nevill A.D. Armstrong also reported that in 1902, a certain Bob Riddell trapped over four hundred marten on the forks of the Macmillan, a tributary of the Pelly River.[7] The valley of the Pelly with its easy access by light steamer upstream from Fort Selkirk and its extensive spruce forests—still among the best in the Yukon—was a sought-after area for marten. It seems certain that the valley was overharvested during those years.

Such overharvesting was both brief and local for one important reason; men kept leaving the Yukon. Between 1901 and 1911, nearly three out of every four Yukoners left the Territory. The richest gold

claims had been worked out of their highest-grade gravels. Ownership of the claims passed to those who could afford to make the
enormous capital outlays for hydraulic machinery. Individuals
necessarily "high graded" the richest portions of their claims, sold
out, then took seasonal wage employment. Those who did not leave
in the fall may have tried their hands at trapping, since the two
livelihoods, placer mining and trapping, were complementary
seasonal activities. In the winter of 1902-3 there may have been
dozens of such men. But if placer mining using hand methods was
an economically risky occupation, trapping was even more so for
the inexperienced and unskilled. Despite the few success stories
on the Pelly that winter, there must have been many more failures.
It was not the sort of work that men used to mining or wage labor
could take to easily. For the next fifty years, Indian people provided the largest part of the Yukon's fur production.

Prices for raw furs increased abruptly after 1900, then remained
steady until about 1905, after which they increased again.[8] The
depression of the middle 1890s had ended, helped no doubt by the
tremendous interest and investment surrounding new gold fields
in the Yukon and South Africa. This new demand for consumer
goods and furs helped to establish the Yukon's most famous partnership in the trading business, Taylor and Drury Ltd.

Isaac Taylor and Bill Drury began their fifty-year partnership in
1898, in the goldfields at Atlin, British Columbia. Drury noticed
that the miners were willing to sell their remaining "outfits" at low
prices before they left the country. The North West Mounted Police
for two years had enforced a regulation that all newcomers to the
Yukon district needed a year's complete outfit of supplies and tools.
Drury, joined later by Taylor, bought some of these outfits and
started a brisk business in mining supplies. They soon moved into
fur trading, and built their first post at Little Salmon on the Yukon
River, about twenty miles upstream from the present town of
Carmacks.

Recalling the early days, Bill Drury said in 1950,

Fifty years ago it was more or less a matter of barter. There were
great quantities of fur in those days but prices were low. We
bought thousands of marten at $6 average, muskrat for 8 cents,
mink for $1.25, lynx for $2.50, foxes $3 to $5 ... A good black
fox might fetch up to $1000.[9]

Helped by rising fur prices and profits, they expanded their business, established posts at other locations along the river system, and eventually bought their own small steamboat, the "Thistle." At one time they operated as many as twenty posts in the Yukon; their firm was always the largest single buyer of Yukon furs until the market collapse of the late forties.

Taylor and Drury Ltd. used a credit and barter system in their dealings with Yukon Indian trappers. Eventually they offered good prices for furs, but they marked up the cost of trade goods so that the profit margin remained the same.[10] Their most isolated posts avoided the use of cash by offering tokens of various values which could be redeemed for designated trade goods when these became available. They offered credit—often termed "jawbone" after western American usage—advancing goods against the next season's catch. The company was essentially a family institution. Always locally owned, it was never seen to be taking excessive profits; yet the business did not fail during times of lowered prices for furs. The fact that the partners still were working in 1950, when both were over eighty years of age, says a great deal about their methods and attitudes as merchants.

One explanation for the success of the company is that the partners maintained a sort of equilibrium with Indian trappers. Their company provided the trappers with trade goods and a market for their furs, yet it did not exploit its obvious advantages to an excessive degree. They were helped immeasurably by the ease of shipment to the coast, the telegraph, and the use of their own boats, for these things allowed them to follow the market closely and to take risks that larger, city-bound firms could not. Taylor and Drury were in direct competition with traders from Vancouver and San Francisco who paid spot cash for furs and with others from the East who bought through the mails. Some trappers, Indians included, shipped their fur to auction themselves, bypassing the Yukon merchants entirely; but there were not many who could afford to wait many months to collect their earnings.

An entertaining anecdote written in 1926 by Isaac Taylor's wife Sarah illustrates something of their relationship with Indians:

In 1901 Mr. Taylor in taking a short trip of seventy miles down the river in a small boat from one post to another, had occasion to stop at a point where a band of Indians were camped, having a package containing a woman's skirt. This was to have been delivered to an Indian by the name of Charlie for his wife. On inquiring Mr. Taylor was informed that there was Big Salmon Charlie, Laberge Charlie, Hutchi Charlie and Shorty Charlie. Not knowing who the package was intended for, Mr. Taylor said "Too much Charlie." The Indian addressed immediately replied, "Taylor him wood-camp, Taylor him telegraph man," and pointing to Mr. Taylor said, "You Taylor, too much Taylor."[11]

Other stories used to circulate among older Yukon Indian people telling how the partners were outwitted in trading incidents, or made fun of, or even insulted. The men and the firm were part of the landscape, molded and pulled by the opinions and gossip of the unique, closely-knit Yukon community. A full history of this firm needs to be written, for it seems to depart from the usual models of mercantile exploitation of trappers. As the population declined, Yukon Indians took larger roles in the Territory's stagnating economy. Actually, despite some direct and indirect opposition, they regained something of the role they had filled in the previous half-century. While it is true that they were excluded from the society of the administrators, were unable to vote, and forbidden by law from having alcohol, the society relied on their labor and on the local commodities they supplied—furs, cordwood, fish, and game meat. Some Indian people had taken the Gold Rush in stride, learning English, the use of money, and entrepreneurial skills with great rapidity. By working at many different livelihoods, some men were able to gain sufficient capital to go trapping on a scale comparable to non-Indians, with all the necessary dogs, steel traps, sleds, boats, and generous outfits.

Anthropologist Richard Slobodin has written about the experiences of people from the Peel River district in the northeastern Yukon in the years after the Gold Rush. A group of men, known locally as the "Dawson Boys," were famous "tough travellers." They journeyed hundreds of miles to Dawson City each winter by dog team, to sell furs, game meat, and fur and leather handicraft items, They also maintained their sophisticated acquaintance with "bars, pool halls, brothels, motion pictures, drug stores, banks, pawnshops, and other specialized emporia."[12] They were not victims in this abrupt cultural change, for they had goods to sell in a willing market, and afterwards, money to spend. Many pictures were taken of their colorful arrival in Dawson wearing their best parkas and decorated mitts and mukluks. If the fur dealers and butchers could not legally buy any of the Dawson Boys a drink, they certainly were treated as local celebrities. Nor were they changed by the non-Indian society. Back in their own camps in the Peel River district,

> ... they returned with the knowledge of travellers; at the same time it was these men who remained the carriers of traditional culture. Far from having been hopelessly corrupted by frontier life in its rawest form, the "Dawson Boys" provided much of the social and economic leadership of the [Fort MacPherson] band in the 1930s and '40s.

Another example of this adaptation to a new society is found in the southern Yukon. Jim Boss was the ranking man of a community on Lake Laberge at the time of the Gold Rush. His family came into the Laberge district from the south and east and were probably interior Tlingits. Instead of being overwhelmed by the Gold Rush, he used his considerable entrepreneurial skill to profit handsomely from the river of humanity that passed his camps. He trapped, netted, and sold fish, operated teams of horses, ran a road house, and involved himself in many different ways in the Yukon economy. Another side of his character is revealed in a letter in 1902 to the superintendent of Indian Affairs in Ottawa. He asked for a land claims settlement for the people in his area so that prior rights to the land could be recognized. He is quoted as saying, "tell the King very hard we want something for our Indians because they take our land and game."[13] Nothing came of this letter, nor of his efforts to obtain a grant of land for himself near Laberge.

Jim Boss continued with his many businesses. A government report for 1915 shows he operated one of the Territory's fifteen fox farms.[14] After his death, his descendants along with many other Yukon Indians continued a lifestyle that included elements from both the Indian and the larger, North American culture. They found that non-Indian economic concepts such as occasional wage employment and capitalism were not necessarily incompatible with their culture. This separation between economic livelihood and cultural traits typified the involvement of Indian people in the fur industry and colored their notions of efficient resource use. Their considerable ambition led them to capitalize on their natural resources, while their culture virtually prevented them from diminishing the fund of the resource. To be a good, hard-working trapper, or a "good rustler" or "tough traveller" were Indian cultural virtues, while acquisitiveness and waste were the opposite. Fredrick Congdon's remarks about Indian trappers which opened this chapter should not be dismissed as a hopeful liberal sentiment.

It had been known since the turn of the century that the Yukon basin contained a higher proportion of black and silver foxes among ordinary red foxes than other places in the north.[15] Black and silver fox pelts obtained the highest prices of any Canadian furs: in fact, some of the prices have never been equalled, even with the inflated dollars of the late 1970s. Stories of pelts sold for over a thousand dollars can still be heard from older people anywhere in the Yukon.

The fox of the Yukon district is the same species of fox distributed throughout western Canada. It is usually yellowish-red, with a distinctive white tip to its tail and dark, almost black feet. Two other color phases are recognized; cross fox, which is reddish with dark bluish-black areas down its back and haunches, and silver fox, which is bluish-black all over, with or without the distinctive (and valuable) silver guard hairs. The characteristic feature of the true black or silver fox is that it has no reddish cast to its fur. Foxes can be reared easily enough in captivity, for their diet is not specialized. What is important to the breeder is the genetic makeup of animals with the silver coloration. For a few years before World War I the excitement and interest attending fox genetics must have resembled that surrounding the famous black tulips of Holland in the eighteenth century. A breeding pair that gave a pure silver strain was worth up to $25,000 according to a prospectus issued by Colwell Fur Farms Ltd. of Whitehorse in 1914.[16]

Raising foxes as a commercial venture began after 1890 in Prince Edward Island, where farmer could easily obtain low cost protein from fish processing plants. A technological factor was the new availability of woven wire fencing for fox pens.[17] Sometime in 1912, although the date is uncertain, Prince Edward Island breeders decided to import pairs of black, cross, and red varieties from the Yukon to use as breeding stock. This started a flourishing industry; three hundred live foxes were exported in 1913.[18] The government publication about the Yukon Territory in 1916 devotes nine pages to fox genetics; more ink than the same book devotes to agriculture and forestry. The Yukon animals were preferred because they were larger and better furred. Trappers often saw the animals in open areas near riverbanks. In the late spring when one or the other of the parents would be staying close to the dens, trappers would put box traps over the den mouth after sealing the other entrances. For a few years, catching foxes in this way to supply breeding stock to fox ranches was an important industry.

Not surprisingly, the Yukon Territorial Council began to regulate the fox business and take a closer interest in the economics of the fur industry. The Fox Protection Ordinance of 1914 made it illegal to catch or "molest in any way" foxes under a year old. All owners of live foxes had to be registered and needed permission from the commissioner before they could export the animals, unless they had been born in captivity or were taken two years or more previous to export. It became illegal to trespass near fox pens, wherever situated. Curiously, the 1914 prospectus of Colwell Fur Farms Ltd. lists Commissioner George Black, a senior government official, and two territorial councillors among its directors. It said further, "Legislation recently passed in the Yukon Territory which prohibits the shipping out of live foxes from its borders until held in captivity for two years or more, works to the decided advantage of this company, by practically cutting off all competition for many years to come."[19]

Since George Black was an important shareholder while at the same time, as commissioner, he wielded powers over the export of foxes, his interests seemed to be in conflict. However that concept meant something different in the Dawson City of 1914 from what it does today. The ordinance did foster a strong Yukon-based fox industry quite apart from the fact that it benefited some of the members personally. Of course most of the trapping of live wild foxes was done by Indians, for they had better knowledge of the animals and the terrain. The new law went against their interests, for most Indian families could hardly afford to build the elaborate pens needed and to feed the foxes for two years.

The 1916 government report listed seventeen fox farms, the largest being J.P. Whitney Black and Silver Fox Company of Whitehorse with sixteen black foxes and thirteen cross foxes. Most farms were at Whitehorse or on the nearby Tagish and Marsh Lake system, close to abundant supplies of whitefish and salmon, when in season. Another group of farms was at Carmacks, or Tantalus as it used to be called, where both salmon and caribou were available. Most farms operated into the twenties, after which many switched to raising mink before abandoning the business. Some farmers lost stock through disease or neglect, while others did very well indeed. The 1926 publication about the Yukon by the Department of the Interior reported that "at the spring sales of Lampson and Co. in London, in 1922-23 the pelts of silver foxes from Whitehorse fox farms brought the top prices in competition with thousands of other pelts sold at the same time."[20] Despite the interest in fur farming, it was never as important as wild fur to the Territory's economy.

After World War I, the role of trapping and fur in the Yukon changed due to a soaring demand for fur that began in the 1920s. Even before the war ended, the fur market started to move upwards. Prices climbed to record levels. One estimate used an index figure of one hundred for prices in 1899. In 1916, the index for furs was three hundred; in 1919, 1009; and in 1920, 1132.[21]

The *Canada Year Book's* figures show that the country's production more than doubled in value, from barely eight million dollar's worth to more than twenty million. The Yukon's own production was given as merely two percent of the nation's annual total value, a ranking the Territory was to keep for many years. Naturally enough, the new prices attracted a lot of attention to the fur industry, just as a great increase in the number of big game hunters in 1919 and 1920 enhanced interest in that aspect of the Yukon's wildlife. Before examining how the Yukon government responded to this interest, it would be useful to take a brief look at trends in the fashion industry, to help explain a renewed interest in fur garments.

In the decorative arts, reliance on forms derived from static, animistic objects using light lines and subdued colors, such as characterized Art Nouveau, was replaced by a discovery of movement, of new colors and shapes. The Art Deco style owed its origin to the astonishing and successful productions of the Ballet Russe in Paris in 1909. Even while the fashion industry was being influenced by the show's costumes and use of color, it began to use the medium of photography to communicate those new designs to ever-larger audiences. The development of half-tone photographic reproduction in mass-circulation magazines began after about 1905 and became the principal means of advertising clothing designs. Photographs of variations in accepted patterns of dress could be made to seem acceptable, by the simple artifice of photographing models wearing the new designs in fashionable places, such as Ascot in England, or Biarritz in France. This was something quite new in advertising, and it plunged the design houses into a competition that has not ceased. Photography helped fashions to change at a faster rate. And yet in that interval between 1905 and the years of the First World War, the uses of fur in clothing did not change.

Short fur continued as linings and trimmings, while fox and marten continued in strong demand for collar, stoles, and muffs. The new fur dyeing industry allowed furs to be worn in any color for evening wear, and white fox enjoyed renewed interest as a daytime fur, worn more for decoration than function. The First World War slackened the demand for fur as fashions adapted themselves to more economical and hence "patriotic" uses of material. This is shown by the sudden rise in women's hemlines in 1915, a phenomenon which has been related to women working for the first time in industrial occupations. During the war years people made do with what they had. There was no desire to replace durable old furs. But once the war ended, everyone who could afford it rushed to catch up with the new, style-conscious age. The consumer goods market bloomed as never before, and carried fur along with it.

The Yukon Territorial government reacted to the boom in fur prices by regulating the fur harvest and by collecting new revenues from it. Before 1920 the only means of control available to the territory was to close the trapping season on a specific animal. After that year, in which substantial changes to the Game Ordinance were approved, the government took a much more active interest and set seasons, harvest limits, and other controls over trapping. However it was prompted to make such changes by agencies outside the Yukon. In 1919 Territorial Council approved the Fur Export Tax Ordinance, which was a means of collecting taxes from the newly-prosperous fur industry. Royalties per pelt were set at approximately five percent of the pelt's market value, payable at the time of export from the Territory. Other jurisdictions in Canada may have approved similar legislation at the same time, for the federal government began compiling fur statistics on an annual basis. Unfortunately, the Archives records for the Yukon are incomplete for 1918-19, so the extent of federal pressure on the Territory to impose such a tax cannot be understood. However the senior government made substantial revisions in the Yukon Act in that year which recognized the now-tiny population and reduced federal expenditures in a drastic manner. The Yukon had to earn its own way, and furs were to prove an important source of revenue.

The Yukon government found itself responsible for managing

an increasingly valuable natural resource. Commissioner George P. Mackenzie had to answer letters such as a plea from E.A. Stephens and Company of Denver, Colorado, offering 2 1/2 cents each for the names of trappers—such was their eagerness to buy fur.[22] He also had to keep the Yukon's laws and policies similar to other jurisdictions, which took a very close and even possessive interest in Yukon affairs. In April, 1919, E.W. Nelson, chief of the U.S. Biological Survey at Washington, advised the commissioner of some information he had obtained.[23] He wrote that Funston Brothers of St. Louis had just purchased 1625 beaver skins from the Yukon. Since the Territory had closed the season on beaver in 1918, Nelson wanted to know whether this fur had been taken illegally. Mackenzie replied that it was not illegal fur because the 1917-18 catch would have taken a year to reach market.

The Yukon's commissioner and Alaskan Governor Thomas Riggs communicated frequently about wildlife matters and the question of smuggling pelts across the border. Alaska had closed its beaver season for five years and its marten season for three years. Riggs feared that Alaskan fur from these animals was being taken to the Yukon and sold there as a local product. Mackenzie's reply, if any, was not filed; but less than a year later, Riggs' letter had become a subject of discussions at the ambassadorial level between the two countries. A long, rambling memorandum written by Maxwell Graham, Canada's director of Parks Animals, arrived in Dawson City. It illuminates the relentless logic of the new, centralized wildlife bureaucracy in Ottawa. Graham wrote,

> ... as the territories [Alaska and the Yukon] are not merely contiguous but identical in their fur products and resources, the reasons that demand a closed season in Alaska are likely to obtain in almost if not exactly the same degree in the Yukon Territory.[24]

Dominion Parks Commissioner J.B. Harkin attached his own, bristling letter which concluded, ''I would be obliged if you would send me a report on the action so far taken to carry out the desires of the United States Department of State.'' In his reply, Commissioner Mackenzie explained that the Yukon beaver season had been closed for some time, and that members of Territorial Council saw no need to close the season on marten as well. But he agreed that the game laws of the three jurisdictions, Alaska, the Yukon, and British

Columbia, should be similar so as to discourage smuggling across the borders.

The problem created by an illegal trade in furs over the Alaska-Yukon border seemed to be confined to the Porcupine River area. Indian and non-Indian trappers always moved freely over the border to take advantage of competitive fur buyers at Ramparts and Fort Yukon. It seemed that some trappers from Fort Yukon took their skins upriver to the closest RNWMP post and paid the newly-instituted fur export taxes. Then the trappers returned to Fort Yukon and sold those skins as Canadian fur, producing the tax receipts to prove it. There had always been a great deal of travelling between Fort Yukon and the great muskrat area at the Old Crow Flats, and the border was a meaningless concept—merely a cut line through the bush. The trappers resisted the efforts of those at Dawson City—or in Washington and Ottawa—to have them confine their trade to one side of the border. Mackenzie wrote later, "To entirely prevent this practice is, I think, impossible, but every effort will be made to cooperate with Alaska officials in the matter."[25] In 1920, Alaska renewed its closed season on marten for another three years. The Yukon Council did not follow their example, because trappers and fur buyers argued that marten and mink were apt to be caught in the same trap. In other words, to stop trapping marten, they would have to stop virtually all trapping. This was a questionable excuse, for marten and mink rarely frequent the same area, but it was politically adequate for Ottawa. The bootlegging issue died away for many years, probably because the RNWMP officers on the Porcupine River learned who the trappers were who were likely to be importing illegal fur.

Not until 1914 did the Yukon administration show any great interest in its fur resources, and that interest came about because of a sudden increase in fur prices. By 1920, the administration was learning to both manage and collect revenues from its wildlife resources, and to respond to a bureaucratic equivalent of a nudge from other jurisdictions with an interest in Yukon wildlife policies. However, this new interest in fur happened simultaneously all over the continent as the market for consumer goods developed right after the First World War. The Yukon was home to some of the world's best long furs; for trappers in the early twenties, the future looked very bright.

7

Years of Prosperity

The quality of Yukon wild furs attracted wide attention during the 1920s. Inquiries and requests came to the Yukon commissioner from fur buying houses all over the continent. In August, 1920, the A.B. Schubert and Company of Winnipeg, "The Greatest Fur House on Earth," according to its colorful letterhead, offered prizes of up to $250 for photographs of fur collections, live animals, or animals in traps.[1] This contest may have been the reason behind numerous pictures taken then of Yukon trappers with their pelts displayed around them on porches, railings, and clotheslines.[2] Whatever the reason or origin for the custom, photographs of proud-looking men, women, and children posing before hundreds, even thousands of dollars' worth of furs became familiar keepsakes of many Yukon families, chronicling the good years of the twenties and thirties. The late twenties in particular provided a seller's market, a time of great prosperity for trappers everywhere in the North.

Things were going so well for the Yukon fur trade that it soon became fossilized in its own success, its vitality squeezed away. Stagnation began to encircle trappers even while fur prices remained high, a condition which revealed itself in many ways. The success of individual trappers was a central, core reason. Beyond the trappers, and scarcely influenced by them, the Yukon government attempted to manage the fur bearers through regulations, taxes, and closed seasons. In turn, the government was influenced by fur traders, who sought to expand their businesses by increasing the amounts of credit they offered. The traders and the marketplace beyond them influenced government to change the trapping laws. These laws and their increasing enforcement enclosed ever more tightly the freedom of action of individual trappers. The rings of constriction were intensified by the offering of credit. As long as prices remained comparatively high, this process did not reveal itself to the people involved.

The meteoric rise of fur prices in 1919 and 1920 was slowed by a miniature depression in 1921 and recovered strongly to peak in the late twenties. The Depression had a pronounced effect on the demand for furs, but it was not so great that individual trappers suffered; it was a two to three year lull in an otherwise healthy market. Peaks in prices of 1927-28 were matched by declines in 1932-33 so that the average prices from 1920 to 1940 do not show great variation. To put it another way, trapping continued to be a viable livelihood during that time, even though fur farming became less attractive. During the Second World War and for a year or two afterwards, prices followed the earlier trends and even increased, only to fall away to very poor levels after 1947-48.

Varieties of fox ranged in price from $15 for red fox to $100 or more for silver until the middle thirties, when the prices for fox of all kinds declined to low levels.[3] Marten averaged around $20 in the twenties falling to about $11 during the Depression years, but recovering strongly to $25 just before World War Two. Lynx fluctuated between $20 and $30 each. Beaver dropped from about $20 down to $8 during the Depression, then recovered; muskrat also suffered a severe drop in prices before regaining the normal, average price of $1.20. Large, matched pelts of top quality might have been worth more than twice as much as these average values for the most important fur species. Average prices may be misleading for another reason. Fur traders maximize their profit by obtaining as much fur as they can. To do this they will be liberal in their grading of the trapper's catch so long as the market is buoyant. But if the market declines, they will tend to be conservative or they will not buy at all.[4] The needs of clothing fashion also will change from one year to the next. This meant that trappers selling to an independent, competitive fur buyer could expect wild fluctuations in the prices offered, higher and lower than the values compiled and published annually by the Dominion Bureau of Statistics.

The twenties were well-known as an age when fashions changed more rapidly than any time before or since. Furs received a lot of attention because they were a luxury in an age appreciative of the qualities for which they had always been in demand. The fur market reflected surges in consumer spending on all luxury goods, despite a drop in demand for durable goods, home furnishings, and wool fabrics.[5] Department stores became a force in merchandising of consumer goods by their ability to stock all the sought-after accessories to clothing of the day, and more broadly, to cater to every whim of the buying public. In Canada the Hudson's Bay Company was no exception; by the mid-twenties it owned large stores in most western Canadian cities and changed its emphasis from that of a trading company into one of an aggressive merchandising firm. Their furs still played a key role, for the Bay was by far the largest supplier of furs to Canada and Britain. But this improved marketing grew in response to the demand, and a reason for the consumer demand may lie with the soaring popularity of films.

Before the First World War, fashion communication relied on photography; afterwards, the static, posed photographs of mannequins could not convey the post-war fascination with movement and suppleness, nor could the black and white photos show the new colors. Fashion magazines turned to line drawings and blocks of color. The artists typically drew their figures with elongated limbs and small heads to focus attention on the clothing. Memories of the Great War were still painfully fresh, so fresh that anything from the recent past—colors, hemlines, garment shape, even scents, and makeup—anything old became passé in a world growing used to the new medium of film, a new appearance of reality. Movies showed not merely the new fashions but the new lifestyle. Even if that lifestyle had little to do with ordinary reality, it was close enough to the dreams of the average person to provide an excuse to change, and the pace of change accelerated through the decade.

It would be hard to think of the twenties without recalling cloche hats, short, tubular skirts, and the classic coat of 1928—knee-length beige wool, plainly buttoned, with a red or silver fox collar rolled above soft lines of the neck and shoulders.[6] Some short furs such as muskrat appeared worn outside and not as linings, but trimmed with more costly furs. Mink became another "daytime" fur. Enhanced prices made it feasible for the first time to match and painstakingly sew small thin skins like muskrat and mink into attractively uniform panels. White fox gained status as an evening fur. Deep shawl collars of long, uniform furs appeared towards the end of the decade and continued into the thirties. Another characteristic fur garment of the twenties was the raccoon coat, the low-cost imitation of the more desirable variegated furs like wolf, lynx, or coyote, all very popular with young men. Fifty years later this style would return bringing with it exceptional prices for these pelts.

In January, 1927, San Francisco fur merchant Louis Levy wrote to Yukon commissioner Percy Reid about the market. He said,

> Lynx, Red Fox, Cross Fox and Mink are in very strong demand, and in fact all furs from the Yukon are bringing around 25% more than last year at this time ....I handle all Shorty Chambers' furs, and have Johnny Johns the native buying fur around Carcross country. Am handling Thayer's furs from Carmacks. These traders are up against Taylor and Drury who are hard competition, and we can pay more than they do, as I get better prices and can pay more.... Business has been very good for the past four months and all indications point to a good season. The country is prosperous and people are spending lots of money.[7]

Levy was one of a dozen fur buyers who wrote to the commissioner on a regular basis with inquiries about licenses and game regulations. It would seem that the Yukon administration did not actively promote the fur business. Levy's letter shows he knew Reid personally which was hardly unusual in a territory containing merely four thousand people. All the Yukon commissioners during the twenties and thirties, George Mackenzie, Percy Reid,

G.I. MacLean, and later, George Jeckell, made it their business to know personally as many of the traders, salesmen, and other businessmen with Yukon interests as they could. It was an old Yukon habit, a throwback, like so many of the Territory's customs, to Gold Rush business ethics and camaraderie. But simply having information on market trends, and knowledge of successful trappers and traders did not automatically produce good management of the Yukon's fur resources.

During the 1920s the government at Dawson City began to take its lead from other jurisdictions in the management of its fur resources, in spite of great differences between the Territory and other places. A low population and the vast land area effectively prevented overharvesting. Besides, most trappers were Indian who were unlikely to trap for cash, or in excess of their own perceived needs. A whole generation born at the time of the Gold Rush reached maturity during this decade. They had been exposed since childhood to the technology and cultural notions of the larger, North American society, while their parents made the adjustment as adults. Younger people took to the new trapping lifestyle with alacrity and were very successful. The government chose not to interfere in the relationship the trappers had with the fur buyers such as Taylor and Drury, while the resource itself was left to the watchful eye of the Royal North West Mounted Police (after 1924, the Royal Canadian Mounted Police).

O.S. Finnie, director of the Northwest Territories and Yukon Branch of the Department of the Interior, was the senior official responsible for dealing with Yukon affairs in the twenties. This man, more than any other, was to prod the sometimes sleepy Yukon administration into life, more to keep up appearances with agencies outside the Yukon than to lead it to new heights of self-determination. In fact, Finnie reacted with some irritation whenever the Yukon chose to go its own way.

Finnie wanted the Yukon's wildlife laws to be in harmony with those in Alaska, the Northwest Territories, and British Columbia. As he was also the *de facto* commissioner of the Northwest Territories, he could enact there whatever game regulations he chose, provided, of course, that the Hudson's Bay Company did not use its political influence. The Yukon commissioners were nominally Finnie's subordinates. Acting through the commissioner, Finnie could merely "submit" or "recommend" policy to the elected Territorial Council. Yet the Council, a tiny, three-man nucleus of democracy, evidently was not overly-conscious of its importance and did its best to agree with the federal requests especially as they concerned wildlife and fur bearers. They showed a similar accommodation of Alaskan requests.

In June, 1924, Commissioner Mackenzie was informed by E.W. Nelson of the U.S. Biological Survey in Washington about Alaska's new fur laws. He asked to have the Yukon marten season closed for 1924-25, saying that improvements in transportation to the Alaskan interior following the completion of the Alaskan Railroad in 1919 had "enabled trappers to clean up beaver and marten more rapidly than ever before." One is reminded here of the controversy surrounding the sale of game meat to the railway construction camps, which left the U.S. Interior Department sensitive to Alaskan wildlife issues. Nelson justified the Alaskan closure on these grounds and not on any direct evidence of depletion, and went on to state:

> While anticipating the hardship that this may place temporari- ly on Indians and others who are more or less dependent on trapping, at the same time such hardship is really in their best interest and is absolutely necessary if they are to have a future income.[8]

In his reply, Mackenzie explained that he had recently obtained powers to close the season on any fur bearer and that he would do so with marten. However since the beaver season had just re- opened after a five-year closure, that would remain open. To Nelson's short treatment of Alaskan Indians, Mackenzie replied at some length:

> I am firmly of the opinion that if the trapping of fur was left exclusively in the hands of the natives we would have little trouble in conserving the supply of fur bearers. The white trap- per as a rule is the menace to the fur bearing animals and not the Indians. We have heard a great deal in this country about the combination of prospector and trapper. As far as my experience goes, the [white] trapper is rarely a prospector. In most cases he poisons the fur bearing animals unless closely watched.[9]

By proclamation on July 5, 1924, Mackenzie halted all marten trapping for a three-year period. Just before he signed the notice, he received a letter from J.H. Mervyn, a trader established at Lansing on the Stewart River, who protested the plans to close the marten season. Mervyn agreed that there had been a decline in marten populations but attributed this to some natural cause, not to trapping. It was his observation that marten populations had been on an increase for the past two years. His letter had no effect. Nor did a telegram from Fort Yukon, signed by nineteen men, probably over half of whom were Indians, which also said marten populations were high in their district along the Porcupine River.

The files do not show any petitions to Council or RCMP reports about a scarcity of marten, nor was there a falling off in the numbers taken in previous years. This might lead one to conclude that the main reason behind the closure was the Alaskan situation, which request came in turn from Washington, not Juneau, Alaska's capital, and had more to do with the perceived potential of overharvesting along the railway. There was simply no evidence on which to base the decision. Ironically, O.S. Finnie in Ottawa did not enact comparable legislation in the Northwest Territories. Hence traders like Mervyn and others close to the Northwest Territories border had to seek permission to buy marten from Indians from the Mackenzie valley, who occasionally travelled into the Yukon watershed to trade.

A similar situation came up again four years later. O.S. Finnie informed MacLean in May, 1928, that the beaver season in the Northwest Territories would soon be closed for a three-year period and asked that the Yukon do the same. MacLean replied some two months later that he had discussed the idea with members of the Territorial Council and several trappers.[10] They all told him that beavers were seriously depleted and that a long closed season would be a good idea. This sounds questionable because there had been a long closure on beaver trapping from 1918 to 1924, and the harvest after that had averaged around normal levels of three thousand to thirty-five hundred pelts. Commissioner MacLean then closed the beaver season by a proclamation on September 1, 1928.

There was an immediate reaction. On the same day that the closure was published, William S. Drury of Taylor and Drury Ltd. wrote to the commissioner complaining about his actions. Drury explained that the firm's post at Ross River had already equipped trappers for the coming season with items they needed to take beaver; now they could not do so. He went on,

Last year we paid out over $30,000 for beaver. You can readily see how the loss of this huge sum, which is practically all spent in the territory, will depreciate the buying power of Indians and trappers and make different policies necessary. Trappers within [the Yukon] bought this last summer, hundreds of dollars' worth of beaver traps, canvas for portable canoes and many other items entirely for beaver hunting. We also gave out thousands of dollars' worth of credit which we shall have to work hard to collect ...[11]

Drury went on to propose a quota system rather than a closed season, to be instituted next year, in 1929. Evidently the firm had purchased about a third of the Yukon's 1926 total of 3,570 beaver.[12] His arguments carried a lot of weight. MacLean promptly rescinded his proclamation, then wrote back to Drury,

I shall be pleased to discuss the fur question with you the first time I am in Whitehorse, as I desire to be informed on all questions affecting the territory, and the fur business is developing into one of the main sources of livelihood.

Ironically, a few months later O.S. Finnie also conceded that the closing of the beaver season in the Northwest Territories had been premature. A serious influenza epidemic swept the lower Mackenzie district in the summer of 1928, causing the deaths of an estimated three hundred people.[13] If the weakened survivors had been prevented from taking beaver even for food, their hardship would have been very great. A cabinet Order in Council withdrew the closure. Finnie's centralized administration had failed to meet or even to understand local conditions in the Northwest Territories and the Yukon.

The question of using game meat in fur farms provides another example of conflict between the Yukon's views on game management and the Ottawa view. Fur farmers had been using game meat to feed their fox and mink for a decade before the practice received legal sanction in 1925. In that year, a police constable newly arrived in Carmacks complained to his superintendent about fur farmers in the settlement who had been taking game meat year round under the generous provisions of their market hunting licenses. The zealous officer interpreted the law to mean that the meat was to be used for human consumption and not for animals, and no doubt made himself thoroughly unpopular in the process. The commissioner secured an amendment to the Game Ordinance which allowed both caribou and moose meat to be used for fur farm animals providing a special permit was obtained and records were kept.

A year passed before the amendment reached the desk of O.S. Finnie in Ottawa for the customary review by the senior government of all Yukon ordinances. He complained to the commissioner that the law was unnecessary and a waste of game.[14] A few months later in its 1926 session, Territorial Council obligingly amended the law to exclude moose from the permit, but left provision for caribou to continue to be used without restriction. For the next few years the Carmacks fox and mink farmers were the only ones to take the permit requirements seriously. They filed annual returns as to the caribou they killed and used in this way, generally about twenty-five animals a year among the five farmers. However, the 1926 amendments did not end the matter.

In June 1930, Finnie tried again. He wrote that the Game Ordinance had been "reviewed" by the deputy minister of the Interior, also by the Advisory Board on Wildlife Protection and they had agreed that the section allowing the use of caribou meat should be removed from the law. His letter concluded "it is felt that there can be no set of circumstances which justify slaughtering caribou in the closed season for the purposes of feeding fur bearing animals in captivity."[15] Council did not change the law and Finnie did not press the matter, even though he had power to do so. On this or any other matter he could have instructed the Yukon commissioner to introduce an amendment or even threaten to abolish the Council and call a new election. However an amending bill might have been defeated, creating an embarrassing situation for the Ottawa administration. The law stayed on the books until 1938. As for the farmers, only two or three continued to apply for permits, while others may have used fish or imported meals to feed their animals, or simply ignored the law. The latter was more likely.

Beyond the examples of closed seasons on fur bearers and the use of game to feed mink and fox, there were other, larger issues concerning game management which concerned the Yukon. These were the levying and collection of fur export taxes, the management of the fur trade industry and preliminary planning for trapline registration. As its policies matured, they tended to have regressive effects on the very trappers who provided a revenue source of increasing importance.

Between 1920 and 1947, the Yukon Territory collected between eight and twelve thousand dollars each year from export taxes on its fur production. What appears today to be an almost insignificant sum represented about ten percent of all Yukon-derived government revenues from such things as business licenses and property taxes through the 1920s.[16] It was a revenue source that declined in importance in later years, but until the Second World War, taxes were an important issue among Canada's wildlife managers. All jurisdictions tried to keep these taxes at comparable levels to avoid opportunities to profit by bootlegging furs into another province or territory where the fees were lower. Such laws were a constitutional anomaly, for they restricted interprovincial trade, normally a federal prerogative.

Each pelt of some twelve different fur bearers had to be cleared past a government inspector before it could be shipped outside the Yukon. At one time, the RCMP used to search the baggage of passengers embarking on the British Yukon Navigation steamboats for furs on which the taxes had not been paid, a task many found very disagreeable. Generally the fees were about five percent of the pelt's value. They were collected at some point along the series of transactions between the trapper or fur farmer and the market for his furs: not surprisingly, the collection point was controversial. A resolution of an interprovincial game officers' meeting in Edmonton in May, 1933 proposed that the taxes be collected from the "first purchaser" of the fur.[17] The alternative was to collect from the exporter, but this would have required single large payments, greater cash outlays, and greater incentives for evasion. Evidently it did not seem feasible to have the fur exporters raise their prices on the outside markets. The first purchaser idea was the one used in the Yukon and it had a regressive effect on fur producers, for it reduced their earnings by five percent, depending on the amount of the tax. It was symptomatic of the attitudes of the centralized scheme of management.

The business aspects of trapping became of interest to the Yukon government nearly a decade after other jurisdictions had taken the lead. The game officers' convention of 1933 approved a number of other resolutions regarding the fur industry, among them ones calling for trapline registration, wolf bounties, closer enforcement of seasons and catch limits, management of game sanctuaries, and others which show that fur had become a subject of serious discussion by governments after decades of neglect. Indians, it was suggested, should be required to comply with all trapping laws including licensing requirements. Trapping was becoming a very good livelihood over a long term, so Indian trappers were then seen to be indistinguishable from white entrepreneurs who earned a living in the same way. All these ideas must have given Yukon Commissioner George Jeckell some concern, for clearly the 1920 Game Ordinance was behind the times. It took him several years to work some of these concepts into Yukon game law. In 1938, a new Game Ordinance brought the fur industry firmly under government control, but the matter of trapline registrations was deferred for over ten years.

Among the new sections in the Ordinance was one requiring fur dealers to be licensed and to operate only at designated posts. Such a requirement helped make fur buying more of a monopoly situation for the established traders, Taylor and Drury in particular. The existing debt or jawbone relationship was thereby strengthened with the added proviso that game officers, Indian agents, and RCMP officers gained powers to examine trader's books, presumably for evidence of fraud. At one level it might seem that Taylor and Drury wanted to eliminate their competition and therefore urged the measure's adoption by Territorial Council; however, the industry was very well established by then and a return to the near-anarchy of the early twenties could have been dangerous to Indian trappers and Taylor and Drury alike. The danger lay in upsetting the trapper-trader relationship which enabled trappers to be financed for the coming season. Then too, the government wanted its taxes and licenses collected in a reliable fashion, just as the traders wanted to collect their debts. Granting conditions suitable for a monopoly seemed to be a workable solution.

During these years in Dawson City, Mayo, and Whitehorse there were several traders who worked competitively. Companies such as Northern Commercial and Taylor and Drury extended credit based on the personal reputation of the trapper and his relationship with the trader. They paid cash for furs, deducting whatever was outstanding against the trapper's account. Credit enabled a trapper's family to obtain groceries during the time the man was away, to be repaid later. It frequently happened that the stores were not able to recover their debts. Losses had to be recovered from the next year's profit. For this reason they tried to avoid cash as much as possible. There was much sympathy for this attitude within government; the belief was that the Indian trapper would use cash in some manner administrators would have judged inappropriate, such as partying. Unfortunately this attitude ignored the fact that the most successful entrepreneurs at the time of the Gold Rush and later, such as Jim Boss, worked on a cash basis.

Trappers needed both foodstuffs and equipment to begin a winter's work. The number of items needed might increase each year because they were available, affordable, and went a long way towards making the trapper's work easier. He needed traditional staples such as flour, sugar, beans, tea, tobacco, and other foodstuffs, as well as traps, snare wire, ammunition, canvas, and so on. When fur prices increased and trapping became more rewarding, his needs included more manufactured goods such as modern repeating firearms, tents, items of clothing, tin stoves, lamps, and equipment for his dog teams such as harnesses and sleds which he might not make himself. If he was well equipped by the standards of the twenties and thirties, he might be able to increase his production to the point where he could afford a boat and an outboard motor or "kicker" which one might argue was the biggest technological advance in the Canadian north since the arrival of firearms.

The technology available to the trapper remained at a plateau for decades and consequently, so did his methods of production. In fact, the most important changes came after 1950, with the use of motorized toboggans or Ski-Doos, chain saws, and new humane traps such as the Conibear. A typical trapline had about fifty traps, although some might have had two or even three hundred. The trapper usually had a partner to help him so he might have owned two dog teams as well, besides which the difficult task of thawing carcasses, skinning them, and stretching and cleaning the hides was one likely to be shared. Outpost cabins would be used, for two or three days may have been needed to check the traps on a big line. The term "trapline" can be misleading. The area covered in one season might not be covered in the next; also, the trapper might make choices about what species of animal he wanted to catch and vary his route accordingly. The boundaries of his area changed according to his needs and success, sometimes even week by week. Then too, he might have decided in the fall to concentrate one type of fur and rule out entirely his chances of catching others.

In the thirties, a man whose principal livelihood came from trapping might have between five hundred and a thousand dollars invested in his outfit. This investment would enable him to buy the best equipment available, which would then improve his efficiency. Besides, when the cost of freight was included in the price of trade goods, it was a foolish economy to purchase anything less than the best obtainable. For example, ordinary steel traps cost from ten to twelve dollars per dozen in those years. Newhouse traps were preferred because they had double springs and long chains. The toggle or anchor could be placed farther away from the set trap, an advantage when setting for wary animals like foxes. But these traps were much more expensive, often twenty to twenty-five dollars per dozen. Capital for this investment could have come from several sources. Most Yukon Indian men had other sources of income in the summers, such as from work on the steamboats, cutting cordwood, big game guiding, commercial fishing, market hunting, and other wage and contract work. These earnings, along with equipment borrowed from relatives, could help a man to complete a trapper's outfit. However as the thirties wore on, credit became more and more important as trappers tried to increase the size of their outfits and their production of fur. A softening of the fur market in the Depression may have triggered this.

Trappers near the isolated posts with no choice of fur buyers could avoid a monopoly only by traveling to the larger centers at considerable cost in time and money to themselves. Thus the convenience of trading for goods—or tokens if the goods were not available—usually outweighed the higher prices and advantages of selling for cash in the towns. The trappers got some benefit from the jawbone system because it insulated them from fluctuations in fur prices and allowed them to assemble their outfit more easily.[18] The trader gained in turn because he could influence the trapper to concentrate on a particular kind of fur, or sell for particular goods, such as those which would keep him trapping instead of taking on another livelihood. Pelts offered in payment for more traps could hardly be used instead for a steamboat ticket to a higher-paying job as a big game guide: traders in isolated posts could have a great deal of influence on these kinds of choices.

On the other hand, competition among fur buyers meant that established traders lost business and money, the latter often through bad debts. These debts plus faltering prices forced the posts to tighten up their credit policies, making it even more difficult for trappers to equip themselves and improve their lot through their own efforts. They had to trap more animals, increase their efficiency, sell their catch as soon as possible and collect less than full value. In the end, the trapper was bound to the post for most of his needs without means to go elsewhere.

Monopoly control of the fur trade in a district held the possibility of overcoming the worst abuses of the credit system, providing that the trader followed liberal policies. Many did, and suffered along with the trappers when prices declined. There is some truth in the following quotation from a 1930s history of the Hudson's Bay Company:

> The whole history of the fur trade in America points to the conclusion that only through monopoly can it be conducted with efficiency and justice ... The Hudson's Bay Company furnishes us with the only example of peace and justice and efficiency ... No matter what the charges brought against this company ... conditions have never been so bad as with competition.[19]

It expressed the conventional wisdom of at least a century, that monopoly was not a bad thing, so the actions of the Territorial Government in creating the 1938 Game Ordinance are therefore understandable.

The years of the great Depression were not difficult ones for most Yukon residents. The economic heartbeat provided by the gold placers in the Klondike basin and the small silver mines in the Mayo area kept the trains and steamboats running. But the fur market did falter and things were not as good for Yukon trappers as they were in the late twenties. This price slump laid the foundation for the Game Ordinance of 1938 and its protectionist measures.

The Depression left an indelible impression, particularly in western Canada. And while millions went without luxuries such as furs, appliances, and automobiles they could afford to buy five years before, there were enough buyers of furs to keep the bottom from falling out of the market. Statistics in the *Canada Year Book* prove that more furs were purchased in the thirties than the twenties.[20] This may be due to lowered prices making fur garments more affordable, particularly in light of the growth of the mink farming industry throughout the continent. During the thirties it was as though people wished to make statements about themselves and dressed better—or at least more expensively— than they had previously. It was far from being an egalitarian decade in the sense that people might not wish to appear wealthy: it was quite the opposite. For the first time those who could afford it bought full-length silver fox coats without worrying about appearing to be ostentatious or vulgar. Indeed it was as though people wished to wear fur to show others that they were not broke. Until this attitude took root, fur dealers endured several bad years; even the Hudson's Bay Company lost money on its furs between 1931 and 1934.[21]

During the thirties, fashion designers turned to photography and away from the line drawings of the 1920s magazines. Early in the decade with the advent of sound in films an edge of realism pushed aside Hollywood fantasies. One might say that people became more individualistic, or felt included in some way, especially when the radio audience was growing so rapidly, and this individuality saw its expression in new clothing styles, especially new ways of wearing furs. The shapeless dresses of the twenties were stuffed into trunks as women wore bias cut garments which fitted the body closely. This gave a tailored appearance to photographed mannequins that was very difficult to imitate. Vitality and movement were no longer fashionable; everything became focussed on the body's potential for movement as shown in the attitude of the shoulders and hips. As this gained popularity, clothing became almost bizarre. Fur garments showed striking patterns and proportions which photographed very well indeed, especially in the surrealistic settings chosen by the best fashion photographers.

It seemed that furs were used more for their appearance than for warmth, durability, and light weight. Many fur bearers have contrasting light and dark areas in their pelts; some such as skunk are strongly striped. Coats in the thirties were often made up with the skins sewn in geometric designs, zig-zags or concentric circles. Other coats showed the individual skins with which they were made, something a furrier normally tries his best to avoid. Full length coats of small furs such as muskrat appeared along with "little furs," jackets or shawls, made of a few carefully-matched skins sewn to a good fabric. Styles changed every winter. Something of a nadir was attained in 1938 with the arrival of the "bulky look." To a person accustomed to modern styles, it would seem that handfuls of wadding were packed into the shoulders of both men and women's outer clothing, extending them out over the arms like a yoke. Some of these more remarkable designs were supplemented by the hats women wore; illustrations show hats made of a fox head peeping over the mannequin's head as though searching for the rest of its pelt, coiled around the neck. In such times the market for furs must have seemed to be on a solid footing. Anyone interested in furs and the Yukon government not the least would have good reason to plan for a stable fur industry. Those reasons held for many years, until after the Second World War. But they were wiped away by new attitudes towards dress which appeared in the late forties when furs went into a long decline.

Some other aspects of the Yukon's management of its fur bearers need to be examined. We have seen that the government used closed seasons to regulate harvests of certain animals, and collected taxes from pelts sold both as a revenue source and also to maintain statistics. But it seemed hesitant to follow management ideas of other jurisdictions because they seemed to be inappropriate to the Yukon situation. The attitude of the administration, and of Commissioner George Jeckell in particular, seemingly allowed divisions within the Yukon community on local matters, yet defended the local fur industry from encroachment by others. This can be pointed out by a 1930s dispute over hunting and trapping areas conflicting with mining, in which the government sided with the miners. But on another occasion, besides the fur buying restrictions already mentioned, the administration protected local trappers from a new threat.

The dispute over trapping lands arose near Teslin, and concerned the complaint of Joe Squam, a ranking man in that community. Squam exercised authority similar to ownership over parts of the Nisutlin and Wolf River valleys, except that it was usufructory ownership in the sense described in Chapter 1. He had been used to seeing prospectors pass through the district every year. In 1919, some of these men had used poison to take wolves, with the result that one Teslin man, known as "Mister Hall" (Billy Hall, Sr.), had several of his dogs poisoned. Hall complained to the police and had the satisfaction of seeing the men convicted, fined, and paying him fifty dollars in compensation.[22] Joe Squam certainly knew of this episode when he made his own complaint to the commissioner about prospectors and non-Indian trappers in 1931:

> I am an Indian Chief here and have to look out for my people's interest ... we resent having white people come and scatter poison bait on our trapping ground. If this poisoning are kept up we shall soon not have any furs to catch and as our living depend on trapping fur, this is a serious matter to us.[23]

Jeckell did not reply to this letter. In 1932 the mining activity increased. A small company sent in a crew of a dozen men to old placer gold workings on Iron Creek, a tributary of the Nisutlin, while others explored streams in the Englishman's Range adjacent to the Wolf River.[24] Unemployment, renewed interest in gold mining with gold now at $35 per ounce, and the potential of trapping during the winter made this isolated part of the Yukon seem attractive to men who had no livelihood, even when they had to pay $100 each for a nonresident's trapping license.

Joe Squam wrote another letter, this time to the Superintendent General for Indian Affairs in Ottawa, for official recognition and protection for his land rights. He wrote,

> I am sending you a sketch of my trapping and hunting ground. I have hunted and trapped over this ground since a child. I wish you could grant me the right to hunt and trap on this ground. I do not wish you to understand that I want to exclude anyone ... Everyone around Teslin Lake recognises my trapping ground, but others may come in who will not do so.[25]

His letter and the accompanying map passed through the Indian Affairs office, the Dominion Lands Board, and then returned to the Yukon for an opinion from Commissioner Jeckell, who replied,

> I have brought this communication to the attention of the Indian Agent, Rev John Hawksley, and he has given me certain information relative to this Indian who appears to be a Chief without much standing in his Band.

> I would not recommend the creation of special preserves in this Territory for the Indians for hunting and trapping, as such action would greatly hamper the exploration and development of the mineral resources of the Territory.[26]

This bureaucratic finesse put an end to Squam's complaint without answering any of the issues raised. Squam had two wives, which was then not unusual in Teslin. But it could scarcely enhance his reputation with the Anglican missionary there, or with the Rev. Hawksley, who in all likelihood never set foot in the place. Squam's complaint was with white trappers and not prospectors, that they were trapping on his ground and using poison. Jeckell ignored these things. There was no room in his interpretation of his duties for solving the problems of individual Indians; that was the responsibility of the Indian agent, and if the agent was unconcerned, so was Jeckell.

The Yukon administration moved quickly to protect the trapping industry and individual trappers in particular from outside threats. Early in 1937, the RCMP at Fort Smith in the Northwest Territories became concerned about the activities of non-Indian trappers working near the headwaters of the Liard River, a heavily forested plateau brought within easy reach by aircraft on skis.[27] One trapper in particular had been causing them concern. The federal government quickly amended the game regulations in the Northwest Territories to prevent trappers from using aircraft and urged the Yukon to do the same. Territorial Council dutifully amended the Game Ordinance at the spring session. It became illegal to use aircraft for any wildlife-related use except transporting a trapper's outfit between camps. They also created a nonresident's trapping license apart from the old nonresident's hunting license which permitted trapping, and set the fee for this new license at $300—clearly a deterrent tax.

In all the excitement and investment attached to the mining industry's long history in the Yukon Territory, the contribution made by trapping to the economy between the wars was often slighted or overlooked. Yet trapping, not mining, supplied the economic glue that held the Territory together. Trapping provided the most important livelihood for the Indian people. Trading posts and the commerce to supply them reduced the costs of mining exploration. Fur export taxes supplied important government revenues. The government never seemed to appreciate the industry's potential, and managed it in an erratic fashion, moving one way then another in response to outside or local influences. The luxury of space with abundant game and fur bearers exempted them from the necessity of careful management. As well, the government seemed over-protective of its resident fur buyers and sanctioned credit policies which ultimately worked against individual trappers. But the prices paid for Yukon furs remained good and they insulated most trappers from the short-term effects of the 1938 Game Ordinance amendments. Most Yukoners lived well in the twenties and thirties; the prosperity of those decades for Indian people was not to be repeated.

8

Ten Dollar Traplines

Trapping had for decades provided the principal means of self-support for hundreds of Yukon families, both Indian and white. All aspects of trapping together with big game guiding made wildlife the most important single Yukon industry after mining. Indeed one could argue mining was less important because it employed nonresidents, mostly, on a seasonal basis, and royalties and other direct benefits did not stay in the Territory any more than they do today. So far this history has examined how the government managed its fur resources in times of relative prosperity; now it must turn to the late forties and a time of collapse in the fur market. This served as a hard test of the political maturity of a government with forty years of experience in managing the only natural resource under its legislative control. The single issue of the registration of traplines showed that the Yukon government failed this test in the same manner as it failed to plan for an expanded big game industry.

It was an unfortunate coincidence that trapline registration began during a time of low fur prices. The government's new policies of administration resulted from closer ties between the Yukon Territory and the rest of Canada, and the spread of "outside" concepts of management. Plotting trapping areas on large scale maps, collecting fees, and issuing certificates seemingly brought order to a system which appeared chaotic to new arrivals in the Territory. George Jeckell's retirement as Yukon commissioner in 1947 removed the most formidable obstacle to new ideas, but those ideas lacked a vital ingredient, the deep conservatism needed to shape them to the Yukon mold. The change in administration saw the expansion of the Indian Affairs bureaucracy and its interposition between Indians and the local government. The trapping industry became a casualty; it was divided, conquered, and left to stagnate at the very time that the government should have been making every effort to protect it.

The onset of low prices was not sudden. Starting in 1947, first one, then another kind of fur dropped ten to twenty percent each spring while muskrat and mink held steady.[1] Those two species together were not as important to the Yukon as marten, lynx, fox, and beaver, but these species were hit hard. The effect of the market drop was therefore uneven; people far to the north who depended on muskrat hardly felt any change while those who trapped long furs were wiped out. There was no warning to Yukon trappers that their future earnings were in jeopardy. They had seen the market falter three times before; in 1921-22, 1931-32, and 1939-41, and they had managed those years without difficulty. They were confident about the long-term health of the fur business. To this day, people cannot identify any one year that the market failed, yet in the short space of three years, people had to abandon the lifestyle that went with trapping.

The Second World War dominated every aspect of commerce including fur. The decade cannot be discussed in the same way as earlier ones, for it was marked by a complete change in emphasis on dress by the continent's consumers. The Christian Dior "New Look," the failure of the British fur market to re-establish itself after the war, and changed garment manufacturing techniques all had a role in this decline. Perhaps also buyers felt a reaction to the styles and attitudes of the thirties, for even though prices became very low, they never placed sufficient demand on furs to stabilize the prices. Low prices and overproduction of ranch furs worked in a vicious circle which dropped prices down in a spiral each year until 1958 when they bottomed out. Even in the recovery of the late 1970s furs had not attained their relative values in the 1920s for long furs.

Christian Dior initiated the greatest changes in women's clothing fashions after the war. His Paris 1947 "New Look" diverged markedly from 1930s and wartime uniform styles as they had natural shoulders and waists and used much more material; this latter point was important because Dior's designs were sponsored by French industrialist Claude Boussac, who was building his textile empire with Marshall Plan development capital. For reasons which remain elusive, furs did not suit these new designs, especially the long bulky furs such as lynx and fox, and their prices dropped abruptly in the same year. One might believe that short, uniform furs like mink and muskrat made garments which were smaller in silhouette and therefore more stylish.

The decline of the fur market included other factors. During the Second World War, Britain stopped fur imports and the Hudson's Bay Company annual auctions—long the world's largest—had to be suspended.[2] New York replaced London as the largest buyer of Canadian fur. Before the war Britain imported between eight and ten million pelts; by 1949 sales dropped to less than five million. By contrast, U.S. buyers purchased five million in 1939 and over eighteen million in 1949.[3] Over half of this latter total, and of its value as well, were represented by mink, both wild and ranch-raised. Clearly Britain lost its centuries-old supremacy in the Canadian fur trade. Fur producers, trappers, and fur farmers became subject to the vagaries of the volatile American garment trade. British furrier knew marten, fox, and beaver, especially beaver: American furriers, blessed with a good supply of muskrat and other light, short furs from the southern states, knew how to dress, design, and sell furs in ways different from the British. Even freight costs seemed to weigh against London. It was cheaper for Canadian dealers to ship small, less-expensive skins to New York than to London, when the pelt's value was balanced against its weight, so in a time of a falling market, dealers took advantage of every economy they could make. London's famous design district along Saville Row was bombed heavily during the war:

without stretching the point, one could argue that the bombing ruined many livelihoods in Canada as well. Britain's textile industry could not keep pace with its competitors abroad. Weakness in the garment industry led to shortages of investment capital to build plants, develop new styles and clothing designs, and keep the furriers buying Canadian furs.

The change in the fur market was more severe in its effects because it followed a time of unusual prosperity. The building of the Alaska Highway created many opportunities for people to obtain wage or contract employment. "Cost-plus" wartime contracts offered high wages that in turn raised wages and contract prices in other work. The excitement and prosperity which came with the road were translated into a renewed interest in trapping by both Indians and non-Indians, but their optimism proved shortlived. Auctions began to return poor prices; traders tightened up defensively. The usual credit offered by Northern Commercial, Taylor and Drury's, and others was not repaid as promptly as in former years and soon dried up. Either furs were graded lower or they were not bought at all. Trappers who had to increase production to make ends meet could not outfit themselves to do so, because they could not get the credit.

A man without a large outfit would not make the effort to trap if he knew he would make only poor returns for a season's hard work. Only those men using good equipment and working districts with mink and muskrat in relative abundance could afford to continue trapping. Those without merely set a few traps along the new roads, never more than a day's travel from their ordinary residence, in a desperate and usually futile attempt to earn a few extra dollars. Others would go out with their .22's hoping to get a few squirrels, worth scarcely twenty-five cents each to indifferent buyers. For men who had sold large number one silver fox pelts in the twenties for hundreds of dollars each, the new poverty must have carried a crushing burden of humiliation, all the more galling because it was beyond their experience and understanding.

For an Indian family in the southern Yukon in the late forties, the decline in trapping coincided with an increase in government subsidies to them; but those subsidies contributed to, rather than relieved their economic distress. After 1944, the Family Allowances Act paid between five and eight dollars per month for each child to the child's mother, "except for Indian and Eskimo [Inuit] children of the Yukon and Northwest Territories, for whom payment is made in kind because of lack of exchange facilities ..."[4] Women obtained a source of income independent of their family group or marital status. Their children attended residential schools operated by the Anglican Church, and later by the Indian Affairs Branch.[5] Improved highway access increased the enrollment of Indian children in schools and those schools tended to draw families to nearby settlements, for the collection of family allowances required enrolling children in schools. Administrators used the threat of withdrawing the allowance to force parents to enroll their children. Between 1942 and 1949 the number of Indian children in Yukon schools increased from 26 to 227 while the number of schools increased from two to eight.[6] Welfare expenditures doubled during the same period.

Before 1947-48 families suffered through financial or economic hardship as a unit; afterwards it was the men, the trappers, who lost the most. Recalling those years, one man said, "the government became my wife's old man. She don't need me anymore."[7] Women stayed in town because they had their own income sources and because they wanted to be near their children. They did not go with their husbands or fathers or brothers to help on the traplines, so the trappers then had to do the painstaking job of skinning and cleaning the pelts themselves, which meant they could not trap as large an area as before or check the traps as frequently. Similarly, many men preferred to be with their families rather than trap. The occupation started to lose its high status of former years because of its poor returns. Yet another consequence of the Highway was that some men sold their dogs—or had them stolen by U.S. soldiers. Dogs represented an important investment. A skilled lead dog that would work hard yet be smart enough to stay out of the set traps was very valuable, even irreplaceable. A lot depended on a trapper's dogs. After 1947 it became too expensive to feed dogs during the summers, so the teams were broken up and sold, or simply shot.

It can hardly be overstated that the collapse of the fur market in 1947 and 1948, coming as it did on the heels of dramatic social changes brought by the Alaska Highway, brought complete economic dislocation on the scale of a disaster to Yukon Indian people. Into this climate the Yukon government imposed its policy of trapline registration.

The idea of trapline registration was to avoid disputes over trapping areas. Without it, one trapper might move into another's area and take fur from it, so the original user was deprived of income, or at least potential earnings. Registration put a legal obligation on the newcomer to recognize the usufructory tenure of the trapper who was there first. The original user, if he wished, could take a sustained yield of fur from his area. A newcomer ignorant of this yield, or who had vastly greater income needs, might conceivably overtrap and destroy the livelihood of the first man. That was the theory. In the Yukon, such tenure had been recognized and protected for years by the RCMP. People quickly learned which areas were open and which were occupied because there were so few non-Indian trappers, and communications along the Yukon River system kept everyone in contact. If newcomers ignored prior use and conflict became evident, the police quickly resolved the matter.

In 1941, Taylor McGundy, an Indian man who has lived all his life near Carmacks, complained to the RCMP about a certain man. He wrote,

> I am write a few lines about W[.] as he trapping rat between here and Montague Valley. As he do not want nobody to trap rat. The reason I write this letter there is only one place for all the Indians of Carmacks to hunt rats every spring so now if he takes all of that valley Indians of Carmacks got no place to go ... Really we don't like to see him go all over the country and kill rats before the season open, we like to see police do something to him quick.[8]

The police investigation which followed resulted in a trial and conviction, for the man had indeed been taking muskrats out of season. He was also advised to go trapping somewhere else. This case was one of about five similar investigations between 1930 and 1947 in which Indians complained to the police about non-Indian trappers. The police knew that they could not order a man out of another's trapline because the law did not have such a provision until later, but after 1938 they could "arbitrate trapline disputes." If a trapper was especially troublesome—and several were—the police could enforce every provision of the law with more than their usual zeal, and thereby encourage the man to go elsewhere.

Yukon Commissioner George Jeckell knew about these cases, since reports of all police investigations on game matters came to him. Perhaps he thought that assigning areas to trappers would prevent a recurring problem. When he was "outside" in Vancouver, B.C. on annual leave in 1943, he met with F.R. Butler, of the British Columbia Game Commission in his Vancouver office. They discussed the B.C. system in some detail and Butler afterwards sent Jeckell a long letter in which his administrative experiences were set out.[9]

Butler reported that the B.C. system came into use in 1926. It caused few disputes while borders of individual trapline borders were being decided. Indians and non-Indians received identical treatment. Their respective areas were plotted by government agents on large-scale maps with mile-wide buffer zones around each. Areas granted were large enough to ensure the trapper did not need to cover the whole of it each year. At the request of some Indian communities, the Commission also created group trapping areas in which no one trapper had exclusive use. Butler concluded his letter on a hopeful note; "Since the regulations ... have been in effect it has been noted that trappers have become more or less fur farmers and have been endeavouring, in the majority of cases, to conserve fur on their respective traplines.

The B.C. model was the one that Jeckell had in mind. Unfortunately he did not appreciate that the system had been initiated when fur prices were relatively high. Trappers in 1926—and in 1943—did not need to trap their entire area each year to make a good living. There were no disputes about the size of the B.C. lines because they had been large enough to provide livelihoods in that seventeen year interval from their registration. Jeckell did not introduce similar legislation in the Yukon in the 1940s because he could not see a way of paying for the required additional personnel.

During the forties, those issuing licenses at Dawson City, Whitehorse, and Watson Lake began asking persons taking out the licenses where they planned to trap. RCMP Corporal G.I. Cameron at Fort Selkirk and Territorial Agent Larry Higgins at Whitehorse went so far as to prepare their own sketch maps of trapping areas and keep them on file. They were following the B.C. system in practice, if not in law. An example shows how this was accomplished. Late in 1946, a non-Indian purchased a trapping area near Snag, in the White River district, from another non-Indian man for five hundred dollars.[10] The buyer purchased his license in Watson Lake, so of course Higgins knew nothing about it. As soon as he learned of the man's intentions, Higgins wrote to the would-be trapper and said he would have no rights to the trapline if a prior claim was proven. In explaining the matter to Acting Commissioner J.E. Gibben, Higgins wrote; "This confusion over traplines is an inevitable and common occurrence and is due mostly to a lack of knowledge of the geography of a region."

Gibben's reply is revealing. Besides acting as Yukon commissioner, he was the judge of the Yukon Supreme Court. He wrote back to Higgins that the 1938 Game Ordinance protected the rights of a trapper to his trapping area provided he was able, "to establish that he had acquired the beneficial use of the trapline without infringing any previous rights and that he is prepared to make full and continuous use of the area for trapline purposes."[11] Moreover, the Crown did not recognize any trapline sale since "the vendor has no vested interest in the area." In the opinion of Gibben, and therefore of the Yukon administration, usufructory tenure to a trapping area was protected by law only provided there was both prior and continuous use of the area for that purpose. Also, a trapline grant gave no automatic rights to big game hunters over it.

This would have to be judged a fair policy, yet if it was no longer economical to trap and the trapper did not use his area, any claim to tenure seemed wiped out. This problem of prior and continuous use without regard by the administration to fur prices was to be the greatest weakness in the trapline registration system which followed. Indeed, it was to cause anxiety and bitterness for the next thirty years.

More discussion about trapline registration followed the advent of record-breaking prices for beaver in the 1946 sales. During 1945-46 fiscal year, beaver averaged $50.80, double the usual price.[12] Since there is always considerable variation in pelt size and quality, large blankets may have sold for nearly $100. Naturally, prices like these caused intense interest in trapping beaver, an interest which soon became a concern, then a worry about trapping areas and the survival of the animal in some districts. Consequently the government closed the beaver season for three years in 1946, but beaver were only an indirect reason for trapline registration plans which followed. A more important reason was that those prices drew the attention of many non-Indian men to the possibilities of trapping as a livelihood, even though the market had started its decline. Government administrators worried about these newcomers usurping Indian trapping lands.

One of these administrators was Jack Meek, the Whitehorse Indian agent. In 1946, he had occasion to visit RCMP Cpl. G.I. Cameron in Fort Selkirk and there he learned Cameron's system for recording traplines in his district. Meek came away convinced of the method's usefulness and saw it as someday applied to the whole Territory. He described it in a letter to his department in Ottawa and urged the adoption of such a system. He added, "Most of the Indians with whom I have talked on this subject are wholeheartedly in favour of the system and action is now very necessary, due to the encroachment of Whitemen on the traditional trapping grounds of the Indians."[13] Meek's letter reached R.A. Gibson, who then passed it back to Yukon Commissioner J.E. Gibben. The tone of Gibson's covering letter showed that the Northwest Territories and Yukon Branch of the Department already had begun searching for policy alternatives and expected Gibben to be doing the same.

There were many similarities between this problem and those described in Chapter 4 concerning the need for a park or wildlife refuge along the Alaska Highway in 1942. Meek was a member of the Yukon Fish and Game Association, so he helped to write provisions about traplines into the new, 1947 Game Ordinance, but they were not as extensive perhaps as he might have hoped they would be. The new law contained provisions for registering trapline districts, within which seasons and limits could be regulated, but it did not allow for registration of individual traplines. Secondly, the government had no appropriation to pay the salary of the official needed to manage such a program.

The issue of trapline registration did not arise again until 1949. In the intervening two years Commissioner Gibben moved the Yukon Territorial Government closer towards the goal of operating its own game department. He discussed the idea with G.I. Cameron, whose RCMP experience in managing traplines seemed an excellent qualification for such a position. Territorial Council approved the necessary appropriation at its spring 1949 session.

Cameron then resigned from the RCMP after twenty-four years of service in the Yukon, and left Fort Selkirk with his family for Whitehorse. He set to work immediately drafting trapline regulations. Ottawa officials must have been in agreement with the proposed registration program for they approved the appropriation for Cameron's salary and operating budget. The Yukon's operating and capital budgets were not left in the hands of the commissioner and Council.

But other forces became involved. The Yukon Fish and Game Association for several years had been asking for money to import elk into the Yukon Territory. Geoff Bidlake, the long-time Whitehorse resident and Association director, had made an acquaintance with Them Kjar, warden of Elk Island National Park in Alberta, and his name was pressed forward as a suitable person for the new director of Game. This man's lack of trapline administrative experience was regarded as unimportant. A brisk exchange of letters between Gibben and Ottawa concerning the appointment ensued.[14] Gibben gave the position to Kjar and demoted Cameron's appointment to that of assistant director. The additional salary used up every cent of slack in the budget and made it impossible for the men to carry on their programs effectively.

Thirty years after the events of September, 1949, Cameron concealed or dismissed as unimportant the disappointment, even bitterness, that he must have felt when Kjar arrived. Kjar's tenure as director cast a long shadow over the Yukon's wildlife policies for the next decade, when the fortunes of trappers hit their lowest depths in a century.

Them Kjar took over Cameron's work of drafting up new trapline regulations. Sometime later in 1949 he decided to include a ten dollar annual registration fee which was to be collected from every trapper. Probably he sought simply to add to the government revenues to balance the new Game Branch costs to a degree. Then in January, 1950, Jack Meek suddenly realized that the trapline registration system which he had been advocating for years would work to the disadvantage of Yukon Indian trappers. He wrote to his Ottawa headquarters, "I resent strongly the assessment of $10 for Indians when the trapline situation in the Yukon is in such an undeveloped stage... I consider it premature to assess Indians $10 when the administration has little or nothing to offer."[15] Soon this letter and attached memoranda found their way to Commissioner Gibben. Thus the director of Indian Affairs wrote, "the opinion of Mr. Meek not only coincided with the opinion of the Branch administration, but reflects directly the official Department policy." The superintendent of Indian Reserves and Trusts' letter suggested that Indian trappers would be treated more fairly by granting them certificates of preemptive right to their trapping areas, which they might obtain after a five year period following application. But Gibben did not heed this advice. He wrote to Kjar that he believed the fee was not exorbitant, because the trapper received, as he put it, an "exclusive right of use of Crown Land."[16] The regulations were approved and printed.

Kjar intended that all the traplines would be plotted and registered by September, 1950. However considerable opposition to the plan first had to be overcome. Trappers at Teslin and Old Crow sent in telegrams signed by dozens of people complaining about the ten dollar fee. They were not objecting to the concept of registration, just how it was being carried out. Meek sent these telegrams to Commissioner Gibben, adding, "... a fee of $10 has been arbitrarily set, the spirit of compromise has been missing, have any trappers, Indians or white, been interviewed in this matter?"[17] But Gibben meanwhile, had left the Yukon to be replaced by A.H. Gibson, an administrator sent in by Ottawa to oversee the Territory's painful transition towards a more modern administration. Gibson gave Kjar his head rather than interfere in a subject that was new to him. Kjar rejected Meek's complaints and left the fee unchanged. He and Cameron began to travel to the small communities to register traplines first hand.

In 1951, in the first full year of the new system, some four hundred and twelve traplines were registered.[18] By 1954, the number rose slightly to four hundred and twenty-nine. In 1959, a year after the fur market hit rock bottom, however, only one hundred and ninety registered traplines remained. Government officials acknowledged that no trapper could be compelled to register and pay the annual fee. The system became lopsided. Tenure rights weakened each year. Some Indian trappers sold their areas to others for cash, and the government honored the transactions. What had begun as a sincere attempt to bring order to the trapping industry entered its second decade as an administrative nightmare of conflicting claims to the traplines.

Complaints about the ten dollar fee were the most visible symptom of the illness of the Yukon trapping industry and the government's clumsy attempts to manage it.

9

Communications and Attitudes

The history of the Yukon Territory before 1950 derives its unique character from a pattern of changes experienced in its communications with the rest of Canada and the United States. The Gold Rush of 1896-1900 and the telegraph linkage to the rest of the continent after 1902 brought the Territory into the Canadian federation and gave it a measure of self government. That brief period of prosperity and fame could not be sustained during the decline of gold production which followed. But decades of economic stagnation and isolation ended abruptly with the building of the Alaska Highway in 1942 and connection with the continental telephone network two years later. The Territory's inhabitants had to make a difficult transition into a more modern society. By 1950 the transition was sufficiently advanced to alter the nature of Yukon society. Changes in communications reveal themselves through the Territory's response to outside influences on wildlife policies.

If no gold had been found in the Klondike, it is likely that the Yukon's development would have been very similar to that of the Northwest Territories. However, the Gold Rush caused a massive investment in communications and transport, just as the thousands of gold seekers and businessmen caused a movement towards self-government. Even though the rush subsided and a less labor intensive form of mining came to be used, the region's new political autonomy and its transportation and communications systems survived more or less intact for the next fifty years.

The long period of stability from about 1911 to 1941 allowed a strongly protectionist attitude to flourish in the Territory's politics, which saw expression particularly in the way the inhabitants managed and utilized wildlife. The role big game species and fur bearers played in the Yukon's economy was a very large one, but it was influenced by the means of communication between the Yukon and the rest of Canada. Changes in those means have seen changes in wildlife use and values, in that a local cultural or economic notion of wildlife management persisted only as long as an "outside" notion could not enter the Territory and supplant it. Changes in communications technology allowed new attitudes to superimpose themselves on the older attitudes and values.

The history of the Yukon Territory can be divided into four periods which correspond to abrupt changes in communications. Before 1869, its Indian inhabitants traded furs directly or through middlemen to obtain European manufactured goods. They used foot paths and river routes, trading in all directions outward from the Yukon basin. The second period, from 1869 to 1900, saw the virtual capture of this earlier trade by owners of American river steamboats, which were financed largely through supplying placer gold mining operations. The third stage occupies the largest part of the 1900-1950 period. Heavy investment in shipping, the White Pass and Yukon Railway, and the upper Yukon steamboat fleet were quickly followed by the federal government's construction of a telegraph line hundreds of miles south to the continental system. The period since 1947 is the fourth stage. It saw the expanded use of the Alaska Highway and linkages to the continent's telephone system. Each of these stages is mirrored by a distinctive pattern of wildlife use by the Territory's inhabitants.

In the long period from 1900 to 1947, two aspects of the Yukon's character stand out: the mixed Indian-white composition of its population and the abundance of its wildlife resources. Even though Indian people played no direct part in politics, they were closely involved in the Territory's economy. Long-term white residents could not attract outside capital, consequently many of them depended on the goods and services provided by Indians. The relationship between the groups was more symbiotic than parasitic or exploitative. Thirty years of economic stagnation encouraged intensive use of wild animals for their fur and meat. The Yukon's forests and rivers harbored nearly all of the valuable fur species as well as abundant moose and caribou. Families of mixed parentage often were among the most persistent in utilizing wildlife for its cash value, especially in the big game business. Opportunities for contract or wage work in the towns or along the river system freed trappers from dependence on white fur traders. Those traders in turn had to be quite competitive with each other in order to collect some of the Yukon's rich harvest of furs.

Besides the mixed character of the population and the abundance of wildlife, one other feature set the Yukon apart from other northern regions. The massive investments in the railway and the steamboats were retired much earlier than elsewhere because of the nature of the Gold Rush and its need for shipments of heavy mining machinery. Freed of its burden of debt, the system operated for decades on the strength of its light but continuing trade to Dawson City and the silver-lead camp at Mayo Landing. The Government of Canada constructed the telegraph line and operated it at a loss much of the time. Central and southern parts of the Territory enjoyed a transportation and communications system that fur trading alone could never have supported. For all these reasons, Yukon history since 1900 does not compare easily with that of the Northwest Territories; or in fact, with any other part of northern North America.

The historical problems posed by the Yukon Territory and its economic use of wildlife can be examined through the nature and means of its communications with the rest of Canada and the United States. These means influenced the marketing of wildlife exports, but they have also permitted the importation of certain cultural notions of use. The British and Russian trading empires reached their limits within the Yukon basin. Transportation of some furs over the footpaths to their posts was scarcely profitable and expansion of this trade was not possible. European technology reached the Yukon through the Hudson's Bay Company in the north and through the middlemen trade with coastal Tlingit peoples in the south. Such trade was incidental to subsistence wildlife use by the indigenous peoples. After 1869, San Francisco merchant companies traveled deeply into the Yukon basin using steamboats and increased the local value of furs. In turn, Indian people acquired new technology and adapted to changing prices, currency, and an ensuing influx of gold prospectors. The steamboat era changed with the founding of Dawson City, and the opening up of an enormously expanded market for wildlife products. Those Yukon Indians who survived introduced diseases and social dislocation made the successful transition from subsistence use of wildlife to a much more exploitative mode.

The long period initiated by the narrow-gauge White Pass and Yukon Railway from Skagway to Whitehorse and the telegraph saw a prosperous fur trading era established. Associated with this was the trade in game meat and hides and the development of the big game guiding industry. These several markets allowed the Yukon's wildlife to be harvested at levels which never threatened its numbers in the long term, yet which brought prosperity to many. A strongly localized or nativistic attitude evolved towards game management and found expression in the form the game laws took and in a resistance, enhanced by isolation, to outside notions of management. Travel in and out of the Yukon and telegraphic communications with the administration there were both costly and slow. Outside conceptions of wildlife management lost their sense of urgency and relevance. But even if they had been successfully introduced into the Yukon, they soon would have been diluted in the vastness of the space, the abundance of animals, and the fragmented centers of population.

Roads and telephone trunks linking the southern Yukon Territory with Alberta began a new order of wildlife use. The population of Whitehorse increased dramatically and gave birth to a new political institution, the territorial pressure group. The Yukon Fish and Game Association transferred the locus of game law from the hands of the commissioner at Dawson and placed it in Whitehorse, where the new, post-highway community quickly shaped the law to resemble those current in other jurisdictions. Travel promotion by radio and films enhanced the highway's fame and the big game industry grew rapidly as a consequence. Similarly, the telephone greatly extended the decision-making powers centered in Ottawa, permitting federal programs for Indian people to be instituted and expanded. Trapline registration was a natural consequence. These effects of the highway combined with the collapse of the fur market enhanced economic class divisions in every community reached by the new roads. The demise of Yukon River steamboats after 1955 was virtually anticlimactic, since that date corresponds to the extension of roads and telephones to Dawson City and the close there of the railway, steamboat, and telegraph era. In the new Yukon, wildlife became an export commodity; its use as a local staple all but vanished.

Wild animals inhabit lands not used by man for the production of commercially important commodities. Although the animals can provide staples, their value in relation to the land they occupy and use soon becomes less than that land's ultimate value as a location for agriculture, or forestry, or mineral and fuel production. As the lands still available for wild animals diminish, so must the varieties and absolute numbers of the animals, and so must the material well-being of persons who obtain their living from wildlife. This historically relentless process is global in scale.

A counterbalancing effect has been provided by the growth of the conservation ethos. The near-extinction of the plains buffalo stimulated the idea of wildlife preservation. By 1900, both Canada and the United States recognized the usefulness of national parks for preserving wildlife. These and other legal barriers to the killing of wild animals owed their general acceptance to the efforts of a small but very influential pressure group that became international in scope. The laws they helped to create showed biases of property and wealth that overbalanced political opinion against local or usufructory stewardship over wildlife. The values of educated and metropolitan classes replaced those of wildlife users in husbanding animal populations, particularly in national parks and sanctuaries, so that the end result was the same as the extinction of the animals: they were no longer available to the wildlife users. The wildlife preservation idea led to the imposition of external, centralized cultural values on the people and animals of a small area. Such methods, it is true, had the effect of preserving the animals, but the core problem posed by wild lands and

---

animals versus agricultural and industrial staple production has not been solved.

Virtually the entire population of the Yukon from 1900 to about 1941 were wildlife users. Their powers of self-government allowed them to resist the imposition of many outside ideas about wildlife, which ideas in any case bore little relevance to the Yukon situation. There, the disproportionally large transportation network and other factors encouraged the economic use of game in ways which had ceased to be acceptable to many people in southern Canada and the United States. This separation of values existed between the various Yukon commissioners and their immediate superiors in Ottawa. The origins of the Yukon government were Canadian in structure and development, but their grassroots spirit and sophistication were egalitarian, having been influenced by the liberal traditions of California. Consequently Yukoners put little faith in law as an administrative tool, especially as it was wielded by the federal government. The elected Territorial Councillors relied on the wildlife users to preserve the resource and seemingly placed little emphasis on enforcement. They approved a succession of game laws in response to various pressures, but as long as the Territory remained relatively isolated, those pressures were never strong enough to shake councillors from their lethargy.

The rapid growth of the civilian population in Whitehorse after 1945 caused this *laissez-faire* attitude towards wildlife industries to diminish as it indeed diminished decades before in the rest of the continent. Only then did the Yukon begin to receive game sanctuaries and more restrictive laws. The problem between wildlife users and those who made other uses of the land was solved in a spatial way, with legal borders, rather than in a temporal way by reserving hunting and trapping rights for prior users. Even though Indian people retained the right to hunt for subsistence year round, their livelihoods from wildlife-related work were made subordinate to new definitions of hunting lands. This was the result to be expected from a more spatially-oriented communications mode that used roads and telephones in place of the older, temporal mode which used steamboats and the telegraph. Outside notions of appropriate resource use and conservation gained more local immediacy and weight. It became easier for them to invade the Territory and apply new definitions to the land.

Yukon Indian people before 1947 were active and willing participants in the Yukon economy. Their roles as commodity producers and service contractors were essential ones. Widespread labor shortages and strong demands for furs, combined with their cultural abilities for adaptation, prevented their exploitation as a group by non-Indians. However, they had no direct control over Yukon government policy. Individual cases of discrimination were frequent. Also, fur traders in isolated settlements took advantage of their monopoly position by using questionable credit practices combined with elevated prices for goods. Yukon society was characterized by many family linkages across cultural lines and the interdependence of the two groups. The fragmented nature of the total population, scattered as it was along the Yukon River system, preserved older perceptions of time and resource use long after those perceptions had disappeared from the larger society to the south. There was no requirement for Yukon Indians to adapt to more modern administrative concepts of space, labor, and land use. Their continuing role as commodity producers was compatible with their existing culture. So long as wildlife staple production held a central place in the Yukon's tiny economy, they did not have to become wage earners.

Indian people were isolated and impoverished by changes to the society that began in the early forties. The non-Indian population increased and the influence of long-term white residents, with their linkages to Indian people, was diluted in a sea of new faces, many of them unfriendly, even hostile. New social programs and compulsory schooling for Indian children made deep and lasting changes to family structure. By an unhappy coincidence, the market for long furs collapsed at exactly the same time and further contributed to these social changes. A pressure group introduced intentionally discriminatory amendments to the Game Ordinance. The abandonment of Yukon River steamboats came later, requiring many people to relocate to unfamiliar settlements. All these changes placed most Yukon Indian people in severe difficulties from which they have not emerged, thirty years later.

Two further aspects of the Yukon's history of wildlife use require summary and analysis—the influence of fur fashions on Yukon trappers, and the problem posed by hunting and trapping rights. They have direct application to wildlife history matters in other jurisdictions in the continent which have similar wildlife and will show that the Yukon's case has evolved along similar lines.

Trappers of wild fur were influenced by distant changes in communications that strongly affected the value of their product. Demands for certain furs and consequent price changes were very susceptible to the means of communications of those fashions. Early use of photography in magazines initiated a surge in demand for some furs prior to World War I, and then immediately afterwards in 1919. Steady growth in the fur market throughout the twenties had its peak in 1928, when the use of long furs was advertised through the new medium of film. In the thirties, fashion photography became important once again, while the new fitted clothing encouraged block purchasing by department stores and aggressive merchandising using radio. This centralization ultimately placed restrictions on fur purchasing, and required greater use of credit by trappers to make their production match changing demands of the market. After 1947, the Dior "New Look" manufacturers used advertising specialists versed in print, radio, and film media to promote successfully designs which caused a drastically reduced demand for long furs. British designers' influence weakened, bringing down with them a long-stable market, while the New York market for short furs grew rapidly.

Yukon trappers were insulated from the volatility of the fur market for over forty years by their remoteness. Even though prices were known and communicated throughout the Territory, there was no interest in forecasting prices over a long term. Abundant fur, competitive buying, and a low capital investment made it unnecessary for a trapper to try to predict market trends and adjust his harvest accordingly. But the old harvesting practices proved inadequate after 1947. Trappers had to shift their emphasis to shorter furs if these were available, or else seek other livelihoods. The effect of the sustained market decline was irresistible.

Hunting rights have been an aspect of land tenure and use for many centuries in both Europe and North America. These rights have been cancelled everywhere in two ways; the animals themselves have been exterminated, or the rights to hunt them have been expropriated. There has been a tendency to deprive wildlife users of their rights to use animals for their meat, hides, and furs as the numbers of animals decline. With few exceptions, this tendency has originated outside the harvest area and its origins are cultural, not economic. A complicating factor are biases which sometimes reserve the enjoyment of wild animals to the upper classes while suspending the normal process of the lower classes maximizing the land's value through wildlife staple production. More specifically, a local value is replaced by one imposed from outside, backed by the force of law.

In the Yukon, those who hunt for a living have never possessed sufficient power to insist on boundaries between their lands and their uses for them, and those lands that are open to exploitation by other means. This problem has been focussed by the creation of Kluane National Park Reserve after 1942 and the closure of the land contained therein to hunting and trapping. The park originally was an idea of conservation interests in the United States, acting through an unprepared and compliant Canadian government. The people who used the area's wildlife were ignored, as were the earlier appeals of Indian men such as Jim Boss and Joe Squam, by the same government. It does not strain one's imagination to see the parallels between the Yukon situation and that of medieval England and the royal forests.

The Land Claims process begun in the 1970s is the first program that has the potential of enhancing the economic well-being of Yukon Indian people. That decade also has seen the emergence there of a distinct non-Indian community, which seeks an alternative to the customary pattern of resource development followed in the west and north. The history of the Yukon since the Gold Rush shows that the waves of ordinary resource development and staple production have collapsed in the Territory as they have in the past. Their energy simply failed to overcome the great barriers of distance, terrain, and cold. Yet modern communications have drawn every part of the Yukon into the mainstream of global communications. Isolation in a temporal sense is no longer possible. The old practice of the Canadian government of subsidizing transportational infrastructure could well destroy the uniqueness of the Yukon, by exposing its rich resources to the same patterns of development occurring everywhere else. Those patterns are centuries old and irresistible as long as wildlife users are unable to protect their land. For the sake of preserving the Yukon's rich diversity of wildlife, one might hope that a new Yukon community could build a breakwater against the waves of development, though the whole world be clamoring for entry.

Appendix

"Here I Am Yet!"

*It is always a delicate matter to approach some of the Territory's oldest
residents with a tape recorder and ask them to tell you about their early
days in the Yukon. First, every consideration must be made so that the
interview is convenient for them. Secondly, there is the matter of
payment, for the interviewer will gain some benefit from the interview.
Finally, the interviewer must make every effort to prepare for the session
by knowing his material and drafting up some specific questions to
initiate the conversations. If a rapport is struck, then everything flows
out smoothly with results which are both a comfort to the person
interviewed and a delight to the researcher. Such were my experiences
with Mr. John Joe, the late Mr. Frank Goulter, and Mr. Johnny Taku
Jack.*

*These interviews took place after a draft of this manuscript had been
completed. Consequently I knew, or thought I knew, the events and
personalities described previously. I suppose I was looking for some
anecdotal material, yet it soon became clear that each man's story
should have a place of its own in this book. Although they had little
knowledge of most of the events I have described, they could talk for*

159

*hours about the people involved. Many other stories like these could—
and should—be recorded. They can be woven in and around more
conventional historical themes and bind the whole into an enduring
fabric. What follows does confirm the archival record, but also
shows how limited that record is in giving us a glimpse of the Yukon's
past.*

John Joe

---

*John Joe was born near Hutchi, in the south-central Yukon, in about
1884. He has lived most of his life at M'Clintock Bay on Marsh Lake,
about thirty miles east of Whitehorse on the Alaska Highway. For
several years he worked as a big game guide and until 1947 was a chief
guide or "outfitter." The events surrounding his 1947 season have been
described earlier.[1] He was asked about some well-known Yukon people
and began with Jim Boss.[2]*

Jim Boss's father was related to my grandma. He got a brother
named Tom Tom Ned. He's got a sister too. The sister has children
from Lake Laberge people. My grandma was raised at Klukshu,
Dalton Post, Kluane, Hutchi. They move down here. That old man,
my grandma's brother, he married here to Tagish people, he send
word back to Champagne and my mother and her sisters, they all

come here in 1896. I was about twelve years old. Not many Indians that time. A few here, a few at Tagish, Marsh Lake, Champagne....

Before that, Indians all the time used to be at Tatlmain Lake [central Yukon]. They got into trouble all at once and spread out. All go away from there, some go this way, one family go that way. Later on, they meet these coast Indians and shack up with them. Yukon Indians too, they go down and shack up down there.

Coast Indians, they take wife from here, take them back. That's the way it worked. When white man come, white man beat them out, they don't come back any more.

Jim Boss's mother has a relation in Hutchi, called in white man's way Hutchi Bill. She comes from there. My grandma and her brother and Jim Boss, they are all relations. That's where all the people come from. Jim Boss's grandpa was from the coast, he was a really old man. Indian hunt gopher [ground squirrel] all the time here with a snare, so this Jim Boss's grandpa, he wants to try it himself. He set a snare and fiddle with it, then he lay down in the sun and take off his shirt. He thinks, "Maybe I've got a gopher," so he goes back to see. When he goes back he can't find his shirt. He looks all over; he can't find his shirt. Soon he thinks a Bushman [Sasquatch or Bigfoot] took it. He goes back to camp without his shirt. "What happened to you?" they ask him. He says, "Bush people took my shirt!" They go back and they find it because he's looking in the wrong place....

The first guns they brought in were muzzle loaders. They were going to shoot one with all the Indians looking. They made a mark up on a tree, they were going to shoot at it. That gun never go off. All the Indians are laughing.

When the Hudson's Bay Company come, Indians have to pay fur to the top of the gun. Indians get gun, Hudson's Bay get all the fur. Next year he come back, bring a longer gun. Indian say it was too long, now.

Klukshu, that's where I was raised. There was no white man at that time. We go down from Hutchi to Klukshu to dry salmon, down to Dalton Post. They say Jack Dalton come, the summer of 1892. My mother and the other women, they're calling something. My mother hold my arm, I must be small then. She call when they come to the river. Jack Dalton. He's got a woman with him, a white woman. They've got a couple cowboys too. They're taking sheep too, they ride on to Carmacks where they build a raft.

I had no parents, my mother died in 1897. People come with the Gold Rush. They get sick, Indians, six of them die right here [M'Clintock Bay, Marsh Lake]. One time I went up the river looking for salmon, I come back and they are all sick. That man, Major Wood [NWMP commander at Tagish, 1897], put medicine on their arm. He moved up and down their arm like this with a needle. Their arm all swell up like that. Hot day in June. Holy Smoke. Me, I run away into the bush. Here I am yet!

One time at the head end of Fish Lake we were drying meat there. We hear a bang. Something is blown up, down there at Lewes Lake. They drain that lake so they can build the railway across it [the White Pass and Yukon Route, 1899]. Nobody had heard anything about it, they didn't know if the railway was coming or not, but it had come that far. They ask an old man when he heard it. He said, "The earth's going down. You pray!" [laughs]. Later I work on that railway when they build out behind the Pueblo Mine.

The police at Tagish, they used to look for whiskey. They push iron rods into sacks of flour. One time a big scow came down all full with barrels of whiskey. Police make them pour it out. Some of the people got drunk that night. Indians couldn't drink at that time. They put them in jail anyways, they hold court. They ask, "Where did you get that whiskey? White man give you that whiskey?" He says, "We draw it from Tagish Lake!" He says, "There's a couple of barrels of whiskey in Tagish Lake!" What can they do? They let them go....

Tom Dickson, I know him, he used to be sergeant at Tagish.[3] There was a girl there, Louise Ned, Louisa they called her at that time. She's a big girl. Somebody raise her, her parents died at Tagish. That Tom Dickson, he got her down the river to the canyon [Miles Canyon] and cached her where McCrae is now. From here people go down in a small dugout canoe. Person see smoke, big sign there with all different writing on it, and under a tree there's a little smoke coming out. "Who is that?" I said, so I land there. It was Louisa; that's where Tom Dickson is keeping her. That's when she begins to stay with him. My mother saw her, she knew her and said "What are you doing here?" Louisa laughs and says, "I'm waiting for somebody!"

Just above the bridge in Whitehorse [Campbell Bridge] there's a slough there. There was a trading post and a telegraph office [ca. 1900], the first building in Whitehorse. The trader there was named "Swifty." People buying from him and he give credit to Indians too. One Indian named John McGinty, he got credit. John McGinty came back to the store and the man said, "Well John, what about this bill here? You owe that much there." John said "Oh, that's my brother. He died not long ago, a few weeks ago...."

Billy Hall's father, a Teslin Indian, I knew him. Mister Hall. He was an old man, a funny old man too. Old Mister Hall. They tell him first time they are making a law about game. They tell him "White man say you're not going to kill cow, just bull moose." Mister Hall says, "Well, who they say going to marry cow moose?"

One time my boy, Ronald Joe, is working for the army [U.S. Army, 1942]. I told him the army is coming. I rented my boat from here and my camp up there. They said they wanted to build the road this way [i.e. past M'Clintock Bay], but I tell them "Lots of rocks!" Rocks don't stop them. Then I cut piling for that bridge there [Yukon River] and for Tagish Bridge. They couldn't find any big trees. When they were coming through they were pushing trees every way, all over like this. I ask him "Are you sweating?" He says "No." I said "You're sure working hard!"

I had some land in town. They bothered me for it. After that they put a gas station there. In those days I paid $12 a year for land. George Black was around in those days. Now you pay over $100 for the same thing. "How come we don't pay so much before?" I ask them.

I used to get three hundred rats sometimes along the river here [between M'Clintock Bay and the Yukon River Bridge, about ten miles]. In summer when the water is low, the muskrat are digging tunnels for winter. From there they can feed along the river bottom in wintertime. Now they build a dam and keep the water high, clean out a big bunch of willow along the bank and the muskrat are all gone. They can make little houses along the top of the ice, but they can't stay there all winter. They get cleaned out. At the same time, they build a bigger dam at Whitehorse. There used to be big king salmon come up through here. Used to be a salmon camp near here and all Indians used to come there to dry salmon for winter. We had two big long traps. One time we got fifty salmon in one night. It was like Klukshu.

I remember Them Kjar. He came here. He was poisoning wolves over at that island [two miles away, in Marsh Lake]. He got some wolf there and a fox too. He quit doing that. One time he showed me one of those little pills, he said one of these would kill five grizzly bears. He's the one who tell me "You're going to find it's going to be like Alberta here," he said. "Going to get cleaned out of all the moose, going to be like Alberta, no game, no moose," he tell me.

About the trapping, I've said before I used to lose money at it [fur trading], so it's no good. Sometimes the less they give me I tell them, "Go hunt your own fur." A lot of times we know it was pretty low, but we just let it go because we've got no place else to go.

I used to fish there below where the dam is. I've done lots of fishing there and here. That man stop my rats, stop my salmon, stop my money too. Now I make nothing. What I do get comes from the government, that's all. That's what I live by now."

Frank Goulter

Frank Goulter was born in Kingston-on-Thames in January, 1877. He joined the British Army in 1894 and saw service in Ireland and India. In 1899, his unit, the 76th Battery, Royal Artillery, was sent to South Africa at the onset of the Boer War. He was in South Africa for three years and saw action at many important battles including the relief of Kimberley and the British victories at Pardeburg and Bloemfontein. He returned to Kingston-on-Thames on his release from the army, but soon decided to migrate to Canada. He joined the North West Mounted Police in 1903 and was sent on Yukon service, after serving for a time near Calgary. In the Yukon he was at Whitehorse and Carmacks, finally taking his release after five years' service in 1908. Two years later he built his home beside the Yukon River in Carmacks. This interview took place in December, 1978, when he was still living there with his wife of over sixty years, Ida May Mack Goulter, and his son, Frank Jr. He passed away in June of 1981.

Taylor and Drury's came about a year or so before I got here
[Carmacks]. They came in "ought two" I think. Their place at Little
Salmon was run by a man named McCauley. Jack McCauley was a
good man amongst the Indians, he could do business with the
Indians when nobody else could. There were no Indians here then
[at Carmacks], they were camped around Little Salmon. There were
four policemen here and the Indians never came around where the
policemen were. There were a few at Big Salmon and at Selkirk
too.

I never knew much about credit. McCauley may have given a
little credit to the Indians although I never knew that part of the
business. All I know about it is in those days, the Indians used to
get out and trap. When they came in, in the spring, that's when
they sold their fur. They give Indians credit and they get him on
the books. That pays. When one Indian get on the books, he stays
there. He's always owing something. Taylor and Drury up the
Pelly, they used to use tokens.

They weren't fair in their trading. They've done the same with
me. They wouldn't meet you half-way. I got in there with old
Drury to raise foxes. I had to kick him out. Damned man. I was
shipping foxes, skins, to him and he was shipping them out to
London and he wasn't telling me what he was getting for them.
One thing after another. I wasn't going to stand for that. I told him
I'd be on my own. It was me that built the fox ranch, you see.

The first foxes we got we bought from an Indian for $500, two
little silver grays. I sold them that fall for $4000 to Pugh, in
Carcross. Pugh was sending them to Prince Edward Island and to
the fox ranches down there. He paid good money for foxes. I got
started in foxes in 1912. I was doing pretty good until the Frome
Brothers [?], they were millionaires already in the States, they got
started on them, built big pens [in P.E.I.], had them running all
over the place. What they were raising was pretty poor stuff, but
they knocked out all the little fellows like me, out of it altogether.
The foxes that I'd been getting and selling for $150, $200 a skin
wasn't worth $24 after they got through. I couldn't raise foxes at
$24, so I had to quit. They had to quit too, I'll bet they lost a lot of
money, those fellows. That's another thing I turn old Drury down
for. He was buying foxes for Whitney and leaving me without any.
Drury was a poor fellow.

I was trapping before I was fox farming. I trapped through the
old Chico country, that's the trail passing from the Twin Lakes
country through to Laberge [lower Laberge]. That's where they used
to come over in the old C.D. days [Mackenzie and Mann, Canada
Development Company], they used to come over to

Montague. I was trapping in through there and over to the other side, where Hutchi River comes in, and at Montague itself. In those days, Montague used to be good fox country, still is now, I think.

I don't like big traplines. The farthest I used to go was from Montague over to the other way. I guess about thirty miles. You've got to go to it all the time if you're going to do any trapping at all, especially in cold weather, you can't do any trapping in cold weather. It wouldn't take many traps. It wouldn't do any good to have a big trapline, you can't get around it. Probably about a hundred traps I guess I used. I've done better with a short line. I've done better right around here. This business with the long lines, used to lose so many animals. Poor devils of things used to freeze, left for the squirrels, ravens, God knows what, and if there's a wolverine around, he cleans them up too. It doesn't do. These Indians used to set out traps and they wouldn't look at them for about a month. All they'd find was a fox tail or something like that.

I can't remember anything about the police and feeding caribou to the foxes. Nobody complained about me—but I complained about the police! I forget his name now, but he went out there and shot a bunch of caribou and left them. He shot seven caribou and left them. Nobody complained to me about feeding caribou, I fed caribou all the way along. They must have taken out those permits you talked about after the caribou had gone. That was the last of the caribou. They never came again. They used to come about every twenty years. I've seen them twice, no more. They come now, a few, out in the Nansen country, but they don't come here. Used to see thousands of them around here at one time. When they were changing the game law I don't think they knew a damn thing about it.

When I was in the police one time there came an old gink loaded down with big number four traps and he was going to one particular hill and he was going to use poison too, we heard. He got down the river and I took a walk down there and I see some of his sets. He had a bunch of tallow or something on a stick, a few inches above the snow. The rabbits were awful thick that year. By God, he must have poisoned a thousand rabbits and never caught a thing, setting these traps about, number fours, big enough for a black bear.

Poison is something I never used. Damned stuff. It isn't as though it poisons the poor devil of an animal, whiskey jacks get hold of it and they die and then squirrels get hold of it and all kinds of things get hold of it and die, ravens even....

There is a really good songster here, that's the white winged cross-bill, you see him feeding on the fir cones, the seeds in the fir cones. It's a pretty handsome bird and a good songster too. There are several cross-bills, but that's the only one that visits here. I got into quite an argument with old Ingersoll, the naturalist that used to write for the *Family Herald* years ago. He had it down as no song, just a mere twittering, but I knew different. It's a wonderful singer, prolonged and quite canary-like. So I wrote about it and some woman backed me up in the north of Saskatchewan, so Ingersoll had to give way to it. I got him on two or three of these birds. I got him on the siskin. He was saying that the siskin resembles the English one. It doesn't, it's a prettier bird than that. In all the time I've spent in the country I've seen a siskin only twice....

I knew John Hawksley, the mission man.[4] That was the man who was telling me about buying a fine double-barreled shotgun from an Eskimo in the Mackenzie country. He wanted that gun in the worst way. This was a mission man talking. He said, "Well, I had this knife, it was one of those that had a corkscrew in it, a chisel and one thing and another—I suppose you've seen that kind!" "Yes," says I, "shoddy things." He said, "I was pulling the blades out of it and he stopped me, he wanted it, so I swapped him the gun for it." I said, "That, to me, is a pretty cheap way of doing business!" "Oh," he said, "I didn't know that he had much use for the gun." I said, "I guess he had much less use for the knife." I didn't go with it at all. These mission men have always given me a pain.

Another one was Swanson. He was a damned liar and I had to tell him so. That rat, I came pretty close to hanging one on his chin, I was pretty riled. He came over one day, it was raining. I said, "Here, take my mackintosh." It was given to me by a lad who used to work for Taylor and Drury's. He went off to the War [World War I] and he gave me his mac and his fishing tackle. So I lent it to him. It didn't come back, he had it for two or three weeks, so I said to him—but he was already worked up for what I was going to say—I had hardly got it out of my mouth and he was saying "You didn't loan me anything, what are you talking about?" I said, "Damn it man, you mean to tell me you forgot you borrowed my coat?" "I never borrowed anything" he said. "Well," says I, "You are a damned liar, a stinker...." He quit the country not long after that, I don't know where he went and I don't care. He was as poor as a churchmouse and had a right way to sneak anything and some of the yarns he would tell weren't fit for the red light district. That was a gink that was more holey than righteous, he was full of holes. Then there was old Stringer [Bishop Isaac Stringer], always showing up at mealtimes. They were a beautiful bunch.

I didn't know Clarence Sands, he died in Whitehorse some years
back.[5] I knew his people, they came from Kingston-on-Thames.
Clarence was evidently named after the street on which Sands had a
big drapery store in Kingston. That was his parents. He came during
the Gold Rush and married a Swedish woman. I don't know much
about him, but I would have liked to have met him.

There were fur buyers outside who would write to you, but those
were the kind of buyers you want to watch out for. You put in a
price, you ship it to them and you won't get what they say. There
was one outfit that called themselves the North American something
or other. I shipped some mink there to them. Damned things, the
price I got was no good and it's no good trying to get the furs back
again either. There's only one place to ship furs and that's the sales.
There you'll get the proper price or they won't sell it them. But
shipping to buyers is no good. Look at old Bill Drury. He couldn't
meet you halfway; he wanted you to give it to him.

In 1919 was when I got the highest prices for my furs. They did
drop down after that too. I remember when muskrat went up to five
dollars and dropped down to nothing at all again. Old George
McDade he had some and I had some. I sold mine for about three
dollars a piece, he was going to hang onto his because they were
going up to five dollars. In the meantime he hung onto them and
lost out. That's the worst of fur, you could never bet on it. Now I
think they are paying enormous prices for lynx, and lynx is a poor
skin anyway for garments. It doesn't carry much leather. I know
that at the prices they are paying they're not worth it. On lynx with
this acid tan, it continues to work away. I'd give the furs two years
before you could put your finger through it.

All the water-loving animals are the best when it comes to
making leather: beaver, otter, and mink. However the longer you
keep mink [in mink farms] the thinner the leather gets. Wild mink
is one of the best of the furs. I remember old Bill Drury got a
whole bunch of mink over at the Pelly there. He had to take me
over there to show me and he was picking out the big fellows. But
I said the size was all very well but the best ones are the medium
ones. The big ones have a kind of coarseness that you won't find
in a medium. Mink is a weasel. I used to raise ferrets when I was
a kid, so I had no difficulty with mink, they're just about the
same.

The Pelly country was the best marten country. You'd see in the
spring the Pelly trappers coming down to Selkirk. Old man Barr and
a few more, used to be another man, I forget his name, he used to
buy for a New York firm of furriers, he used to buy up all the
marten. That country may have had a setback when there was a lot

of trapping, but it isn't long in picking up again if they let it alone for two or three years.

Trapping is a sorry kind of business. I gave it up anyway. Cruel. You'd set a bunch of traps out and cold weather would come. Seventy below zero, something like that. You'd get back and find the animals cold and stretched out, some of them would be all curled up and covered with snow, frozen solid. A sorry job. I quit it. I didn't trap any more; I raised them instead.

Johnny Taku Jack

Johnny Taku Jack was born in April, 1903, near Atlin, B.C., a small community a few miles south of the Yukon border. He spent most of his early life there before going to work on the Yukon River steamboats in 1926. His father was Taku Jack, a well-known and respected man who served as head man for the Atlin band of Atlin Tlingit Indians at the time of the Atlin gold rush. His mother was born in the Atlin area, but his grandmother was originally from the Alaska coast. Johnny Taku Jack is of the Cro-hit-'tan clan which means the "Noon House," in the complex Tlingit Indian kinship system. He learned fluent English in his years as a railway section foreman, steamboat officer, big game hunter's cook, carpenter, and maintenance supervisor. He has lived mostly in British Columbia, in Atlin, Telegraph Creek, and Cassiar, but his taped recollections about trapping and big game hunting apply equally well to other Indian men in the southern Yukon.

I was born near Atlin. Yes, that's where the old Indians in the summertime 'till late in the fall had a regular camp ground where the Indian village is now, and then late in the fall they all split up and go here and there. They used to be just like the white people a long time ago. Each one of those Indians got a place to trap and nobody interfere with him. Therefore they were in peace with every one of the trappers. There's no fighting over fur land wherever there's fur.

In these days I'm talking about there used to be traders coming in from Juneau, Alaska. They were Indians. They used to trade for rifles, blankets, buckets, knives, and all that stuff. That's what they were using that fur for. And before that time started the Indians used to use fur clothes in the winter time. Everything is in fur. They were just like the Skidoo suits they use today.

When the white people came in they didn't use those clothes any more. There's a big demand for the fur and they have to sell their fur instead of making clothes out of it. There used to be a lot of people saying—even the women saying something like: "This fur is sure spoiled when they have to sell it then in the end they've got nothing." A long time ago one set of good fur clothes last them two to three years if they take good care of it.

They used to go down to the coast to trade the fur for what they want and in fact, they get the stuff cheaper down the coast than they do when it comes up in the interior because they have to just about pay for the trip they are making up here too. One day when some Indians take a good catch of furs they go down the Taku River with somebody and they buy boats down there. They used to make dugout canoes down there on the Taku or near Juneau. They buy their own boats and come back up. They use sail. They put a sail on and mast and when there's a good heavy wind they can go from the Tulsequa right up the Taku River to the forks of the Nakina and the Inklin River. When there was no wind they'd have to use line, they'd line the boats up the river.

They used to buy rifles and make their own powder and shells. They buy the black powder by the cake and lead and stuff like that they used to buy; they make their own bullets or balls. That was for the muzzle loaders.

At that time the Indians don't use very much whiteman's food but if they come up they might bring some flour, like a twenty-five pound or fifty pound bag. That thing would last a whole year because they don't know how to cook it or use it.

They used to buy clothes, shoes, and stuff like that but mittens and moccasins they made themselves, but in summer they use shoes and regular travelling boots. They never used dress clothes at that time because it was just virgin country; no gold strike, no white people.

When they go trading down the coast they sometimes bring back sealskins and stuff like that. Then they trade with people the other way, like with Teslin people or Whitehorse people or farther down the river to Moosehide [Dawson City]. What kind of berries they don't have on the coast and what kind of thing they don't have inland, why those are the things that they trade with one another. Soapberries, pitch, spruce gum—they don't have anything like that on the coast. People used to pick boxes and boxes full of gum and trade them off down there, you see people everywhere chewing away.

When I was a young man, at that time the younger generation pretty well have respect for their father and mother and when we catch any furs like that we let our father handle it and sell it for the reason that as an older man he gets a better price selling. But when there's a younger generation selling anything—I remember selling a big mink one time for three boxes of chocolate bars while that thing was worth seven, eight, ten dollars maybe. We don't speak good English in those days, we don't know what was ticking. It was great when you got a few candies for the fur.

So that's the reason the older people tell us to give them the fur to sell it for us, we don't keep the money. If I get a pair of overalls and a shirt I'm just as happy as ever because my father and mother used the money to buy clothes or grub; flour, beans, rice, and stuff like that. We were happy to get that, were well satisfied too, not like nowadays. Kids have to be fifteen years old to run out on the street and be on his own, not like the old days, have to be twenty-five years old before he can start going out by himself. You had to prove you could take care of yourself.

Ever since I was a kid at Atlin I started off with snares, trying to catch rabbit and even minks, weasels. It takes practice. You may set when you ask an older man how to do it. You have to regulate the size just right and you never miss. We use deadfall. In the old days they used to use sinews, thread, to make a big mesh net which they used for beaver. They used a rattle on a pole at one end where the net is tied. The rattle was made of caribou hooves. At five o'clock, about that time, the beaver are coming out. They set the net away from the house so that you won't catch the young beavers. Have to hurry and catch the beavers before he cuts the net and gets out.

When we kill the beaver we are not supposed to feed the meat to the dogs because the beaver is just like people. Amongst the fur, the wild animals, the spirit of the dead beaver goes back to the spirits of the live ones and tells them they are feeding our meat to the dogs. For that reason they get bad luck and can't catch any more beaver. The beaver meat is the kind we don't eat all the time, just once a year when the trapping season is over. That's the only meat that's not poor. Bear is good then too.

Long time ago the people from Teslin used to come down to Atlin and spend pretty near the whole summer at Atlin. That's how I met up with George Johnson.[6] George was older than I was. At that time he'd done a lot of trapping, he got a lot of fur too. He was a good manager of everything. He built a boat on Teslin Lake called the "Nakina" with an inboard motor in it, just like you'd get outside, a really good boat. George and his brothers, William and Shorty Johnson, were really capable guys.

When he got that car most of the time he used it on Teslin Lake when it froze up. He used it to take the trappers out, tie the dog sleds on behind it, and then take them out with a supply of groceries. It worked pretty well. He had to be very careful. Some places had spring water and shallow ice. They always had the idea of marking those places, even of going around with a dog sled to do it. When the wolf and the coyote had a good price he used the car to chase them. He killed a lot of wolves and coyotes when wolf was under a fifty dollar bounty. He made a lot of money. In one year he pay back the car and then some.

He gave out credit to the young fellows. Then later he got the idea of blazing out a road three, four miles to Fox Point, so he says to these boys, "Well, you boys owe me some money. How are you going to pay when you got no money? You fellows will have to grade out the road for me. Shovels, I've got lots of shovels, axes, we are going to chop that road open." And so they did, where the Alaska Highway is today, near Teslin to Fox Point, that's where George Johnson built his road. They used to go to Fox Point for their games and picnic parties. Indians at that time got lots of money and no place to spend it and that's the only way they have fun. They built the road that far and took the whole village there in one day for the picnic.

When I had a trapline at Atlin I used to sell my fur at Taylor and Drury's in Whitehorse; but we had to pay the royalty on it before we sell any fur. I used to take fur from Cassiar to Vancouver when I first go on holiday, but I have to have export papers from the government offices. They had those tags or seals to keep a record of how much fur is coming out of each trapline.

I believe this was a very good idea because before that there were poachers from the Yukon and poachers from B.C. and there's always this trouble.

I got money from beaver and dry land furs such a mink, weasels, muskrat, otter, beaver and marten, fisher, coyote, wolf, fox—all that stuff we used to get money for. It was the way amongst Indian people that they say the otter is a queer, wicked animal. They believe it was bad luck if you catch otter. We don't believe that because there was good money for otter so we kill them.

There was three traders in Atlin. John Sands used to buy for Louis Scholls. Clarence M. Sands was another buyer since 1910, something like that.[7] After 1925 another trader built a store, named John Garrett. There used to be a fur buyer from the Taku River named Billy Strong, used to have a trading post on the Taku River.

We generally tell them we're not going to sell them the fur unless we get a good price for it. The trappers send word to one another where they're paying high prices for the fur. Like if Teslin paying a good price for the fur they tell one another. We used to tell the fur buyers in my home town, in Atlin, we expected a good price because we know the prices outside of Atlin. The three buyers would give us bids; sometimes they would go over the Teslin price.

Old man Louis Scholls used to supply the Indians with groceries when they go out trapping whether they sell to him or not. He was a very good man so we always pay for everything he give to us. One year he outfit the Indians out to trap, this is the young fellows. But the older men they had their own money, they had money left over from last year, from the year before, they don't spend it, they hang onto it. When they go trapping they buy their own supplies. For myself, when I was twenty, twenty-five, I had no money and I go to Louis Scholls and he outfit me, tell me "you go and find out how much you will be getting for your fur, because," he said, "I'll give you a hundred dollars more than the other buyers will give you on your fur." We always tell the truth, saying we got so much better on the fur and he give us a hundred dollars over it, because he like to see the fur coming in. No doubt he's making money on it, but he gets the fur. He gets pretty near all the fur that comes in, even the older people who were trapping before, even they get a hundred dollars extra. So the other buyers have to compete with that, have to put up with that.

They cut pretty near half of the fur price off if the fur is greasy. Some beaver they bring in have a lot of grease or fat on it and the trapper says, "What's the matter, that fellow got a better price than I did?" The trader shows them what the other fur looks like. If there's a lot of grease on it that burns the hide; it's supposed to be clean.

In the early days beaver was really cheap. The beaver and otter skins went up when the Japanese invade Attu Island; we hear that was because they use the short fur to line the fliers' clothing. That's when the beaver went sky high, marten went up as well. One hundred and fifteen dollars for a marten skin, pale or brown just the same, they all came in one price. Beaver went up to $79 just for one pelt.

I went out hunting and trapping, I went out twenty days and came back. I had $2200 worth of beaver skins and that is more money than I ever made in five years of trapping. Twenty-four hours after I sold my furs the Hudson's Bay Company got a telegram saying no more beaver than $25 a pelt. Some trappers came in with seventy beaver, they don't get half a much as what I made.

The word got around fast. When I was coming back I saw Fred Callison. I was taking a rest because I was tired. He said, "If I was you Johnny I'd keep going. Do you know what the beaver is now? I sold there and got $79 dollars." I said, "O.K. I'm going tonight." So I left and sold them. Just in twenty-four hours, the time I would have stayed in Callison's ranch that price went way down.

In the old days if they had four or five beaver streams in their line they never used to clean them up all at one time. They used to take one stream per year and next year go on to the next. In four or five years he would come back to the first stream and have four or five litters. But nowadays these young fellows it's money, money, money. They'll take everything and they clean out their trapline.

In my time when I was a young fellow, the best price I ever get was nine dollars for a blanket beaver. That's in 1924, 1928, and we go hundreds of miles for that. But nowadays they don't because....it's the government; I do blame the government for that. They go and give money out to teenagers because they say "We're hungry, we've got no money, nothing!" They give them lots of money. They give them money right out. They like liquor and stay in the beer parlor.... It doesn't matter how much money is in the fur nowadays, they say it's not enough. At the same time the young Indian fellows they don't know how to trap. The reason why is because their father and mother don't show them how to trap.

Trapping is just like anything else, you have to practice at it which way you can make money, and you have to figure things; how many traps you're going to set. If you set a bunch of traps, you lose that many days to take care of the other traps you have set. For my part, the way I used to trap myself, fifty traps was good enough for the winter, that's including from number 0 trap to number 4 and I never used more than that. Fifty traps can keep you very busy.

Every three days I run the traps. Anything beyond three days he might cut his paw off or something else will come along and tear up the hide and you lose it. By using fifty or sixty traps you've got lots of work to do on that I've heard it said that some people had two hundred traps set out and at the end, during the winter, sometimes he lose ten skins—the animals get away or the fur is damaged.

When we go trapping, we are always happy to get what we trap before we lose it. That's how a lot of us Indians find out if we use fifty-sixty traps, even only forty traps, we do as much trapping as we did with two hundred traps because we don't lose any. But for beaver trapping, I do believe the more you put out the more you're going to get.

Sometimes when I was in the Taku River we set out beaver traps over forty miles. My partner and I were in a boat. We put sinkers on the traps. When they jump over they fall down into deeper water and are drowned. It's guaranteed you'll catch every beaver you get; even if you get him by the claw, it's drowned. The more traps you put out the more you get because you don't lose it. It's not like a dry land fur animal.

They say the government doesn't allow to sink beaver, that it's cruel. Well I do believe it's cruel to trap beaver on dry land and it suffers for two or three days. And another thing, if you shoot a beaver while he's in the trap they say you can get pinched for that because they don't allow using a rifle on the beavers. So if it's a live beaver we have to use a club on it and I think that's cruel; but that's the law, we have to follow it.

The only thing that don't fight the trap at all—and I have pity on them too—is the lynx. You could catch them even by one toe, one little claw with the trap hanging on it, it would sit there. We kind of hate to kill that animal when we catch one because he's not fighting, he'd just sit there and growl at you....

In the early days there was a fox farm twenty miles north of Atlin. They catch rabbits for the fox farm and they kill a moose. At that ranch they go through ten or fifteen moose a year. One time in the fall time of year, this man go out hunting and he thought he saw a bear and took a shot at it, but it let out a yell because it was his partner, shot dead. He thought it was a bear because this fellow had a black sweater on. They took him in and prove everything was accidental. They sold that farm after that. They used a lot of fish besides moose, rabbits, and caribou.

Old man Taku Jack complained a lot about that. But the white people used to get after the Indians because they said they were killing too many moose. At that time Chief Taku Jack started kicking about the fox farm, saying they were taking too many fish. He said the Indians were using the moose for their own use, but the fox farmers were taking all the game and fish only to use as feed in the fox farm and nobody was kicking about that. The only thing they told Chief Taku Jack was they said he was "dictating" to his band about the white people; and if he goes dictating then they get five years or ten years in jail for that. The Atlin band was afraid to say something about that because they don't want to end up in jail about it. The only one who drove home the attack was Chief Taku Jack.

There's tons of fish coming out of Little Atlin Lake and tons of fish coming out of Big Atlin Lake and they even go up to Squanga Lake where the fish spawn. They even go to the spawning grounds. Same thing on Atlin Lake, that Fourth of July Bay, that's where the whitefish spawn, up that creek in the fall, and that is where the whiteman put up a net for their fox farm. That's the reason why old man Taku Jack was hollering about it. At that time they are raising mink too. Nowadays the fish are coming back the way it was.

One time on the south end of Atlin Lake a whiteman named C.B. Cole had a trapline in there. He had some poison. Some people go through there and their dogs pick up the poison and got killed. He give some money to these people to keep quiet about it so they did. They were paid for the loss of their dogs. They all got careless with the poison. Some of the white people tell the Indians that you can set poison on the lakes, and ravens and some other birds, camp robbers, they wouldn't go out onto a big lake to pick those things up. That was not true because whenever a raven pick up poison they'd fly about four, five miles before they drop. Some of the people say they push it under the ice and as soon as the water hit it, it's no longer poison, but that's not true.

The number of coyotes seem to be increasing. Out there on the Cassiar Road there's some hippies; they're feeding those coyotes there. Last July [1978] they hear some noise out there, they look out and here's the coyote back with six little puppies. He said he had to feed them, also the little puppies. There was something good to eat so they walk right up with their ears back, shaking their tail, and taking food from the man's hand. In Cassiar, up the mountain at the mine, the foxes know when it's time to eat, they line up to catch the sandwiches they throw at them.

I worked for George Ball out of Telegraph Creek and I worked for Hudson's Bay Company too, then I worked for the late John Craig. I liked that work [big game hunting] fine. I learned that whole Telegraph Creek country. The hunters were all very good to the cook. I did the best I could for them. I kept my clothes clean and all that sort of stuff, kept the kitchen very neat, and I baked bread, made doughnuts, and baked cake for them. Some of the hunters, if it was their anniversary or birthday I made a cake for them. Out of five or six hunters I would get away sometimes with five or six hundred dollars—just tips—besides my wages.

I cooked for one lady, a DuPont lady. I got a $200 tip from her for a forty day hunt. Then I cooked for Fisher Body Builder, Mr. Fisher. I cooked for him and then at the end I got a $150 tip. The car body builder, that is. Then I cooked for another guy named Edward Kerr, he was one of those guys who make binders for those big books, kind of a hardboard like. I cooked for him and his wife. His wife was a Jew so I had to cook two different meals. She didn't like the game meat, she said it was too strong and of course I guess it's in the religion too. In the end she did eat game meat. When we got back to town I find an envelope that's got a $300 tip in it. That's the top recorded Telegraph Creek tip from the hunters.

On my last trip I told them I'm not going hunting and cooking for $10 or $15 a day, I'm asking for $20 a day if I have to, so he gave me $20 a day. When I got there there was two Mexican guys. One was a lawyer and the other was a doctor. I got $400 for a forty day trip. That's just their tip. They say they've been all over the country hunting and that's the best they've ever had because both both of them gained weight!

One time in Telegraph Creek area we went out through the summer, I know there was sixty moose, just moose taken out of the country, just antlers. They saw the meat—the smell is too strong. They don't want the meat. They just cut the antlers off and the rest lay there to rot. Sixty moose in one year. As far as that goes there was forty-eight moose come out of Atlin this year [1978]. It's the same thing, the moose is just scattered around the country. Here's one Indian in Lower Post kill a moose out of season, he gets a $250 fine. He didn't throw that meat away, he took it home to his family. He got pinched for that because he's got no permit. Since I was a kid, my father Chief Taku Jack, he had an awful time with the game warden.

What moose we kill, if I'm alone I go and gather up help from the village, I tell them all I want is a bit of meat out of it then they divide it amongst themselves so if the next Indian kill a moose like that, I get meat out of it too. That's the way we used to do those things. All the time the white men get a license to get moose and take the antlers off and just leave the rest. There's a lot of stuff that's going to waste absolutely which it doesn't have to. There's lots of other ways the government could make money, lots of other ways, but the way this thing is, is ridiculous.

Notes

1 Old Laws—New Attitudes

1. United States Environmental Law Institute, *The Evolution of National Wildlife Law* (Washington, D.C.: U.S. Superintendent of Documents, 1977), p. 8.
2. William Holdsworth, *A History of English Law*, 7th ed., Vol. 1 (London: Methuen & Company, 1956), p. 4.
3. William Nelson, *The Laws Concerning Game*, 4th ed. (London: 1751), p. x.
4. Austin L. Poole, *From Domesday Book to Magna Charta*, 2nd ed. (Oxford: University Press, 1955), p. 339.
5. J.E.A. Joliffe, *The Constitutional History of Medieval England* (London: Adam and Charles Black, 1937), p. 80.
6. Ibid., p. 140.
7. Justice William Manwood, *Treatise on the Forest Laws*, 4th ed. (London: 1717).
8. G.J. Turner, ed., *Select Pleas of the Forest* (London: Bernard Quaritch, 1901).
9. Ibid., p. 125.
10. Nelson, p. 206.
11. Clarence J. Glacken, *Traces on the Rhodian Shore* (Berkeley: University of California, 1967), p. 312.
12. Ibid., p. 310.

13. Ibid., p. 323.
14. Edward, Second Duke of York, *The Master of Game*, William A. Baillie-Grohman, ed. (London: Ballantyne and Hanson, 1904); and William Twici, *The Art of Hunting*, Alice Dryden, ed. (Northampton: William Mark, 1908).
15. George Turbervile, *Book on Falconrie or Hawking* (London, 1611); and *Book on Hunting* (London, 1611).
16. David C. Itzkowitz, *Peculiar Privilege: A Social History of English Foxhunting, 1735-1885* (Hassocks, Sussex: The Harvester Press, 1977).
17. *Oxford English Dictionary* (London: Oxford University Press, 1933).
18. Nelson, p. 247.
19. Holdsworth, p. 103.
20. Charles Oman, *The Great Revolt of 1381*, 2nd ed. (Oxford: Clarendon Press, 1969), p. 121.
21. R.B. Dobson, *The Peasant's Revolt* (London: Macmillan, 1970), p. 186.
22. Glacken, p. 338.
23. R.G. Barry and R.J. Chorley, *Atmosphere, Weather and Climate*, 3rd ed. (London: Methuen, 1976), p. 359.
24. Holdsworth, p. 105.
25. Fernand Braudel, *Capitalism and Material Life 1400-1800* (New York: Harper and Row, 1974).
26. Ibid., pp. 34, 134-139.
27. Nelson, p. 221.
28. Antonia Fraser, *Cromwell: Our Chief of Men* (St. Albans, Herts.: Panther, 1975), p. 460.
29. Nelson, p. 35.
30. Ibid., p. 37.
31. Ibid., p. 40.
32. E.P. Thompson, *Whigs and Hunters* (Harmondsworth, Middlesex: Penguin Books, 1977), p. 64.
33. Ibid., p. 236.
34. Charles C. Tench, *The Poacher and the Squire* (London: Longmans, 1967), p. 153.
35. *Daily Mail* (London), March 16, 1978, p. 11.
36. Tench, p. 141; and Holdsworth, p. 108.
37. Tench, p. 154.
38. United Kingdom, Parliament, *Blue Books*, Vol. LXVII (1871), Parliamentary Papers, pp. 524-700.
39. Edward, Second Duke of York, p. ix.
40. Turner, p. xiii.
41. Calvin Martin, *Keeper of the Game* (London: University of California Press, 1978), pp. 107, 148.
42. Roderick Nash, *Wilderness and the American Mind* (London: Yale University Press, 1973), p. 26.
43. Cited in Henry George, *Progress and Poverty* (London: Henry George Foundation, 1937), p. 70.
44. *Blue Books*, Vol. LXVII (1871), pp. 524-540.
45. Ibid.
46. F.G. Roe, *The North American Buffalo*, 2nd ed. (Toronto: University of Toronto Press, 1972).
47. Roe, p. 377.
48. Ibid., p. 443.

49. Francis Hines, *The Buffalo* (New York: Thos. Crowell, 1970), p. 189.
50. Ibid., p. 191.
51. Ibid., p. 206.
52. *Ordinances* of the Northwest Territories, 1877.
53. A.J. Ray, *Indians in the Fur Trade* (Toronto: University of Toronto Press, 1974), p. 198.
54. Nash, p. 153.
55. R.S. Ontario, 56 Victoria (1893), c. 49; and Canada, 57-58 Victoria (1894-95), c. 31.
56. Canada, House of Commons, *Debates*, June 2, 1894.

2 The Law in the Yukon

1. Harold A. Innis, *The Fur Trade in Canada* (Toronto: University Press, 1962), p. 383.
2. Catherine McClellan, *My Old People Say*, 2 vols. (Ottawa: National Museums of Canada, 1975); Fredrica de Laguna, *Under Mount St. Elias* (Washington: Smithsonian Institute, 1973); and William B. Workman, *Prehistory of the Aishihik-Kluane Area*, Ph.D. thesis, University of Wisconsin, 1974.
3. Workman, p. 523.
4. de Laguna, p. 353.
5. George Davidson, *The Alaska Boundary* (San Francisco: Alaska Packers Association, 1903), p. 63.
6. Clifford Wilson, *Campbell of the Yukon* (Toronto: Macmillan, 1970), p. 15.
7. Alexander H. Murray, *Journal of the Yukon*, Publication of the Canadian Archives, No. 4 (Ottawa: Government Printing Office, 1910), p. 5.
8. Ibid., p. 54.
9. Innis, p. 234.
10. Alan Wright, *Prelude to Bonanza* (Sidney: Gray's Publishing, 1976), p. 61.
11. William Ogilvie, *Information Respecting the Yukon District*, Department of the Interior (Ottawa: Government Printing Bureau, 1897), p. 44.
12. Inspector Charles A. Constantine, "Report of Inspector Charles Constantine, 10 October 1894," in *Report of the Commissioner of the North West Mounted Police* (Ottawa: Queen's Printer, 1895), p. 70.
13. Ibid., p. 79.
14. Morrison, p. 7.
15. Ibid., p. 9.
16. Morris Zaslow, "The Yukon: Northern Development in a Canadian-American Context," in Mason Wade, ed., *Regionalism in the Canadian Community 1867-1967* (Toronto: University of Toronto Press, 1969), p. 185.
17. John W. Dafoe, *Clifford Sifton in Relation to His Times* (Toronto: Macmillan, 1931), p. 152.
18. Inspector F. Harper, "Report of Inspector F. Harper" in *Report of the Commissioner of the North West Mounted Police for 1899* (Ottawa: Queen's Printer, 1899), p. 73.
19. Canada, 63-64 Victoria c. 34.
20. Yukon Territory, *Ordinances*, 1901, c. 2.

21. Harold A. Innis, "Settlement and the Mining Frontier," in *Canadian Frontiers of Settlement*, Vol. 9 (Toronto: Macmillan, 1936), p. 216.
22. See for example A.F. Fraser, *Reproductive Behaviour in Ungulates* (London: Academic Press, 1968), p. 88.
23. Nova Scotia, 57 Victoria c. 2, Sect. 35.
24. See Mr. John Joe's history, in the Appendix, p. 160.
25. Robin W. Doughty, *Feather Fashions and Bird Preservation* (Berkeley: University of California Press, 1975).
26. Canada, 8-9 Edward VII, c. 27.
27. Canada, Committee on Conservation, *Annual Report*, Vol. II (1911) (Ottawa: King's Printer, 1912), p. 110.
28. Ibid., Vol. VI (1915), p. 66.
29. Ibid., Vol. VIII (1917), p. 121; Canada, *Revised Statutes of 1906*, c. 151.
30. Canada, Committee on Conservation, *Conference on Conservation of Game, Fur-Bearing Animals and Other Wildlife*, February 1919, Proceedings (Ottawa: King's Printer, 1919), p. 11.
31. Yukon Archives, Yukon Record Group 1, Series 3, File 12-8, April 1929. Hereafter "Yukon Archives, Yukon Record Group 1" will be cited "YRG1."
32. YRG1, Series 3, File 12-8, April to September, 1929.
33. YRG1, Series 3, File 12-3, June 27, 1919.
34. YRG1, Series 3, File 12-18, March 25, 1939.
35. See fur production statistics, *Canada Year Book* (Ottawa: King's Printer, 1920-1948).

3 Big Game: Heroes and Losers

1. Cited in the preface of G.F.G.R. Schwerdt, *Hawking, Hunting and Shooting* (London: Waterlow and Son, 1937).
2. Cited in the introduction to Edward, Second Duke of York, *The Master of Game*, William A. Baille-Grohman, ed. (London: Ballantyne and Hanson, 1904).
3. Nevill A.D. Armstrong, *After Big Game in the Upper Yukon* (London: John Long, 1937), p. 176.
4. James H. Bond, *From Out of the Yukon* (Portland, Oregon: Binfords and Mort, 1948), p. 99.
5. Canada, Department of the Interior, *The Yukon Territory and Its Resources* (Ottawa: King's Printer, 1907), p. 84.
6. Major Z.T. Wood, "Report of Major Z.T. Wood," in *Report of the North West Mounted Police for 1904*, Part III, (Ottawa: King's Printer, 1905), p. 54.
7. Major Z.T. Wood's report in *Report of the North West Mounted Police for 1901* (Ottawa: King's Printer, 1902).
8. Canada, Statistics Canada, *Canada Year Book 1974* (Ottawa: Queen's Printer, 1975), p. 457.
9. Assuming dressed weights of four hundred and fifty pounds each for cattle, sixty pounds for sheep, and sixty pounds for hogs.
10. F.C. Selous, *Recent Hunting Trips in North America* (New York: Scribner's, 1907).

11. Charles Sheldon, *The Wilderness of the Upper Yukon* (New York: Scribner's, 1911).
12. Wood, *Report* for 1904, p. 30.
13. Selous, p. 9.
14. United States, 60th Congress, 35 Stat. 102, May 11, 1908.
15. Thomas Martindale, *Hunting in the Upper Yukon* (Philadelphia: George Jacobs, 1913), p. 2.
16. YRG1, Series 3, File 12-3, July 1919.
17. G.O. Young, *Alaska Trophies Won and Lost*, 2nd ed. (West Virginia: Standard Publishers, 1947).
18. Yukon Territory, *Public Accounts*, 1918 to 1939.
19. Canada, Department of the Interior, *The Yukon Territory: Its History and Resources* (Ottawa: King's Printer, 1916), p. 220.
20. Canada, *Revised Statutes 1906*, c. 50, sect. 5.
21. YRG1, Series 3, Vol. 1, File 346A, April 1910.
22. YRG1, Series 3, File 12-3, November 7, 1919.
23. See page 35.
24. YRG1, Series 3, File 12-3, May 20, 1920.
25. YRG1, Series 3, File 12-4, October 1920.
26. YRG1, Series 3, File 12-4, November 1920.
27. YRG1, Series 3, File 12-4, May 1921.
28. YRG1, Series 3, File 12-4, December 1921 and March 1922.
29. YRG1, Series 3, File 12-4, December 1921.
30. YRG1, Series 3, File 12-4, December 1921.
31. YRG1, Series 3, File 12-5, June 1922.
32. H.A. Auer, *Camp Fires in the Yukon* (Cincinnati: Stewart and Kidd, 1916), p. 150.
33. Yukon Territory, *Ordinances 1923*, c. 5.
34. YRG1, Series 3, File 12-5, June 1926.
35. YRG1, Series 3, File 12-7, August 1927.
36. See Johnny Taku Jack's comments on George Johnson in the Appendix, p. 172.
37. YRG1, Series 3, File 12-13, June 1934.
38. YRG1, Series 3, File 12-12, May 1933.
39. Yukon Archives, British Yukon Navigation Co., *Superintendent's Annual Report of Operation for 1921*.

4 The Alaska Highway

1. *Whitehorse Star*, Vol. 42, No. 15 (April 15, 1942), p. 1.
2. YRG1, Series 1, Vol. 4, File 466, June 1929.
3. David A. Remley, *Crooked Road* (Toronto: McGraw-Hill, 1976), p. 119.
4. YRG1, Series 1, Vol. 4, File 466, March 7, 1939.
5. *Whitehorse Star*, Vol 39, No. 28 (July 21, 1939), p. 1.
6. In the twenties and thirties, Yukon commissioners were given the title of "Controller." "Commissioner" is used throughout this book for the sake of clarity.
7. YRG1, Series 1, Vol. 4, File 466, March 28, 1942.
8. YRG1, Series 1, Vol. 4, File 466, March 30, 1942.

9. YRG1, Series 1, Vol. 4, File 466, May 12, 1942.
10. YRG1, Series 1, Vol. 4, File 466, May 19, 1942.
11. YRG1, Series 1, Vol. 4, File 466, June 4, 1942.
12. YRG1, Series 1, Vol. 54, File 33226.
13. Philip H. Godsell, *Alaska Highway* (London: Samson Low, 1944), p. 143.
14. YRG1, Series 1, Vol. 4, File 466, August 6, 1942.
15. YRG1, Series 1, Vol. 4, File 466, August 6, 1942.
16. YRG1, Series 1, Vol. 4, File 466, September 8, 1942.
17. Canada, P.C. Order 11142, December 8, 1942.
18. Johnny Johns, *Testimony* before the Mackenzie Valley Pipeline Inquiry, Yellowknife, N.W.T., Vol. 151 (May 5, 1976).
19. Joe Jacquot, *Testimony* before the Mackenzie Valley Pipeline Inquiry, Yellowknife, N.W.T., Vol. 151 (May 5, 1976).
20. YRG1, Series 3, File 12-20, December 17, 1942.
21. YRG1, Series 3, File 12-20, February 25, 1943.
22. YRG1, Series 3, File 12-20, January 8, 1943.
23. YRG1, Series 3, File 12-20, June 9, 1943.
24. YRG1, Series 3, File 12-20, June 25, 1943.
25. Yukon Territory, *Public Accounts* (Dawson: King's Printer, 1940-1945).

5   The Invasion of New Attitudes

1. YRG1, Series 3, File 35561, March 1945.
2. YRG1, Series 3, File 35561, February 1945.
3. YRG1, Series 3, File 35561, September 1945.
4. See for example *Maclean's Magazine* for September 1, 1942: cited in YRG1, Series 3, File 12-20, September 18, 1942.
5. YRG1, Series 3, File 35561, February 1947.
6. *Alaska Sportsman*, III, No. 1, (January 1947): 18.
7. YRG1, Series 3, File 12-22, December 1946.
8. YRG1, Series 3, File 35561, January 7, 1947.
9. YRG1, Series 3, File 35561, February 20, 1947.
10. YRG1, Series 3, File 35561, February 1947.
11. YRG1, Series 3, File 12-22, July 1947.
12. YRG1, Series 3, File 12-22, March 4, 1947.
13. YRG1, Series 3, File 12-22, June 24, 1947.
14. James H. Bond, *From Out of the Yukon* (Portland, Oregon: Binfords and Mort, 1948).
15. YRG1, Series 3, File 12-22, near October 1947.
16. YRG1, Series 3, File 36275, March 1949.

6   Yukon Furs: The Early Decades

1. YRG1, Series 1, Vol. 27, File 9935.
2. See p. 35.
3. Fredrick T. Congdon, *Fur Bearing Animals of Canada and How to Prevent Their Extinction*, pamphlet (Ottawa: Committee on Conservation, 1910).

4. Janet Foster, *Working for Wildlife* (Toronto: University of Toronto Press, 1978), p. 36.
5. Inspector A.E.R. Cuthbert, "Report of Inspector A.E.R. Cuthbert," in *Report of the North West Mounted Police* (Ottawa: King's Printer, 1904), p. 60.
6. Canada, Department of the Interior, *The Yukon Territory: Its History and Resources* (Ottawa: King's Printer, 1907), p. 85.
7. Nevill A.D. Armstrong, *After Big Game in the Upper Yukon* (London: John Long, 1937), p. 56.
8. M.C. Urquhart and K.A.H. Buckley, eds., *Historical Statistics of Canada* (Toronto: Macmillan, 1965), pp. 291-292.
9. Yukon Archives, Tape Series 4, Tape 2, "Henderson" (November 1950).
10. Adrian Tanner, *The Structure of Fur Trade Relations* (MA thesis, University of British Columbia, 1965), p. 51.
11. Sarah D. Taylor, "Toot Toot! The Thistle," in *Zenith Magazine*, July 1926, p. 7.
12. Richard Slobodin, "The Dawson Boys—Peel River Indians and the Klondike Gold Rush," *Polar Notes* (June 1963): 24.
13. Yukon Archives, Manuscript Collection, Box 10, File 1.
14. Canada, Department of the Interior, *The Yukon Territory: Its History and Resources* (Ottawa: King's Printer, 1916), p. 177.
15. Tappan Adney, "Moose Hunting with Tro-Chin,"in *Outing Magazine*, XXXIX, No. 6 (March 1902): 623.
16. Yukon Archives, Pamphlet Collection, No. 1914-17C.
17. *Canada Year Book 1921*, p. 312.
18. Canada, Department of the Interior, *The Yukon Territory: Its History and Resources* (Ottawa: King's Printer, 1916), p. 176.
19. Yukon Archives, Pamphlet Collection, No. 1914-17C.
20. Canada, Department of the Interior, *The Yukon Territory 1926* (Ottawa: King's Printer, 1926), p. 70.
21. Urquhart, p. 292.
22. YRG1, Series 3, File 12-3, September 1919.
23. YRG1, Series 4, Box 4, File 241a.
24. YRG1, Series 3, File 12-3, May 7, 1920.
25. YRG1, Series 3, File 12-3, October 7, 1920.

7 Years of Prosperity

1. YRG1, Series 3, File 12-3, August 11, 1920.
2. See Julia Cruikshank and Jim Robb, *Their Own Yukon* (Whitehorse: Yukon Native Brotherhood, 1975).
3. See *Canada Year Book*, 1921-1940 (Ottawa: King's Printer).
4. A.R. Harding, *The Fur Buyer's Guide*, 2nd ed. (Columbus, Ohio: A.R. Harding, 1942), p. 56.
5. Paul H. Nystrom, *The Economics of Fashion* (New York: Ronald Press, 1928), p. 419.
6. See for example R. Turner Wilcox, *The Mode in Furs* (New York: Scribner's, 1951).
7. YRG1, Series 3, File 12-6, February 7, 1927.
8. YRG1, Series 3, File 12-5, June 27, 1924.

9. YRG1, Series 3, File 12-5, June 30, 1924.
10. YRG1, Series 3, File 12-7, July 13, 1928.
11. YRG1, Series 3, File 12-7, September 20, 1928.
12. Dominion Bureau of Statistics pamphlet, *Fur Production in Canada, 1926,* in YRG1, Series 3, File 12-6, July 1927.
13. YRG1, Series 3, File 12-7, January 7, 1929.
14. YRG1, Series 3, File 12-5, April 10, 1926.
15. YRG1, Series 3, File 12-8, June 13, 1930.
16. See Government of the Yukon Territory, *Public Accounts,* 1920-1930.
17. YRG1, Series 3, File 12-13, November 13, 1933.
18. For a description of Yukon fur trading practices in the recent past, a Master's thesis by Adrian Tanner, *The Structure of Fur Trade Relations* (University of British Columbia, 1965) is a useful source.
19. Robert E. Pinkerton, *The Hudson's Bay Company* (London: Thornton Butterworth, 1936), p. 301.
20. Canada, Dominion Bureau of Statistics (Ottawa: King's Printer, 1930 *et ann.*).
21. *Beaver* (June 1934): 56.
22. YRG1, Series 3, File 12-3, April 1919.
23. YRG1, Series 3, File 12-9, May 16, 1931.
24. Robert Mulligan, *Geology of the Teslin Lake Map Area,* Memoir 326 (Ottawa: Geological Survey of Canada, 1963), p. 76.
25. YRG1, Series 3, File 12-11, November 17, 1932.
26. YRG1, Series 3, File 12-11, November 21, 1932.
27. YRG1, Series 3, File 12-17, March 22, 1937.

8 Ten Dollar Traplines

1. See Dominion Bureau of Statistics, *Production of Fur,* Catalog 23-207 (Ottawa: Queen's Printer, 1966), p. 11.
2. *Beaver,* Outfit 277, No. 2 (June 1946): 40.
3. *Canada Year Book,* 1940 (Ottawa: King's Printer); ibid., 1951.
4. Ibid., 1948-1949, p. 254.
5. See A. Richard King, *The School at Mopass* (Toronto: Holt Rinehart, 1967) for a detailed and interesting account of the Carcross School.
6. Julia Cruikshank, *Testimony* before the Mackenzie Valley Pipeline Inquiry, Vol. 151 (May 5, 1976), p. 23108.
7. Ibid., p. 23110.
8. YRG1, Series 3, File 12-20, April 26, 1941.
9. YRG1, Series 3, File 12-20; letter dated March 8, 1943, filed near January 13, 1944.
10. YRG1, Series 3, File 12-22, January 14, 1947.
11. YRG1, Series 3, File 12-22, January 28, 1947.
12. Dominion Bureau of Statistics, "Production of Fur," *Catalogue 23-207* (Queen's Printer, 1966), p. 11.
13. YRG1, Series 3, File 12-22, May 26, 1947.
14. See Public Archives of Canada, Series RG 85, Vol. 1035, File 20491.
15. YRG1, Series 3, File 12-22, March 8, 1950.
16. YRG1, Series 3, File 12-23, September 29, 1950.
17. YRG1, Series 3, File 12-23, September 29, 1950.

Appendix

1. Supra, p. 96-97.
2. Supra, p. 111.
3. Supra, p. 51.
4. Supra, p. 135.
5. A merchant and fur buyer at Atlin, B.C. in the 1920s.
6. Supra, p. 60.
7. Supra, p. 168.

Bibliography

Adney, Tappan. "Moose Hunting with the Tro-Chin." *Outing Magazine*, XXXIX, No. 6 (March, 1902).

Alaska Sportsman, III, No. 1 (January, 1947).

Armstrong, Nevill A.D. *After Big Game in the Upper Yukon*. London: John Long, 1937.

Auer, H.A. *Camp Fires in the Yukon*. Cincinnati: Stewart and Kidd, 1916.

Bancroft, Hubert H. *History of Alaska*. New York: Antiquarian Press, 1960.

Barry, R.G. and R.J. Chorley. *Atmosphere, Weather and Climate*. Third Edition. London: Methuen and Co., 1976.

Beaver (Winnipeg, Manitoba) June, 1934; June, 1946; June, 1947; June, 1953.

Bond, James H. *From Out of the Yukon*. Portland, Oregon: Binfords and Mort, 1948.

Braudel, Fernand. *Capitalism and Material Life 1400-1800*. New York: Harper and Row, 1974.

Canada. Committee on Conservation. Annual Reports, 1911-1919. Ottawa: King's Printer, 1912-1920.

_____. Commitee on Conservation. Conference on Conservation of Game, Fur-Bearing Animals and Other Wildlife (February 1919), Proceedings. Ottawa: King's Printer, 1919.

_____. Department of the Interior. *The Yukon Territory: Its History and Resources.* Ottawa: King's Printer, 1907.

_____. Department of the Interior. *The Yukon Territory: Its History and Resources.* Ottawa: King's Printer, 1916.

_____. Department of the Interior. *The Yukon Territory 1926.* Ottawa: King's Printer, 1926.

_____. Dominion Bureau of Statistics (Statistics Canada). *Canada Year Book* 1920-1949 and 1974. Ottawa: King's Printer, 1920-1949 and Queen's Printer, 1975, annual.

_____. Dominion Bureau of Statistics (Statistics Canada). "Production of Fur," *Catalogue 23-207.* Queen's Printer, 1966.

_____. Parliament. *Debates of the House of Commons,* June 2, 1894. Ottawa: King's Printer, 1894.

_____. Public Archives, Series RG 85, Vol. 1035, File 20491.

Congdon, Fredrick T. *Fur Bearing Animals of Canada and How to Prevent Their Extinction* (pamphlet). Ottawa: Committee on Conservation, 1910.

Constantine, Inspector Charles A. "Report of Inspector Charles Constantine, 10 October, 1894." In *Report of the Commissioner of the North West Mounted Police,* Appendix B. Ottawa: King's Printer, 1904.

Cruikshank, Julia M. and Catherine McClellan. Testimony before the Mackenzie Valley Pipeline Inquiry, Volume 151 (May 5, 1976). Yellowknife, Northwest Territories.

_____, and Jim Robb. *Their Own Yukon.* Whitehorse: Yukon Native Brotherhood, 1975.

Cuthbert, Inspector A.E.R. "Report of Inspector A.E.R. Cuthbert." In *Report of the North West Mounted Police,* Appendix B. Ottawa: King's Printer, 1904.

Dafoe, John W. *Clifford Sifton in Relation to His Times.* Toronto: Macmillan, 1931.

Daily Mail. London, United Kingdom (March 16, 1978).

Davidson, George. *The Alaska Boundary.* San Francisco: Alaska Packers Association, 1903.

De Laguna, Fredrica. *Under Mount St. Elias.* Washington: Smithsonian Institute, 1973.

Dobson, R.B. *The Peasant's Revolt.* London: Macmillan, 1970.

Doughty, Robin W. *Feather Fashions and Bird Preservation.* Berkeley: University of California Press, 1975.

Edward, Second Duke of York. *The Master of Game,* William A. Baille-Grohman, ed. London: Ballantyne and Hanson, 1904.

Foster, Janet. *Working for Wildlife.* Toronto: University of Toronto Press, 1978.

Fraser, A.F. *Reproductive Behavior in Ungulates.* London: Academic Press, 1968.

Fraser, Antonia. *Cromwell: Our Chief of Men.* St. Albans, Herts.: Panther Books, 1975.

George, Henry. *Progress and Poverty.* London: Henry George Foundation, 1937.

Glacken, Clarence J. *Traces on the Rhodian Shore.* Berkeley: University of California Press, 1967.

Godsell, Philip H. *Alaska Highway.* London: Samson and Low, 1944.

Harding, A.R. *The Fur Buyer's Guide.* Second Edition. Columbus, Ohio: A.R. Harding Publishers, 1942.

Harper, Inspector F."Report of Inspector F. Harper." In *Report of the Commissioner of the North West Mounted Police for 1899.* Ottawa: Queen's Printer, 1899.

Hines, Francis. *The Buffalo.* New York: Thomas Crowell Company, 1970.

Holdsworth, William. *A History of English Law.* Seventh Edition, Volume 1. London: Methuen and Company, 1956.

Innis, Harold A. *The Fur Trade in Canada.* Toronto: University of Toronto Press, 1962.

Innis, Harold A. "Settlement and the Mining Frontier." In *Canadian Frontiers of Settlement.* Volume 9. Toronto: Macmillan, 1936.

Itzkowitz, David C. *Peculiar Privilege: A Social History of English Foxhunting 1753-1885.* Hassocks, Sussex: The Harvester Press, 1977.

Jacquot, Joe. *Testimony* before the Mackenzie Valley Pipeline Inquiry, Volume 151 (May 5, 1976). Yellowknife, Northwest Territories.

Johns, Johnny. *Testimony* before the Mackenzie Valley Pipeline Inquiry, Volume 151 (May 5, 1976). Yellowknife, Northwest Territories.

Jolliffe, J.E.A. *The Constitutional History of Medieval England.* London: Adam and Charles Black, 1937.

King, A. Richard. *The School at Mopass.* Toronto: Holt Rinehart, 1967.

McClellan, Catherine. *My Old People Say.* 2 volumes. Ottawa: National Museums of Man, 1975.

Manwood, Justice William. *Treatise on the Forest Laws.* Fourth Edition. London: 1717.

Martin, Calvin. *Keepers of the Game.* London: University of California Press, 1978.

Martindale, Thomas. *Hunting in the Upper Yukon.* Philadelphia: George W. Jacobs, 1913.

Morrison, David R. *The Politics of the Yukon Territory 1898-1909.* Toronto: University of Toronto Press, 1968.

Mulligan, Robert. *Geology of the Teslin Lake Map Area.* Memoir 326. Ottawa: Geological Survey of Canada, 1963.

Murray, Alexander H. *Journal of the Yukon.* Publication of the Canadian Archives No. 4. Ottawa: Government Printing Bureau, 1910.

Nash, Roderick. *Wilderness and the American Mind.* London: Yale University Press, 1973.

Nelson, William. *The Laws Concerning Game.* Fourth Edition. London: 1751.

Nystrom, Paul H. *The Economics of Fashion.* New York: Ronald Press, 1928.

Ogilvie, William. *Information Respecting the Yukon District,* Department of the Interior. Ottawa: Queen's Printer, 1897.

Oman, Charles. *The Great Revolt of 1381.* Second Edition. Oxford: Clarendon Press, 1969.

Oxford English Dictionary. London: Oxford University Press, 1933.

Pinkerton, Robert E. *The Hudson's Bay Company.* London: Thornton Butterworth, 1936.

Poole, Austin L. *From Domesday Book to Magna Charta.* Second Edition. Oxford: Oxford University Press, 1955.

Ray, A.J. *Indians in the Fur Trade.* Toronto: University of Toronto Press, 1974.

Remley, David A. *Crooked Road*. Toronto: McGraw Hill, 1976.

Roe, F.G. *The North American Buffalo*. Second Edition. Toronto: University of Toronto Press, 1972.

Schwerdt, G.F.G.R. *Hunting, Hawking and Shooting*. London: Waterlow and Son, 1937.

Selous, F.C. *Recent Hunting Trips in North America*. New York: Scribner's, 1907.

Sheldon, Charles. *The Wilderness of the Upper Yukon*. New York: Scribner's, 1911.

Slobodin, Richard. "The Dawson Boys—Peel River Indians and the Klondike Gold Rush." In *Polar Notes* (June, 1963).

Tanner, Adrian. *The Structure of Fur Trade Relations*. M.A. Thesis, University of British Columbia, 1965.

Taylor, Sarah D. "Toot Toot! The Thistle." In *Zenith Magazine* (July, 1926).

Tench, Charles C. *The Poacher and the Squire*. London: Longmans, 1967.

Thompson, E.P. *Whigs and Hunters*. Harmondsworth, Middlesex: Penguin, 1977.

Turbervile, George. *Book on Falconrie or Hawking* and *Book on Hunting*. Second Edition. London: 1611.

Turner, G.J. ed. *Select Pleas of the Forest*. London: Bernard Quaritch, 1901.

Twici, William. *The Art of Hunting* (1413), Alice Dryden, ed. Northampton: William Mark, 1908.

United Kingdom. Parliament. *Blue Books* Vol. LXVII (1871), Parliamentary Papers.

United States. Environmental Law Institute. *The Evolution of National Wildlife Law*. Washington: Superintendent of Documents, 1977.

Urquart, M.C. and K.A.H. Buckley, eds. *Historical Statistics of Canada*. Toronto: Macmillan, 1965.

Whitehorse Star, Whitehorse, Yukon Territory. Vol. 42, No. 15 (April 1, 1942) and Vol. 39, No. 28 (July 21, 1939).

Wilcox, R. Turner. *The Mode in Furs*. New York: Scribner's, 1951.

Wilson, Clifford. *Campbell of the Yukon*. Toronto: Macmillan, 1970.

Wood, Major Z.T. "Report of Major Z.T. Wood." In *Report of the North West Mounted Police for 1901*. Ottawa: King's Printer, 1902.

_____. "Report of Major Z.T. Wood." In *Report of the North West Mounted Police for 1904*. Ottawa: King's Printer, 1905.

Workman, William B. *Prehistory of the Aishihik-Kluane Area*. Ph.D. Thesis, University of Wisconsin, 1974.

Wright, Alan A. *Prelude to Bonanza*. Sidney, British Columbia: Gray's Publishing, 1976.

Young, G.O. *Alaska Trophies Won and Lost*. Second Edition. Huntington, West Virginia: Standard Publishers, 1947.

Yukon Archives. British Yukon Navigation Co. *Superintendent's Annual Report of Operations for 1921*.

_____. Central Records Division, Box 5015, File "Trapline Correspondence," 1950-1960.

_____. Manuscript Collection, Box 10, File 1.

_____. Pamphlet Collection, No. 1914-17C.

_____. Yukon Record Group 1, Series 1, Vol. 27, File 9934, 1904.

_____. Yukon Record Group 1, Series 1, Vol. 6-8, File 466.

_____. Yukon Record Group 1, Series 3, Files 12-2 to 12-23, 1900-1950.

———. Parliament. *Debates of the House of Commons*, June 2, 1894. Ottawa: King's Printer, 1894.

Zaslow, Morris. "The Yukon: Northern Development in a Canadian-American Context." In *Regionalism in the Canadian Community 1867-1967*, edited by Mason Wade. Toronto: University of Toronto Press, 1969.

Index

International Highway Commission, report of 1933, 66
Isaac, Albert, 52, 58

Jackson, F.H.R. (Rex), 90, 95
Jacquot, Eugene and Louis, 51, 58
Jacquot, Joe, 51, 81
"Jawbone," 109, 128, 130
Jeckell, George A., Yukon commissioner, 61; Alaska Highway, 67, 68-74; trapline registration, 122, 143; retirement, 138
Joe, John, 96-97, 98, 160-164
Johns, Johnny, 58-60, 96; Alaska Highway, 80, 86, 96; fur buying, 121
Johnson, George, 60-61, 172

Kane, Bobby, 52
Kane, Jimmy, 52
Keenleyside, Dr. Hugh, Canada Dept. of External Affairs, 70
King, Mackenzie, prime minister: Alaska Highway, 66, 68
Kjar, Them, 91, 93, 100-101, 146, 163
Kluane National Park, 78-79

LeCapelain, Charles K., 77-80
Lee, R.G., 95
Little Salmon, 108
London, Jack, 43

MacBride, W.D., 89, 98
Mackenzie, George P., Yukon commissioner, 52, 116, 121, 123-124
MacLean, G.I., Yukon commissioner, 65, 122, 124
Market hunting: in Dawson City, 45-48, 61; attitudes towards, 48-49; Yukon Fish and Game Association, 93; in Alaska, 123
Marten, closed season, 124
Martindale, Thomas, 51
Mast, Ivor, 97
McGundy, Taylor, 142

Meek, R.J. (Jack), 93, 95, 145-147
Mervyn, J.H., 124
Mervyn, Norman, 99
Migratory birds treaty, 35, 36
Moffat, Pierrepont J., American ambassador, 70

Nelson, E.W., 123
Nolan, Mike, 96
Nonresident hunting: Yukon attitude, 53; export of game, 54; fees, 55. *See also* Trophy hunters
Northern Commercial Co., 129
Northwest Staging Route, 68, 72

Old Crow Flats, 117
Osgood, Wilfred, 49
Outfitter: defined, 96-97; obtain areas, 102. *See also* Trophy hunters; Big game industry

Pattullo, T.D., British Columbia premier, 66
Pearl Harbor attack, 68
Peel River Indians, 38, 110
Phelps, W.L., 74
Public Roads Administration personnel, 85

Ramparts, 117
RCMP: game enforcement, 82-85; fur inspections, 127-128
Reid, Percy, Yukon commissioner, 121
Riggs, Thomas, Alaskan governor, 55, 116
Roosevelt, Theodore, U.S. president, 43, 106
Ross River, 125
Rungius, Carl, 49

Sands, Clarence, 168, 173
Scholls, Louis, 173
Second World War, in May to July, 1942, 74
Selous, F.C., 49
Service, Robert, 43
Shade, Carson, 94-97

Photo Credits

Front Cover photograph — Detail from "Joe Slaggard and Solomon Albert Returning to Dawson from Headwaters of White River, E.O. Ellingsen Photo 260," MacBride Museum Collection, Yukon Archives #3801. Reprinted with the permission of the Yukon Archives.

Back Cover photograph — "Dan Cadzow's Store with Winter Furs in Front. Peter Timble and Jacob Njoatli. New Ramparts House, Yukon Territory." Dan Cadzow's log trading post was located on the Porcupine River and this picture is known to be circa 1913-17. Alaska-Canada Album/Dan Cadzow Collection, Acc. #65-31-56, Archives, Alaska and Polar Regions Department, University of Alaska, Fairbanks. Reprinted with the permission of the University of Alaska Archives.

Introduction, p. xi — "Family of Taku Jack; Atlin, B.C., ca. 1910(?)." Johnny Taku Jack (see Appendix, p. 169) is the boy fourth from the right on the bottom row. Provincial Archives of British Columbia #HP44731. Reprinted with the permission of the Provincial Archives of British Columbia.

Chapter 1, p. 1 — "Watson Block, Dawson, Y.T., Sept. 1899." The sale of game meat was common during the Gold Rush (see pages 46-48). MacBride Museum Collection, Yukon Archives #3776. Reprinted with the permission of the Yukon Archives.

Chapter 2, p. 22 — "Joe Slaggard and Solomon Albert Returning to Dawson from Headwaters of White River, E.O. Ellingsen Photo 260." These men were probably market hunters (see page 49). MacBride Museum Collection, Yukon Archives #3801. Reprinted with the permission of the Yukon Archives.

Chapter 2, p. 24 — Map of the Yukon Territory in 1942. Drawn by Stephanie Kucharyshyn, Cartography Division, Department of Geography, University of Alberta.

Chapter 3, p. 42 — "Tom Dickson with Mrs. Newmarsh and Lillian Harbottle, Burwash area, ca. 1920." See pages 41 and 162. Harbottle Collection, Yukon Archives #6117. Reprinted with the permission of the Yukon Archives.

Chapter 4, p. 64 — "U.S. Army Corps of Engineers Band, Silver City, Yukon, July 4, 1942." Silver City was the terminus at Kluane Lake of an old mining road from Whitehorse; it became an important construction camp for the Army. MacBride Museum Collection, Yukon Archives #3976. Reprinted with the permission of the Yukon Archives.

Chapter 5, p. 88 — "Hunting Party, Donjek River, about 1945." McPherson Collection, Yukon Archives #4353. Reprinted with the permission of the Yukon Archives.

Chapter 6, p. 103 — "Dan Cadzow's Store with Winter Furs in Front. Peter Timble and Jacob Njoatli. New Ramparts House, Yukon Territory." Dan Cadzow's log trading post was located on the Porcupine River and this picture is known to be circa 1913-17. Alaska-Canada Album/Dan Cadzow Collection, Acc. #65-31-56, Archives, Alaska and Polar Regions Department, University of Alaska, Fairbanks. Reprinted with the permission of the Univeristy of Alaska Archives.

Chapter 7, p. 118 — Furs of the Yukon, Adams & Larkin Photo, Dawson, Y.T." Yukon Archives #2054 and the Vancouver Public Library. Reprinted with the permission of the Yukon Archives.

Chapter 8, p. 137 — "Van Bibber Family," (left to right) "Dad, Mother, Dave, Myself, George, Linch, Lucy." Van Bibber Collection, Yukon Archives #160. Reprinted with the permission of the Yukon Archives.

Chapter 9, p. 149 — Mr. Johnny Johns, April, 1985. Photograph © 1985 by Jim Robb, Whitehorse, Yukon. Reprinted with the permission of Jim Robb.

Appendix, p. 160 — Mr. John Joe, Whitehorse, Yukon, May, 1985, age 101. Photograph by Fred Stewart, Fred's Foto, Whitehorse, Yukon.

Appendix, p. 164 — Mr. Frank Goulter, Carmacks, Yukon, age 102. Photograph taken in 1979 by the author.

Appendix, p. 169 — Mr. Johnny Taku Jack, Atlin, B.C., June, 1985, age 82. Photograph by author.

Cover design by John Luckhurst/GDL.

Typography by Joanne Poon.